The Imagery of
Euripides

The Imagery of
Euripides

*A study in the dramatic use of
pictorial language*

Shirley A. Barlow

Methuen and Co Ltd
11 New Fetter Lane London EC4

First published in 1971
by Methuen & Co Ltd
© *1971 Shirley A. Barlow*
Printed in Great Britain by
William Clowes & Sons Limited
London, Colchester and Beccles

SBN 416 08130 4

Distributed in the U.S.A.
by Barnes & Noble Inc.

Contents

Preface

The original idea for this book grew out of a thesis I wrote for the University of London in 1963, although much of the material has been expanded since then, and the basic method of approach slightly altered. I thought then, and still think, that there is a need to examine more closely than has previously been the case, the poetic qualities of Euripides' plays. For it has been the non-linguistic aspects of his work which have so far appealed to scholars; questions of staging and dramatic technique, for instance, problems of psychological motivation, or the dramatist's intellectual ideas considered in relation to those of his contemporaries. I have spent some time in the first chapter suggesting reasons as to why this dismissal or neglect of Euripides' poetic qualities might have arisen. One of them, in my opinion, is that whenever Euripides' stylistic qualities *have* come up for evaluation, they have been dismissed as inferior because they have been measured by criteria which are applicable to the other two tragedians, Sophocles and Aeschylus, but not to him. It has been assumed, in other words, without any justification whatever, that their aims must also have been his. It is part of my purpose to demonstrate that this is not so, and to do this by taking a restricted stylistic area, that of imagery, and trying to show how it works on its own terms, that is, functionally, in different parts of the plays.

There are two main principles of method operating. The first concerns the range of the term 'imagery', and the second, the relation of imagery to the different dramatic parts or modes. By 'imagery' I mean two things: first, descriptive language which is sensuous but not metaphorical, and second, language which is clearly either metaphorical or comparative. Although the latter is what constitutes the more usual interpretation of imagery, I have spent the major part of the book, from Chapters II–V, on the first purely descriptive type. There are several reasons for this. In the first place, Euripides' use of a pictorial style which is sensuously descriptive but not necessarily metaphorical, is very extensive. It occurs in iambic as well as lyric sections, and is particularly noticeable in the distribution of the compound pictorial epithet. In the second place, this extensive use is on the whole fully justified by the overall dramatic context, and is therefore important for the full understanding of any given play. And thirdly, it seems to me to deserve attention simply because it is an aspect of style other commentators and critics have ignored, whereas simile and metaphor are a well-worn tract, and in most studies are all imagery is thought to be. One chapter only, VI, deals with imagery in this more conventional sense. More detailed study seemed unnecessary because there is no point in repeating what has already been said on the subject. Sensuous imagery in my opinion is the more important of the two categories (although of course they overlap to some extent); it is also the more flexible in range, for whereas the short metaphor is ubiquitous, and likely to occur in the same form in any part of the play, descriptive language adapts its style to the mode in which it occurs, whether lyric or iambic, chorus, monody, dialogue, *rhesis* or messenger speech.

The book is not intended to be more than a starting point for some new thoughts or approaches to Euripides' use of language. I am conscious of how much more still needs to be done. I am deeply indebted to friends and colleagues who have helped me in the course of this work by their comments and suggestions, in particular to Professor T. B. L. Webster, who supervised the original thesis, to Professor E. W. Handley, Mrs P. Easterling and Mrs W. B. Trousdale for reading different stages of the book in draft, to Mrs Carole Phillips for typing the manuscript, and to Dr Doreen Innes, who generously gave up time to help me with the proofs. For such errors as exist, and for such interpretations as I have obstinately clung to in the face of differing views, I am entirely responsible.

SHIRLEY A. BARLOW
University of Kent

List of Abbreviations

Euripides – *continued*

Hercules Furens	H.F.
Hippolytus	Hipp.
Hypsipyle	Hyps.
Ion	Ion
Iphigeneia in Aulis	I.A.
Iphigeneia in Tauris	I.T.
Medea	Med.
Orestes	Or.
Phaethon	Phaeth.
Philoctetes	Philoctetes
Phoenissae	Pho.
Supplices	Supplices
Troades	Tro.

Dioscorides	Diosc.
Heliodorus apud Stobaeum	Heliod. ap. Stob.
Herodotus	Hdt.
Hippocrates	Hp.
περὶ ἄρθρων ἐμβολῆς	Art.
ἀφορισμοί	Aph.
γυναικεῖα	Mul.
περὶ διαίτης	Vict.
Homer	Homer
Iliad	Il.
Odyssey	Od.
Pindar	Pi.
Isthmian Odes	Isthm.
Nemean Odes	Nem.
Olympian Odes	Ol.
Pythian Odes	Pyth.
Plato	Plato
Protagoras	Protag.
Republic	Rep.
Theaetetus	Theaet.
Pliny	Pliny
Natural History	N. H.

Plutarch	Plut.
Sophocles	Soph.
Ajax	*Aj.*
Antigone	*Antig.*
Electra	*El.*
Oedipus Tyrannus	*O.T.*
Oedipus Coloneus	*O.C.*
Philoctetes	*Phil.*
Trachiniae	*Trach.*
Theophrastus	Theoph.
De Causis Plantorum	*C.P.*
Virgil	Virg.
Aeneid	*Aen.*
Xenophon	Xen.
Anabasis	*An.*
Memorabilia	*Mem.*

Lexica

Liddell & Scott, revised edition by H. S. Jones	*L.S.J.*
Allen & Italie, *Concordance to Euripides*	Allen & Italie

Periodicals cited

American Journal of Archaeology	*A.J.A.*
Classical Philology	*C.Ph.*
Harvard Studies in Classical Philology	*H.S.Cl.Ph.*
Hermes. Einzelschriften	*Hermes. Einz.*
Journal of Hellenic Studies	*J.H.S.*
Wiener Studien	*W.S.*

Museums cited

British Museum	B.M.
Nauplion Museum	Naup.
National Museum, Athens	Nat. Mus. Ath.
New York Metropolitan Museum	N.Y. Met.

Abbreviated Book Titles

J. D. Beazley, *Attic Black Figure Vase Painters*	*A.B.V.*
J. D. Beazley, *Attic Red Figure Vase Painters*	*A.R.V.*[2]

Furtwaengler & Reichold, *Griechische*
Vasenmalerei   *G.V.*
Croiset, *Histoire de la Littérature Grecque*   *H.L.G.*
R. Lattimore, *The Poetry of Greek Tragedy*   *P.G.T.*
A. Nauck, *Fragmenta Tragicorum Poetarum*,
2nd edition   Nauck[2]
D. L. Page, *Greek Literary Papyri*   *G.L.P.*
E. Pfuhl, *Malerei und Zeichnung der Griechen*   *M.und Z.*
W. B. Stanford, *Greek Metaphor*   *G.M.*
R. P. Winnington-Ingram, *Euripides and*
Dionysus   *E.D.*

Miscellaneous

Fragment   fr.
The Oxyrhynchus Papyri, ed. B. P. Grenfell,
A. F. Hunt, E. Lobel and others   P.Oxy.
Scholia   *Σ.*

Chapter I

Modes of Imagery

Verse drama is not popular in the twentieth century.[1] There have been attempts to revive it by Eliot, Fry and others, but these have not been wholly successful. Few would describe the *Cocktail Party* or *Venus Observed* as mass entertainment: in fact these plays are more in danger of being regarded as diet for an élite with superior critical sensibilities. Perhaps Brecht comes nearest to making verse approach a more popular form of theatre but he only uses it occasionally and then for special effects.[2] The view of poetry as some kind of intellectual indulgence would have been untenable to the average fifth-century Athenian, since to him poetry was what gave adequate expression to important occasions. It was poets who celebrated athletic successes, praised war heroes, commemorated the dead and honoured the Gods. It was therefore not odd, but natural, that all varieties of Greek drama performed at the festivals in honour of Dionysus, should have been composed in poetry not prose, a poetry moreover, which meant not just one sort of verse, but a wide range of styles and accompanying moods from iambic trimeters which were spoken, to the most complex and varied lyric metres which were sung and danced to musical accompaniment.

But if external conditions in the shape of a live poetic tradition guaranteed for the metrically spoken and sung word a place of prominence it has seldom occupied since, it is also arguable that so did the conventions within the plays themselves. The austerity of a dramatic tradition which allowed no change of facial expression, no elaborate scenery and no lighting, allowed the poet's imagination to walk in ways which are no longer open to him.[3] What words then did, has now become the province of the production manager.

The Greeks' acceptance of poetry as a natural dramatic medium, meant that their ear for those things most characteristic of its form (metre, rhythm, image, musical cadence and the tone appropriate to each mode), was sharp enough for them to detect the finer points of parody in Aristophanes' comedies or the precise degree of new colouring given to old motifs in the tragedians' re-working of their predecessors' work.[4] Style as well as content distinguished Aeschylus from Sophocles and Sophocles from Euripides, but it was all *poetic* style. The kind of questions ancient critics asked related to the handling of divisions within this poetic genre. How did a poet compose his lyrics? What rhythms did he use? How varied was his iambic line?[5] Poetic skill was estimated by the way in which all varieties of verse, the spoken as well as the sung sections, were handled. In this sense Euripides was as much a poet as Aeschylus, and his iambic sections as much to be judged poetry as the lyric.

This obvious point is worth re-stating if only because the word 'poetic' today is bedevilled by quite different connotations. Because it is no longer a *natural* word to use in describing modern drama, its range has shrunk, and our use of it as a term for ancient drama has narrowed. It has become a qualitative not a determinative epithet, often cavalierly applied, and most commonly to the lyric portions of ancient tragedy only. For instance it is given unreservedly to Aeschylus largely because of the importance of choral lyric in his plays and the high degree of metaphor they contain. His genius, it is alleged, is the most purely 'poetic' of all three tragedians, lacking perhaps the technical virtuosity of Sophocles but otherwise consisting of the most 'spectacular flights' of imagination.[6] 'Poetic' seems less commonly applied to Sophocles: 'dramatist', a word which has undergone similar shrinkage, is most frequently applied to him.[7] As for Euripides, 'poet' is seldom mentioned in the catalogue of his qualities. He would really, it has been suggested, have been happier writing in prose.[8] Such critical schizophrenia, which would have been incomprehensible to the ancients, has had unfortunate consequences. It has too often had the effect of isolating the slots into which each dramatist has been put, either making it impossible to attribute to one qualities ascribed as belonging par excellence to the other, or making it impossible for each to move from his place on this ladder of 'poetic ascent' in which Aeschylus is at the top, Sophocles is half-way up and Euripides is at the bottom.

Euripides, who comes out lowest in the critical allotment of raw imaginative power, has suffered most from such invidious comparisons. His lyrics have been condemned and found wanting in the qualities which those of Aeschylus show. 'L'infériorité de ses qualités lyriques est évident', writes M. Croiset. They have 'ni l'enthousiasme, ni l'élan, ni la majesté, en un mot, aucune des hautes qualités lyriques.'[9] His diction, in the words of Lesky, 'is contrasted by Aeschylus' impetus and the noble control of Sophocles.'[10]

In general, it must be admitted, there are some reasons for such judgements. The sheer intellectual excitement generated by the issues fought out in Euripides' plays has drawn off the main energy of critics. However variably his competence in handling lyrics has been judged, the power of his mind to grapple with human problems and to articulate them as dramatic issues has never been in dispute. But it has earned him such terms of praise as 'rationalist', 'irrationalist', 'sceptic', 'voice of the enlightenment', 'realist', as if these things were somehow separable from 'poetry'.[11] As far as the lyrics go, some of the most elaborate and high-flown choral odes are undeniably irrelevant, and this has perhaps brought down hasty judgement on them all.[12] Some of them too are written in an elevated but unambiguous, metaphorless style which exposes them to greater risk in translation. The famed obscurity of Aeschylus which, incidentally, often arises from real doubt as to the textual reading, as much as to the density of his imagination, lends a mystical aura to his poetry which has if anything benefited him in translation.[13] Not so Euripides. Never was Frost's brief definition of poetry as 'that which is lost in translation', more applicable. For the English language is capable of rendering the *simplicity* of his Greek without, at the same time, conveying either the accompanying elevation of the language as it appears, for instance, in the compound adjective which is virtually non-existent in English, or the complex word order which may be vital to the sense.[14]

At the root of many stylistic criticisms of Euripides' work seems to be the feeling that the lyrics, where one looks for 'poetry', are inferior to those of Aeschylus because in them he is not doing with language what Aeschylus did – above all he is not going in for metaphors. His images are tame after the daring flights of Aeschylus. Mr. Delulle for instance, writes:

> Très différente ... de celle d'Eschyles, on imagination apparaît plutôt avec tous les signes de la faiblesse. Elle s'arrête souvent à l'image générique sans atteindre la précision et la rigueur de l'image individuelle.[15]

In spite of the words 'tres différente', Delulle is still judging Euripides' imagery by Aeschylean criteria, that is, by simile and metaphor and the frequency with which they are used. It is perfectly true that viewed solely in this light, his metaphorical range seems thin and impoverished

in comparison with Aeschylus. But since simile and metaphor account
for such a small part of his writing, it is legitimate to ask whether there
are not other kinds of pictorial language which contain no simile or
metaphor, and which still deserve the name image, and also whether
such language does not also occur in other places besides the lyric sections. In fact, not only the lyrics (chorus and monologue), but also nearly
all the messenger speeches and some dialogue contain a wealth of
imaginative writing which makes powerful appeal to the visual sense
and which is not figurative, except in as much as it serves a dramatic
purpose in the wider unit which is the play. I hope to show in the course
of this book that such imagery is evidence of highly individual poetic
talent on the part of Euripides, and that such talent serves a variety of
dramatic functions. These functions may sometimes be the same as those
in dramas by other poets: it will be the means of serving them that
differs. But sometimes also, a totally new dramatic function may arise
as a result of insights particularly characteristic of Euripides. The choruses
mostly belong to the first type: the monologues and messenger speeches
to the second.

The truth is, that whereas metaphor has always been a respectable tool
of the creative imagination, other sorts of picture-making have not.
Ever since Aristotle, the metaphor has been hailed as the only true
yardstick of poetic genius. 'This is by far the greatest of devices', he says,
'because it is the only thing which cannot be acquired from anyone else
because it is a sign of genius.'[16] His view, as Stanford has shown, was
echoed by such ancient critics as Cicero and Quintilian, and has provided
the starting point for definitions of metaphor ever since.[17] Metaphor has
provided an important subject of debate in recent literary criticism not
only in its theoretical aspects,[18] but also in the practice of poetic analysis
by the New Critics and others. The use of it in drama has received considerable attention from Shakespearian scholars. To Caroline Spurgeon,
for instance, 'imagery' is synonymous with 'simile and metaphor': to
Prior, metaphor is the very 'apex' of tragic diction: to Fermor and to
Clemen it is an essential means of communicating dramatic meaning
and of enriching a play's texture.[19]

At the risk of oversimplification in what is a highly complex subject,
one might perhaps single out from many, three characteristics which
have won praise for the use of metaphor in drama: its economy, its
originality and its conceptual element. The following lines from the
Agamemnon seem to me to illustrate these qualities in a high degree.
They describe the impact of Helen's arrival in Troy.

πάραυτα δ' ἐλθεῖν ἐς 'Ιλίου πόλιν
λέγοιμ' ἂν φρόνημα μὲν νηνέμου γαλάνας
ἀκασκαιόν (τ') ἄγαλμα πλούτου,
μαλθακὸν ὀμμάτων βέλος,
δηξίθυμον ἔρωτος ἄνθος.
παρακλίνασ' ἐπέκρανεν
δὲ γάμου πικρὰς τελευτάς,
δύσεδρος καὶ δυσόμιλος
συμένα Πριαμίδαισιν
πομπᾶι Διὸς ξενίου,
νυμφόκλαυτος 'Ερινύς.

And that which first came to the city of Ilium
call it a dream of calm
and the wind dying
the loveliness and luxury of much gold,
the melting shafts of the eyes' glances,
the blossom that breaks the heart with longing.
But she turned in mid-step of her course to make
the bitter consummation,
whirling on Priam's people
to blight with her touch and nearness.
Zeus hospitable sent her,
a vengeance to make brides weep.[20]

Helen is logically none of these things, but each metaphor combines both
a sense of what she herself is, and the circumstances which by her agency
will involve vast numbers of people in destruction.[21] The 'dream of
calm' includes a notion both of Helen's artless and unruffled first
appearance at Troy and the subsequent becalming of the Greek fleet at
Aulis. 'The loveliness and luxury of much gold' or 'the gentle ornament
of riches' as one might translate it, is both what she seems to be and what
is appropriate in a city of Eastern opulence. It is elsewhere hinted that
Troy's wealth was instrumental in its fall. Several ideas are contained
also in the metaphors of lines 742 and 743. Helen's glance is both alluring
and destructive. The metaphor of the arrow is heightened by the oxymoron it becomes when taken with μαλθακὸν, 'soft' or 'melting' as this
translator renders it. Helen's relation to Paris is evidence both of the
blossoming flower-like quality of love, and of its power to break the
spirit – the spirit of Paris and of the Trojan people. Throughout, the
ambivalence that beautiful things have the power to destroy is conveyed

through the economic means of metaphor and oxymoron: several ideas are contained within the compass of each short phrase. The metaphors change shape as they go. Visually they do not present a consistent picture: the natural world in fact is violated by a kind of illogic which jumbles together these different images in rapid succession. But it is precisely such inconsistency, such swift metamorphosis, which conveys the many levels of meaning and the far-ranging implications of Helen's presence in Troy.

Metaphor then assumes an imagination which yokes disparate things, which cuts across the natural world by daring analogies which force the mind and eye to leap out of one context into another at speed. It is not consistently perceptual, only consistently conceptual. How can mere pictorialism measure up to this? My purpose is not to show that the qualities of economy, originality and mental dexterity just described do not exist in metaphor, but that *different* ones may exist in certain kinds of descriptive narrative, or that the same ones may exist in another form.

Originality, for instance, is not the province of metaphor alone, although the assumption has sometimes been that all there is left for the metaphorless description to do is to produce an exact copy, a still life, as it were, of some landscape or visual object as if the poet's task were merely to

> arrest the fleeting images that fill
> the mirror of the mind and hold them fast
> And force them sit, till he has pencill'd off
> A faithful likeness of the forms he views.[22]

But the mind of a poet of any stature is seldom a mere mirror: he produces not a retinal impression, but a personal vision which may transform and distort a scene or an object in such a way as to make one seem to see it for the first time. Indeed, if he does not do this he is not much of a poet. 'The genuine artist' as Wallace Stevens has said, 'is never true to life. He sees what is real but not as we are normally aware of it.'[23] This applies as much to imagery which does not consist of simile and metaphor as that which does. Take for instance William Carlos Williams' well known poem *The Red Wheelbarrow*.

> So much depends
> upon
> a red wheel
> barrow
> glazed with rain
> water
> beside the white chickens.[24]

These metaphorless lines force the physical presence of the objects described upon the reader's attention: in this sense the image seems very close to reality, to what is. Yet it is far more economic a picture than most people's vision would allow, and original in the sense that no other poet has chosen to present this subject in these terms before. The opening four words, by arousing in the reader expectations which are not subsequently fulfilled by the ensuing description, give the poem intellectual as well as sensuous content. The image seems superficial but perhaps it is profound. What are our expectations of the things in life upon which so much depends? Do they differ from what follows here? If so, why? Is the poet saying that truth lies not in the abstract, as we might expect, but only in the presence of tangible physical objects? And so on. Descriptive imagery need not be static mirage or extraneous ornament – taken in context, it is capable of providing empirical experience, or proof of the point the poet wishes to communicate. It may be part of both logical exposition and the expression of emotion. In Larkin's poem *Love Songs in Age*, for instance, the description of the faded song sheets has precisely this function.

> One bleached from lying in a sunny place,
> One marked in circles by a vase of water,
> One mended, when a tidy fit had seized her,
> And coloured, by her daughter –
> So they had waited, till in widowhood
> She found them, looking for something else . . .[26]

In order for the last two lines of the stanza to carry full weight, the image must maintain a consistently visual experience, which metaphor would be less likely to achieve. The woman's thoughts which follow in the next stanza are fed in the first instance by a strong impact made on the visual sense.

If the painter in order to communicate his vision may, without using allegorical signs, interpet the colour, light, texture, surface and line of what he sees, forming objects and landscapes into new perspectives of his own, now isolating them, now grouping them against new backgrounds to form new shapes, so surely may the poet, without using metaphor, create for his own purposes images of a consistently perceptual nature. Rembrandt is not a more superficial painter than Leonardo because he did not use allegorical signs. But it is not basically a question of irrevocable choice at all, but of degree. All modes of imagery overlap to some extent and their use is likely to depend on conventions of subject,

form and genre as well as on individual taste. The artist must be familiar
with all modes of his art whatever his own predominant stylistic
inclinations. Euripides uses metaphor, but often seems to prefer not to.
Pindar, that most metaphorically minded of all poets, sometimes writes
purely sensuously when it suits his purpose. His description of the
eruption of Aetna is a case in point.[27] Or the description of Evadne's
baby lying

> in the long grass and wilderness of thicket, his soft body
> deep over in the blue and yellow brightness of violets.

$$\dot{\alpha}\lambda\lambda' \, \dot{\epsilon}\nu$$
$$\kappa\dot{\epsilon}\kappa\rho\upsilon\pi\tau o \, \gamma\dot{\alpha}\rho \, \sigma\chi o\dot{\iota}\nu\omega \, \beta\alpha\tau\iota\hat{q} \, \tau' \dot{\epsilon}\nu \, \dot{\alpha}\pi\epsilon\iota\rho\dot{\iota}\tau\omega,$$
$$\ddot{\iota}\omega\nu \, \xi\alpha\nu\theta\alpha\hat{\iota}\sigma\iota \, \kappa\alpha\dot{\iota} \, \pi\alpha\mu\pi o\rho\phi\dot{\upsilon}\rho o\iota\varsigma \, \dot{\alpha} -$$
$$\kappa\tau\hat{\iota}\sigma\iota \, \beta\epsilon\beta\rho\epsilon\gamma\mu\dot{\epsilon}\nu o\varsigma \, \dot{\alpha}\beta\rho\dot{o}\nu$$
$$\sigma\hat{\omega}\mu\alpha.[28]$$

The delicate tenderness of the child's body suggested by ἁβρὸν 'soft', is
enhanced by the epithet ἀπειρίτῳ 'boundless' (not rendered by the
translator), which makes the undergrowth in which he is hidden and to
which the epithet is applied, seem to go on for ever. The combination
of emphatic colour epithets, 'blue and yellow brightness' as the translator renders ξανθαῖσι καὶ παμπορφύροις, concentrates all attention on
the small patch of flowers where he is lying. Adjectives, like these, an
accepted part of the lyric poets' equipment, are very important to the
development of the pictorial image in drama particularly in Euripides;
for he borrowed from Pindar many of those which expressed most
strongly the sensuous qualities of objects, their colour, or the light
reflected from their surfaces.[29] He rearranges what he inherits as common stock of the lyric tradition, and invents, by analogy with the old,
new decorative compounds, using them to pinpoint aspects of landscape and scene hitherto unnoticed or differently described.[30] One
could almost say that in Euripides' handling of this one small syntactical
item, are revealed the extremes of his visual horizons, at least in the
direction of the rather decorative style which these epithets presuppose.

In a description of the python coiled among the laurel leaves at
Delphi, for instance, which forms part of an ode of praise sung to
Apollo at the end of the *Iphigenia in Tauris*, the poet achieves in one
brief image by means of such adjectives, the intricate play of light and
shadow upon bright colour.

ὅθι ποικιλόνωτος οἰ-
νωπὸς δράκων,
σκιερᾷ κατάχαλκος εὐ-
φύλλῳ δάφνᾳ,
γᾶς πελώριον τέρας, ἄμφεπε μαντεῖ-
ον Χθόνιον.

And there as a monstrous portent guarding Earth's oracle was a snake. Its back was flecked and its head was deep red and its bronze scales glistened among the shadowy laurel leaves.[31]

Here the effect is of the sun filtering through the leaves in patches of concentrated brightness, making the bronze scales on the serpent's red colour and spotted skin gleam as they intermittently catch the light. The placing of κατάχαλκος 'bronze-covered', between σκιερᾷ 'shadowy' and εὐφύλλῳ 'leafy', exploits contrast of shadow and light, and implies also a further one in the hardness of the scales against the soft leaves. The motif and some of the language is Pindar's,[32] but the disposition of the several epithets, each one of which takes colour from its opposition to another is entirely Euripidean. Interlocking word order and the concentration of visual impression in the compounds which are alone capable of giving two pictures for the price of one, are the essential qualities here. Both, unfortunately, are almost impossible to do justice to in English.

Euripides' adoption of Pindaric compound epithets and the invention of many more by analogy, reveals a new sensitivity to effects of colour and light. Where Pindar tends to use one adjective epideictically to single out and isolate an object so that it dominates its setting, Euripides, as in this passage and many others, clusters his adjectives, so that a final unified impression arises only after a synthesis of diverse or contrasted effects.[33] A coloured or bright object is seen not in isolation, but as it is conditioned by other colours or degrees of light with which it comes into contact. An object does not dominate its setting, but is defined by it. The visual horizons suggested by Euripides' use of adjectives which express carefully calculated gradations of colour and brightness, including words to convey elaborate flecked and dappled effects which no poet before him had used in such profusion,[34] are commensurate with those of the shadow painter who was in the last quarter of the fifth century discovering new ways of rendering perspective and light reflection by means of an extended range of juxtaposed and overlaid colours. In the words of Pliny, 'at last the true art of painting made itself felt, and discovered light and shadow through the differentiation of colours which threw each other into relief, by their alternating juxta-position.'[35] And if it is objected that painting has always done this, it should be said that Pliny is thinking here not of the old four primary colours, but of new shades and new techniques of application in flecks and splashes of paint which involve obliteration of pure outline. There are passages in Euripides' later plays which show a similar concern with communicating the effects of light reflection, and colours which change according to the strength of light acting upon them. Not unlike the description of the python curled under the laurel bush, is the one from the new *Oedipus* fragment where the Sphinx is sunning itself in a tree.[36] Like the python, she is half in and half out of the sun where the leaves cast shade. Her tail is tucked underneath her lion paws, and her back 'shines gold as her wing catches the light, but turns deep blue in the shadow of a cloud.'

ὅταν μεθῇ τε]προσβάλῃ τ' αὐγαῖς πτερόν·
εἰ μὲν πρὸς ἵπ]πους ἡλίου χρυσωπὸν ἧ[ν
νώτισμα θη]ρός· εἰ δὲ [πρ]ὸς νέφος βά[λοι
κυανωπὸν. ὥ]ς τις ἶρι[ς ἂν]τηύγει σ[έλας

The whole effect is 'like the sombre splendour of a rainbow'. This almost technical preoccupation with the relative and changing effects of light comes out in many Euripidean descriptions, of many different subjects – the gleam of blood on a gold necklace, the glare of fire in the darkness, the sun's reflection in a crocus-petal, the shine in a bull's eyes.[37]

These are small examples of a decorative kind taken out of context, but characteristic of them and of more extended descriptions one could cite, is a certain visual consistency lacking in the simile or metaphor. Such descriptions communicate themselves slowly, building up per-ceptually consistent details to create a total impression rather than relying upon the one incisive word which reveals a momentary insight before moving on to the next.

At this point it becomes meaningless to talk out of context, for the pace at which an image is assimilated must relate to the context which encloses it. Any study of Euripides' imagery therefore, must be con-sidered in the light of tragedy where conditions and requirements are obviously very different from that of lyric poetry. There may be occasions, for instance, when the high decorative style is appropriate in itself, as in the ornate 'dithyrambic' choruses of a light-hearted play like

the *Helen*. But it would be a strange sort of tragedy that could tolerate
an unrelieved diet of the sort of pictorial decoration just discussed. It is
more likely that decoration itself might be called upon to serve an ironic
effect rather than a merely beautifying one, as when the notorious
Pasiphae, in a fragment from the *Cretans*, sarcastically describing the
bull as if he were a human lover, evokes a fleeting image of beauty blown
into the air like a bubble to burst against the hard absurdities of the real
truth. In effect she says:

> Do you think I was mesmerised by his beautiful clothes, by the
> light that shone so brilliantly from his eyes and flaming red hair
> that it cast wine dark shadows upon his cheek ?[38]

> ὡς εὐπρεπὴς μὲν ἐν πέπλοισιν ἦν ἰδεῖν,
> πυρσῆς δὲ χαίτης καὶ παρ᾽ ὀμμάτων σέλας
> οἰνωπὸν ἐξέλαμπε περ[κάι]νων γένυν;

Here the decorative style makes more forceful her technique of
'reductio ad absurdum'. Even in this form, however, decorative effects
are not the only kind of images appropriate to the range of content and
seriousness of tragedy. One would expect, and indeed it is so, that the
sensitivity to sensuous detail so apparent in the passages just discussed,
might also show itself in the description of subject matter most appropriate to tragedy, in the deeds of horror messengers relate, or in the
squalid appearance to which heroes are reduced by the force of their
tragic circumstances. The beauty of some of Leonardo's portraits is in
sharp contrast to the savagery of his caricatures, but both are the product
of a common acuteness of observation. Euripides' sharpness of eye led
him to introduce into tragedy more than the sunlit world of Pindar's
lyrics, although this has its place. From Pindar he borrowed pictorial
language and transformed it. From Aeschylus he borrowed subjects and
transformed them by a treatment more appropriate to his own genius.
The essential difference between the two dramatists' stylistic character
may be illustrated by a chorus each wrote on the destruction of Troy and
how it fell through Zeus' agency. Their theme and aim is similar enough
to invite comparison since they both cast the ode in the form of a prayer
to Zeus, and they both use imagery to convey the enormity of the act of
destruction.

> ὦ Ζεῦ βασιλεῦ καὶ Νὺξ φιλία,
> μεγάλων κόσμων κτεάτειρα,

ἤτ᾽ ἐπὶ Τροίας πύργοις ἔβαλες
στεγανὸν δίκτυον, ὡς μήτε μέγαν
μήτ᾽ οὖν νεαρῶν τιν᾽ ὑπερτελέσαι
μέγα δουλείας
γάγγαμον, ἄτης παναλώτου.
Δία τοι ξένιον μέγαν αἰδοῦμαι
τὸν τάδε πράξαντ᾽, ἐπ᾽ Ἀλεξάνδρωι
τείνοντα πάλαι τόξον, ὅπως ἂν
μήτε πρὸ καιροῦ μήθ᾽ ὑπὲρ ἄστρων
βέλος ἠλίθιον σκήψειεν.

O Zeus our lord and Night beloved,
bestower of power and beauty,
you slung above the bastions of Troy
the binding net, that none, neither great
nor young, might outleap
the gigantic toils
of enslavement and final disaster.
I gaze in awe on Zeus of the guests
who wrung from Alexander such payment.
He bent the bow with slow care, that neither
the shaft might kindle the stars, nor fall
spent to the earth, short driven.[39]

Aeschylus is thinking of the event in terms of immediate symbols.
The metaphors of the net and the bow demonstrate abstract things such
as power, unerring aim and the inextricable predicament of the Trojans.
There is no visual relation between these objects, or between them and
what they illustrate. What is common is their function and the function
of Zeus as powerful destroyer. The rapidly changing images convey his
immediate mastery of the city, but they also have implications beyond
this immediate context since the net is an image which Aeschylus uses
repeatedly elsewhere in the play, for the pressures of power.

Euripides approaches his similar theme in the *Trojan Women* quite
differently. He makes one consistently see Troy and its environs in order
to enhance the magnitude of its capture.

οὕτω δὴ τὸν ἐν Ἰλίῳ
ναὸν καὶ θυόεντα βω-
μὸν προύδωκας Ἀχαιοῖς,
ὦ Ζεῦ, καὶ πελάνων φλόγα

σμύρνης αἰθερίας τε κα-
πνὸν καὶ Πέργαμον ἱερὰν
'Ιδαῖά τ' 'Ιδαῖα κισσοφόρα νάπη
χιόνι κατάρυτα ποταμίᾳ
τέρμονα πρωτόβολόν θ' ἁλίῳ,
τὰν καταλαμπομέναν ζαθέαν θεράπναν.
φροῦδαί σοι θυσίαι χορῶν τ'
εὔφημοι κέλαδοι κατ' ὄρ-
φναν τε παννυχίδες θεῶν,
χρυσέων τε ξοάνων τύποι
Φρυγῶν τε ζάθεοι σελᾶ-
ναι συνδώδεκα πλήθει.
μέλει μέλει μοι τάδ' εἰ φρονεῖς, ἄναξ,
οὐράνιον ἕδρανον ἐπιβεβὼς
αἰθέρα τε πτόλεως ὀλομένας,
ἂν πυρὸς αἰθομένα κατέλυσεν ὁρμά.

Thus O Zeus, you betrayed all
to the Achaeans: your temple
in Ilium; your misted altar,
the flame of clotted sacraments,
the smoke of the skying incense
Pergamum the hallowed,
the ivied ravines of Ida, washed
by the running snow. The utter
peaks that surprise the sun bolts,
shining and primeval place of divinity.
Gone are your sacrifices, the choirs'
glad voices singing to thc Gods
night long, deep into darkness;
gone the images gold on wood
laid, the twelves of the sacred moons,
the magic Phrygian number.
Can it be my lord you have forgotten
from your throne high in heaven's
bright air, my city which is ruined
and the flame storm that broke it ?[40]

Strophe and *antistrophe* form a visually compatible whole, which is given
shape by a series of contrasts, linked by a common theme, of sacred
places and sacrifices. The cold green ivy glades of Mount Ida whose

rivers run with snow and glisten in the light of the morning sun, are set against the implied warmth of altar flames and the smoke of rising incense. The morning scene is followed by a night one: songs and dances sound in the darkness and the gleam of gold statues is defined against it. The chorus' imagination of these things contrasts with their absence in 'reality'. This is how things were, but Zeus has betrayed the city. The passage is also full of an irony quite lacking in Aeschylus' treatment. The tone is set by the laconic οὕτω δὴ 'So then . . .' in the first line. By beginning with Mount Ida which is sacred to Zeus, and with a scene of devout worship, Euripides makes Zeus' act of destruction positively blasphemous. He has reversed the usual situation of human misbehaviour towards the Gods: this is divine impiety to man. The strong emotions of anger and bitter regret in these lines come from the tension between the suppressed force of their comment to Zeus (contained in the one strong verb προύδωκας 'you have betrayed . . .' on which the whole of the *strophe* depends, and in the phrase μέλει μοι . . . εἰ φρονεῖς 'it concerns me whether you care' in the last lines of the *antistrophe*) and the extended detail of the imagery (particularly as brought out in the compound epithets) which indirectly reveals the strength of their feelings for Troy. They never once say 'how awful that this happened': they say 'the city was like this; you destroyed it'. It is left to the audience to ask the question, Why? It is a question central to the whole play, and it is the strength of the imagery which makes them ask it.

Euripides' pictorial language differs in kind from that of Aeschylus and must be judged on its own terms. The difficulty, as with all imagery, is in finding an adequate way of classifying the traits and uses of such a style. It has usually been the practice in studies of imagery either to list the content areas of the image, a process which leads back to the poet's own personal predilections almost before he puts pen to paper, or to group images round certain basic ideas the poet is trying to get across.[41] Both methods seem to me to have serious limitations. The first puts undue weight on the personality of the poet, as distinct from the stylistic means he uses to serve dramatic ends. The second begins from a set of abstract ideas which are in themselves undramatic, and again ignores the particular context which must present them.

It may be that one could trace the frequency of sea images, or similes and metaphors taken from painting, for instance, to certain biographical traditions relating to Euripides' own life.[42] It is certainly appropriate that a man who spent so much time looking out on the waters of Salamis bay should reveal such sensitivity to the changing lights and movements on the sea surface. No other ancient poet describes the sea with such fine perceptions of shade as is shown, for example, in a line from the *Helen*, where the grey-blue sea swell is set against the white surface foam of the waves with their darker blue underneath.

γλαυκὸν ἔπιτ᾽ οἶδμα κυανόχροά τε κυμάτων
ῥόθια πολιὰ θαλάσσας. . .

Cross close on the green swell and the dark skinned back of the rollers and the grey splash of the breaking sea . . .[43]

It may also be that the many similes and metaphors drawn from the visual arts[44] reflect the well known tradition that Euripides began painting seriously, before he finally turned to the writing of tragedy; although it has always seemed to me that scholars could have better supported this thesis not by drawing attention to his metaphors and similes, but by analysing some of the passages where he shows an almost technical pre-occupation with textured surfaces and the effects of light on colour.

These things are an important clue to understanding some of the areas in which Euripides' imagination finds expression. But in themselves they are inadequate to understanding the way he works as a dramatist. The business seems more complex than that, for quite apart from a poet's unconscious likes and dislikes, and the influence of his own personal environment, there are more conscious and formal elements which must work upon his choice of image at any given moment. Among these is obviously the particular context of the play in question; another is the part of the play in which he wishes to use the imagery. And here comes an important distinction between simile and metaphor and descriptive imagery. Whereas the short metaphor, for instance, is ubiquitous – equally at home in any part of the drama – pictorial description is more likely to vary with mode. The compound epithet, for instance, is most appropriate in lyric sections; images which proceed in ordered chronological sequence are unnecessary and even unlikely in lyric, but imperative in the messenger speech. Pictorial descriptions of place are more appropriate for instance in the *parodos* which must set the scene, than in the *agon* which consists of intellectual verbal debate.

For these reasons, and because the sense of formal division of mode is so strong in Euripides, I have decided to use it as a convenient means by which to explore more fully the working of Euripides' imagery as it serves his dramatic purpose. This is not to imply that there is no relation between the parts. However much the style may vary formally between them, the source of it remains the same, and the total context overrides, or should, all the separate means which serve it. Imagination at its deepest level means unity and integration, and the ultimate question must be how far Euripides, in his tragedies, achieved this. But it is an ultimate and not a first question.

Chapter II

The Choral Odes: Imagery of Place

The choral odes seem a natural enough place to begin in any study of tragic imagery. It is here that the lyric imagination can work unimpeded by the same limits of time and space which restrict the immediate on-stage action. Where the actors must forward the action in strict accordance with the urgency of present events, the chorus from their detached position in the orchestra can revel in a freer and more leisured imagination, moving in thought backwards and forwards through space and time, recalling past events and far-off scenes, seeing into the future, wishing for a present that is different, and showing the relevance of the times and places they recall to the situation at hand.[1] Their songs give to the drama a three-dimensional quality which is beyond the range of iambic dialogue. They are not bound by the sharp logic characteristic of the set debate, nor the chronological order necessary to the messenger's narrative.[2] Much of the language, inherited as it was from lyric poetry, was rooted in a tradition of great pictorial richness, and the variety of metres conducive to representing a wide range of different moods. The choruses of Aeschylus are proof of the imaginative possibilities such a mode offered in the hands of a great poet.

Sophocles on the other hand reduced the choral role. His odes are shorter, narrower in range, and one finds in them firmly directed moral comments rather than sweeping panoramic visions. Quotable moral precepts such as 'Insolence breeds the tyrant', 'Envy stalks men of wealth and power', 'How are the generations of men like those who have never been born at all', may contain metaphorical elements, but it is not primarily the visual qualities in them which are developed.[3] Such sensuous elements as there are in his expression, are not always developed so extensively that they last the length of several *strophes* or a whole ode. As Sophocles handles them in context they may be called imaginative in the sense of being dramatically integral, but not in the more specific pictorial sense.

Euripides, like Aeschylus, had an eye for the panoramic scene, but unlike him, did not rely upon metaphor to anything like the same extent to conjure it up. Like Sophocles, he occasionally attributes to his chorus extended moral disquisitions, but these are often trite – 'pieces of pavement philosophy' as Kitto puts it –[4] and they do not represent the whole or even the essence of his choral writing. This is to be found elsewhere, in the extended descriptive imagery which serves instead of the developed philosophical or moral comment. Euripides was by no means committed to the idea of a neutral chorus who would offer detached criticisms of the human scene, and in those plays where the chorus are protagonist, and therefore subjectively involved in the main action, the language of visual description presents their own common experience with no pretence of philosophic detachment.[5] The horror of Troy's desolation, or the miracle of Bacchic ecstasy, comes over from the women in terms of their own direct and concrete experience as if they have observed it in an accumulation of small sensuous details: the smear of smoke stains on the city walls, the trace of blood on a stone floor, the long hair of a dancer streaming in the wind, milk and honey oozing from the ground.[6] 'Reality' is as it is established through the physical presence of concrete things and the selection itself of those things acts as implicit comment. Even where the chorus are not protagonists, imagery often does the work of explicit and abstract assessment of a situation. The chorus' vision of a white-sailed boat cutting across the Cretan straits, for instance, is a way of reminding the audience of the significance of Phaedra's Cretan ancestry, that heredity must count for something in the weighing of her responsibility.[7] The image of Death in the *Alcestis* as an old man steering his boat across Acheron, is a way of emphasising in pictorial terms the finality, as the chorus think, of Alcestis' death, condemnation of Admetus for acquiescing in it, and an estimation of Alcestis' worth which is to be wrung from even as grim a figure as this.[8]

Because Euripides did not go in much for the darting metaphor with its quicksilver shifts of view, his choral imagery is more consistently extended than that of either Aeschylus or Sophocles. He had an eye for seeing scenes whole, and the landscapes and fantasy worlds which make up so much of his pictorial imagination derive their strength and conviction from the accumulation of visual detail slowly built up. Setting is a clue to understanding a particular event or action, and imagery of place perhaps assumes the importance it does in his dramas because, more than any other ancient poet, he grasped and explored the significance of environment as an operating factor in human behaviour.[9] Even in the smallest details, and in lyrics of an apparently decorative kind, it is from the described surroundings that one can judge the way in which an action is to be interpreted. These establish the precise shade of tone and mood. Two small examples may serve to illustrate this. In the *Alcestis*, the chorus refer to Apollo's temporary spell of service as a shepherd on Admetus' estate.

δοχμιᾶν διὰ κλιτύων
βοσκήμασι σοῖσι συρίζων
    ποιμνίτας ὑμεναίους.
σὺν δ' ἐποιμαίνοντο χαρᾷ μελέων βαλιαί τε
    λύγκες,
ἔβα δὲ λιποῦσ' Ὄθρυος νάπαν λεόντων
    ἁ δαφοινὸς ἴλα·
χόρευσε δ' ἀμφὶ σὰν κιθάραν,
    Φοῖβε, ποικιλόθριξ
νεβρὸς ὑψικόμων πέραν
βαίνουσ' ἐλατᾶν σφυρῷ κούφῳ,
    χαίρουσ' εὔφρονι μολπᾷ.

Apollo led your sheep over the slanting hilltops playing pastoral wedding songs to them on his pipes. Charmed by your music, spotted lynxes began to graze in the fields, and groups of tawny lions left their mountain forests; the speckled fawn skipped daintily from beyond the high-crowned fir trees, and she too danced to your lyre, Apollo.[10]

The mood of light-heartedness on this Orpheus-like occasion comes from the sense of movement in the natural scene. Animals leave their old surroundings to form a new one. Even were the direct words for happiness lacking, the prominence of dancing, in the image of the nimble fawn and in the position of χόρευσε and the effect of luxurious leisure which three-dimensional epithets of colour produce (δαφοινὸς, ποικιλόθριξ, βαλιαί) and two visually evocative adjectives for the surrounding landscape (δοχμιᾶν and ὑψικόμων), would make it difficult to judge this scene a gloomy one. All the descriptive terms are pitched at the same decorative level; that is, there is nothing jarring or discrepant to induce a feeling of irony or criticism. Contrast another pastoral scene graced by Gods, this time in the *Andromache*, where the chorus are describing the Judgement of Paris.[11] The goddesses are their usual decorative selves, their hands linked prettily so that they look like 'fillies in a beautiful chariot yoke'. Their bodies glisten as they bathe

naked in a mountain stream. In this respect, the presentation is traditionally ornamental.[12] But undermining it are other details of setting less
conventional. The goddesses meet Paris at a lonely cattle station where
he has been living in isolation from human habitation. The words used
to describe this go beyond the usual casual reference to Paris as a herdsman. This place he has had to make his home (ἑστιοῦχον αὐλάν reinforces
σταθμοὺς ἐπὶ βούτα) and its air of lonely desolation is stressed in the
adjective ἔρημον 'deserted' and the rare compound μονότροπον 'solitary
in his ways' which shows how unused to visitors Paris is.[13] The contrast
here in the level of setting casts the traditional scene in an ironic light,
producing some sympathy for Paris in his hovel and a reinforcement of
the theme cue for the ode which is the machinations of vicious women.[14]

The picturing of events as defined in certain ways by their total
physical setting, exposed the poet to greater risks of irrelevance than if
he were to focus on the single isolated act, or change style in mid-course
and pull everything together with a neat pithy maxim. Since each detail
had its place in the architecture of the whole, the irrelevance of one
would imply the irrelevance of all. To take an example. If any part of the
chorus' lengthy description of Athens in the *Medea* is beside the point,
then it all is, because *strophe* and *antistrophe* form one coherent image.[15]
The classic case of pictorial irrelevance is in the *Electra* where the chorus
describe in highly colourful language the Nereids with Achilles'
armour.[16] Another possible case is the very long *parodos* of the *Iphigeneia
in Aulis*.[17] Both these display-pieces are characteristic of Euripides' lyric
style at its most decorative. The sensuous attributes are given full play in
the curving motion of a dolphin round a blue ship,[18] a painted sun shining
in the middle of a round shield,[19] dancing groups of stars, or the interlocking patterns of colour made by four horses in a chariot yoke.[20]
Careful positioning of words indicates objects perceived in a spatial
relation, as in the description of Protesilaus and Palamedes sitting with a
draught set between them,[21] or in the alternately juxtaposed compound
epithets applied to Eumelus' horses. The visual idiom is reminiscent of
certain treatments of similar themes in art such as the figures squatting
over draughts in the famous Exekias *amphora*, the Nereids riding over
the sea with Achilles' armour on a white lekythos by the Eretria painter,
or the personified stars who adorn the Blacas krater.[22] But for all their
pictorial vivacity, these odes, in particular the Electra one, are hardly
justified in terms of dramatic integration. Achilles and his saga have
little to do with Electra's household, either for the purpose of parallel
illustration or ironic contrast. In the *Iphigeneia in Aulis*, the Greek camp

at Aulis is relevant, in the sense that this is the location of the stage set, but many of the figures the chorus describe, such as Protesilaus, Palamedes, Diomedes and the Ajaxes, have no importance as characters in the plot. In short, the test of choral imagery must be whether it is organic. There are patently some instances in Euripides' plays where it is not,[23] but there are more where the texture of the play is enriched by the power of imagery integrally conceived, to evoke mood and underline main themes by intensification or contrast or both.

Imagery of place has an important part to play in the *parodos*, where the chorus must set the scene and prepare for the coming action. Scene setting is necessary as motivation for their entrance into the *proscenium*, and probably in the absence of elaborate scene painting.[24] The austere façade of a building which could be converted according to play, as a palace, hut, temple or cave did not give much clue beyond its own immediate presence. Scene painting even at the end of the fifth century was still somewhat crude, and what visual details there might have been in the set itself, or on panels fixed to it, were likely to have been missed by people sitting beyond the first few rows. For this reason and as explanation for their arrival, Euripides frequently made his chorus place themselves in an immediate environment created verbally by them as they took their places in the empty orchestra, which would of course itself be devoid of scenery. In spite of Grube's assertion that Euripidean *parodoi* usually complete the prologue rather than anticipate what is to come, there are examples other than the exceptions he quotes, where they perform the double function of completed explanation and anticipating by contrast.[25] Three examples where descriptive imagery is differently deployed may serve to show this, the first from the *Helen*.

κυανοειδὲς ἀμφ' ὕδωρ
ἔτυχον ἕλικά τ' ἀνὰ χλόαν
φοίνικας ἁλίου πέπλους
αὐγαῖσιν ἐν χρυσέαις
ἀμφὶ δόνακος ἔρνεσιν
θάλπουσα· ⟨ποτνίας δ' ἐμᾶς,⟩
ἔνθεν οἰκτρὸν ἀνεβόασεν,
ὅμαδον ἔκλυον,

I was down by the shining blue
water, and on the curl of the grass
there in the golden glare of the sun
laid out the coloured wash

3

in the bed of young rushes
to dry. There I heard my lady
and the pitiful sound as she cried out . . .²⁶

These few graphic lines establish the chorus' identity as servants of
Helen and prepare by contrast for what is to come. The ornamental
style describing a tranquil everyday occupation sets up a norm which is
then disturbed by Helen's cry of distress. The new theme is marked by an
abrupt change of pace, rhythm and style at 185–6. The same motif is
used more austerely in the earlier *Hippolytus* as is appropriate for a more
serious play.²⁷ The extraordinary delirium of Phaedra is enhanced by a
preceding image of calm normality. In the *strophe*, the chorus describe
a sunny seashore where they do the washing, and in the *antistrophe* they
depict Phaedra idle, closeted inside the house and muffled up in covers.
The simple physical contrast of θερμᾶς. . . πέτρας εὐαλίου 'warm
sunny rock' in the *strophe*, and κεφαλὰν σκιάζειν 'shadows' or 'veils her
head' in the *antistrophe*, suggests a number of more abstract comparisons
between the life of the average and the eccentric, the hard working and
the leisured rich, the carefree and the careworn. The problem of Phaedra's uncharacteristic love, and the nourishing of it by circumstance are
hinted at in her own speech to the women of Troizen, and the chorus
here prepare for it by the juxtaposition of their own familiar environment to hers.²⁸

Description of place occupies the whole *parodos* of the *Ion*, where a
group of Athenian women who are sight-seeing at Delphi come face to
face with Apollo's temple for the first time.²⁹ They express amazement
that the themes they see on its sculptured *metopes* are already familiar to
them. In language reminiscent of Pindar, they first allude to the two
pediments which shine out on the building with the brightness of eyes on
a face,³⁰ and then go on to the series of sculptured mythical themes.
Heracles' killing of the Lernaean hydra while Iolaus holds up a torch to
give him light, is a subject they themselves have embroidered on the
peplos woven for the Panathenaeic festival at Athens. Athena herself they
recognise as a familiar sight ἐμὰν θεόν 'my goddess'. The style of this
precinct-viewing is different in character from the elaborate imagery of
the *Iphigeneia in Aulis* or *Helen parodos*. Few visual details are supplied
and these take the form of conventional and uninspiring adjectives. The
scythe Heracles kills the hydra with is 'gold', the torch of Iolaus is 'flaming',
πυρίφλεκτον, Athena's shield is embossed with a flashing Gorgon's
head γοργωπὸν, Zeus' thunderbolt is on fire at both ends, ἀμφίπυρον.

On the other hand direct words for seeing (there are nine in the space of thirty-six lines) make up for the lack of more precise description. There may be several reasons for this somewhat pedestrian presentation of one of the great cultural sites of Greece. First, the one the chorus themselves suggest. Since most of the themes must have been familiar to them from other buildings or paintings in Athens,[31] and presumably to the audience as well, all that is needed here is a prompting of the visual memory, and the poet does this through a familiar pictorial shorthand consisting of theme and brief distinguishing description. In this way he neatly stresses both the chorus' identity as Athenians, and their wonderment at seeing Delphi. It is not clear how much temple decoration, indeed if any, was visible to the audience through scene-painting; in any case, introducing them to the temple is not the point here. They have already heard Ion's monody in the preceding scene, and the set would have been visible to them from the start. The purpose of introducing the chorus in this way is to make a contrast with Ion's preceding aria, and thereby enhance his own role which departs from this norm. The chorus are the measure of difference between inner experience of service in Apollo's temple, as Ion's monody reveals it, and the judgement of outsiders which must necessarily be cursory and superficial. (It is tempting to see deeper significance in the Athenians' disarming remark about the temple, 'We won't go inside, we are happy enough to look at the outside.') The chorus are ordinary people to whom Ion's youthful idealism, like Phaedra's excessive love, would seem strange. In both cases the special mood appropriate to the solo role is heightened by comparison with the chorus, and in both cases it is done through the women's description of places.

The function of descriptive language in the *Phaethon parodos*, the third example, is similar, although the means of presentation again differ. Here the scene the women evoke is a romantic idealised one which bears no relation to a particular place.

> μέλπει δ' ἐν δένδρεσι λεπτὰν
> ἀηδὼν ἁρμονίαν
> ὀρθρευομένα γόοις
> "Ιτυν "Ιτυν πολύθρηνον.
> σύριγγας δ' οὐριβάται
> κινοῦσιν ποίμναις ἐλάται·
> ἔγρονται δ' εἰς βοτάναν
> ξανθᾶν πώλων συζυγίαι.

ἤδη δ᾽ εἰς ἔργα κυναγοὶ
στείχουσιν θηροφόνοι,
παγαῖς τ᾽ ἐπ᾽ Ὠκεανοῦ
μελιβόας κύκνος ἀχεῖ.
ἄκατοι δ᾽ ἀνάγονται ὑπ᾽ εἰρεσίας
ἀνέμων τ᾽ εὐαέσσιν ῥοθίοις
ἀνὰ δ᾽ ἱστία . . . .
. . . .
. . . .
. . . .
. . . .
σινδὼν δὲ πρότονον ἐπὶ μέσον πελάζει.
τὰ μὲν οὖν ἑτέροισι μέριμνα πέλει·
κόσμον δ᾽ ὑμεναίων δεσποσύνων
ἐμὲ καὶ τὸ δίκαιον ἄγει καὶ ἔρως
ὑμνεῖν·

A nightingale is singing her shrill symphony in the trees, awake in the early dawn to lament over and over again in grief for Itys. . . . The mountain firs make whispering music for the flocks. Bay horses are yoked and put out to grass: huntsmen are already on the track of their quarry: the swan sings its sweet notes by the water's edge; boats are lashed on by oars as a fair wind foams the sea, and up along the canvas . . . and the sail is brought close to the centre of the forestay. Worries belong to other people. Love and a sense of what is right are making me sing a song to compliment Phaethon's wedding.[32]

It is nouns and verbs here in a series of parallel structures[33] which conjure up associations of morning energy and cheerfulness. There is nothing unusual about any of them although the combination is perhaps Euripides' own. The passage has been praised for the rare delicacy of its feeling for nature,[34] although taken in the total context its effect must be ironic, for while the chorus are revelling in this mood of happiness which they think appropriate for Phaethon's wedding to Aphrodite, he himself is wretchedly miserable at the thought of a marriage which his father has arranged for him against his will.[35] Once again, lyric imagery is adapted to a long-term purpose as well as to the job of creating immediate mood.

Since the *parodoi* come early in the play as a rule, imagery there is not retrospective, but defines the present context. The *stasima* or main choral odes on the other hand, look both forwards and backwards, and a greater complexity of texture characterises the imagery in them. The chorus are free to stray in imagination beyond the locale of the set itself, and beyond the restrictions of present time, in their search for material which will illuminate the tragic situation facing them.

Although the range of the odes in subject, length, style and metre is so great as to make any rigid categorization impossible, it is true that those of a descriptive nature often derive their main dramatic strength from visual associations of place. In the *Ion* for instance, the chorus pay tribute to the various haunts of the Gods, from the ridges of Parnassus traversed by the Dionysian votary to the rocky grottoes of Pan.[36] In the *Helen*, the story of Demeter is told through the vivid visual evocation of the stages of her journey over the earth in search of her daughter.[37] In the *Hecuba*, the Trojan captives indulge their imaginations by wondering what Athens and the Greek islands will look like.[38] The description of some well-known places is almost formulaic, although the use of them is not. Sparta for instance is commonly characterised by the river Eurotas, 'green with reeds',[39] Athens by the Pindaric epithet 'shining', and the presence of the grey-green olive.[40] Delos is graced by the fanning date palm and the laurel.[41] Such associations are worked into the fabric of the play to express moods of reverence, nostalgia, hope or resignation, and to provide necessary background to present events. Broadly speaking, their organic justification is of two kinds, further amplification of the present scene, and relief or contrast from it.[42] Intensification is achieved in the first case by preserving the emotional rhythm of the play unbroken, and in the second by a deliberate break which acts in much the same way as a Homeric simile, which momentarily leaves the scene of battle only to return to it from a different focusing perspective.

Three plays in their evocation of place, illustrate organic imagery of the first kind particularly clearly. In the *Iphigeneia in Tauris* descriptions of the sea provide a recurring visual focus for the main action, in the *Troades* the city of Troy, and in the *Bacchae* the mountains where Dionysian revels take place.

In the *Iphigeneia in Tauris*, it is by the sea, just off-stage, that all the most important events of the play (except the recognition scene) take place. Orestes and Pylades arrive by sea. The ritual of purifying the statue is to take place in the sea: the final escape is launched from there. It assumes a natural prominence therefore in the accounts of the main characters, who, as if to compensate for what the audience cannot directly see, describe it in colourful lively terms. Pylades characterises the place where he and Orestes hid by the point at which the 'sea washes into the caves in a black stream'. The herdsman too spends four lines describing the hollow cut-away of the cliff-line where the foaming breakers rush into the caves. And as he gives an account of the fight his men had with Orestes and Pylades in the water he draws a picture of the sea 'blossoming red with blood'.[43]

In the context then of the stage-setting, and as the place where much of the action goes on, it is natural that the chorus should in their lyric odes turn their thoughts to the sea. It is not only the means by which strangers like Orestes land on their shores, it also keeps them captive. The sea is the boundary of their physical horizon in Tauris, and the prominence the chorus give to it suggests that it is a controlling force in their lives. Their very first words define this existence.

> εὐφαμεῖτ' ὦ
> πόντου δισσὰς συγχωρούσας
> πέτρας 'Αξείνου ναίοντες.

All those who live in the shadow of the clashing rocks set in an unfriendly Sea, sing words of good omen.[44]

Iphigeneia in reply takes up this theme:

> νῦν δ' ἀξείνου πόντου ξείνα
> δυσχόρτους οἴκους ναίω,
> ἄγαμος ἄτεκνος ἄπολις ἄφιλος.

I am the stranger whose home in this inhospitable place is next to the unfriendly sea. I am husbandless, childless, friendless and a citizen of nowhere.[45]

The dangerous Symplegades ensure that few travellers get through, and escape is almost impossible for these marooned Greek women.

'O dark, dark blue highways of the sea' are the opening lines of the first *stasimon*, as the chorus imaginatively develop their vision of the sea as a continuous blue pathway, stretching from the green river Eurotas in Sparta, their own home, to the pillared temple in Tauris where blood runs down the altars.[46] This is a pathway traversed by Orestes and his men, and the chorus are thus led from this colourful opening image to construct in their imagination the voyage these strangers have made.

> ἢ ῥοθίοις εἰλατίνας
> δικρότοισι κώπας ἔπλευ-
> σαν ἐπὶ πόντια κύματα, νά-
> ιον ὄχημα λινοπόροις αὔραις,
>
> . . . . .
>
> πῶς πέτρας τὰς συνδρομάδας,
> πῶς Φινεϊδᾶν ἀΰ-
> πνους ἀκτὰς ἐπέρασαν
> παρ' ἄλιον
> αἰγιαλὸν ἐπ' Ἀμφιτρί-
> τας ῥοθίῳ δραμόντες,
> ὅπου πεντήκοντα κορᾶν
> Νηρῄδων . . . . χοροὶ
> μέλπουσιν ἐγκύκλιοι,
> πλησιστίοισι πνοαῖς
> συριζόντων κατὰ πρύμναν
> εὐναίων πηδαλίων
> αὔραις ⟨σὺν⟩ νοτίαις
> ἢ πνεύμασι Ζεφύρου,
> τὰν πολυόρνιθον ἐπ' αἶ-
> αν, λευκὰν ἀκτάν, Ἀχιλῆ-
> ος δρόμους καλλισταδίους,
> ἄξεινον κατὰ πόντον;

Did they sail their pine ships, with double rutted wake of foam across the surging waves, their vessels set in motion by the wind on the canvas? ... How did they come through the clashing rocks and how through the unsleeping coast of Phineus as they rushed through the sea-spray by the pebble beach of Amphitrite where a chorus of fifty Nereids sings in dancing circles as the wind swells the sails and the rudders creak in their holders across the stern, with the breezes of the South wind or the breaths of Zephyr, as they approach the land haunted by sea-birds, the white headland where Achilles ran the track by the unfriendly sea.[47]

Compound adjectives and verbs here bring out a sense of movement, sound, and texture which enable one to get a physical sense of the journey Orestes made.[48] This suggests danger and excitement and by

implication, energy and courage, on the part of those who undertook
it. The extended description gives the voyage a significance that direct
statement of fact could not give. It not only looks back to Orestes'
arrival, it also anticipates the journey he will again make before the play
is out, this time with Iphigeneia.

Even when the chorus reminisce about Greece, as they do in the
third *stasimon*, they mentally cross the sea first. They wish they could
become a kingfisher which is able to fly above the dangerous chains of
rocks and so reach Greece in safety.[49] Like Ion's gadfly in the previous
stasimon, the kingfisher acts as a kind of lens through which the horizons
of sea and land beyond Tauris may be viewed in long perspective.[50]
Even in imagination, the wide sea separates them from Greece, and their
attention to it stresses the loneliness and isolation they as Greeks feel in
an alien country, as well as preparing for the ending. A painted set could
not do, in this sense, what language does, for a set is static and fixed,
whereas in the language of lyric it is possible to present a scene in several
guises at once, designed to serve several dramatic ends at once. The sea
in description may be filled both with mythical presences and sailors out
on commercial ventures; it may seem both a threat and a means of
salvation, an inhibiting neighbour and a spur to the imagination. If there
is nostalgia in the images prompted by the chorus' thought of it, that is
quite proper, for nostalgia is the driving force of the action. But there is
also hope. Because Iphigeneia, like her friends, is homesick for Greece,
the escape is planned. For past, present, and future, the sea provides the
means of action, and descriptions of it a unified climate for concerted
dramatic emotion.

Descriptive imagery of place becomes dramatic imagery also in the
Troades, where the captured city of Troy is the constant preoccupation
of the chorus' thoughts. Once again they do not abstract these, but
bring alive in sensuously evocative language a sense of the city's life,
past and present, making the scenes themselves act as commentary.
Unlike Iphigeneia's attendants, these women, now refugees, must
nerve themselves to set out for Greece. Troy has been their home, and
tragedy comes from the sense of their loss of it. What the choral odes do,
is implicitly and consistently to build up a sense of the magnitude of this
loss by making Troy seem momentarily real in every detail. The force
of their imagination which is a condensation of lived experience, sharp-
ens and contrasts with the moment at the very end of the play, at which
this reality is finally overcome by two physical facts: embarkation onto
Greek ships, and the firing of the remaining city buildings.

The first *stasimon* begins with an address to Troy itself. The Muse is to help in a new kind of song in its honour, for it will be a dirge for the city's death, ᾠδὰν ἐπικήδειον.[51] Without more ado, the chorus begin with an account of the bringing of the wooden horse into the city and the destruction which followed. The narrative begins with a picture of the citizens clustered on their own Acropolis, looking down at the wooden horse which stands at the gates. It is magnificently attired in gold trappings and the unique compound adjective chosen to express this, χρυσεοφάλαρον, is intended to draw attention to the idol's spendid appearance, and thence by natural implication to the susceptibility of the Trojans to superficial attractions. This scene is followed by a sudden one of movement in which the citizens rush to the gates and drag the idol into the city to the temple of Athena.

> πᾶσα δὲ γέννα Φρυγῶν
> πρὸς πύλας ὡρμάθη,
> πεύκᾳ ἐν οὐρείᾳ ξεστὸν λόχον Ἀργείων
> καὶ Δαρδανίας ἄταν θεᾷ δώσων,
> χάριν ἄζυγος ἀμβροτοπώλου·
> κλωστοῦ δ' ἀμφιβόλοις λίνοιο ναὸς ὡσεὶ
> σκάφος κελαινόν, εἰς ἕδρανα
> λάινα δάπεδά τε φόνια πατρί-
> δι Παλλάδος θέσαν θεᾶς.
> ἐπὶ δὲ πόνῳ καὶ χαρᾷ
> νύχιον ἐπεὶ κνέφας παρῆν,
> Λίβυς τε λωτὸς ἐκτύπει
> Φρύγιά τε μέλεα, παρθένοι δ'
> ἀέριον ἀνὰ κρότον ποδῶν
> βοὰν ἔμελπον εὔφρον', ἐν
> δόμοις δὲ παμφαὲς σέλας
> πυρὸς μέλαιναν αἴγλαν
> ⟨ἄκος⟩ ἔδωκεν ὕπνῳ.

Then the whole Trojan people rushed to the gates to gaze at the ambush of Argives hidden beneath that polished pinewood surface, that which was to be the city's destruction, a favour of the immortal Virgin Goddess. Like the hull of a dark ship they dragged it with circling spun flax ropes into the stone shrine of Pallas Athene. After the exertion and the exhilaration, when twilight came, the Libyan flute rang out and Phrygian songs sounded, young girls singing them light-heartedly in accompaniment to the beat of their dancing feet. Inside the houses, the shining brightness of torch flares cast a dark flickering gleam to drive away sleep.⁵²

No moral comment intrudes upon the narrative, there is only the tangibleness of the scene stressed through descriptive words which suggest sight, sound and texture, that is, flute-calls, singing, and thudding, dancing feet; polished wood, stone floor, flax ropes; subtle hints of the sinister too in the suggestion of blood,⁵³ and in the ambiguous epithet dark/fatal applied to the ship with which the idol is compared. Ships are to the Trojans, throughout, of sinister significance.⁵⁴ The final oxymoron of dark gleams of light in the dusk, suggests the ambivalence of the whole scene, the false rejoicing, and the treachery lurking beneath the bright surface.

The *epode* moves from the public scene to a private one in the palace.

> ἐγὼ δὲ τὰν ὀρεστέραν
> τότ' ἀμφὶ μέλαθρα παρθένον
> Διὸς κόραν ἐμελπόμαν
> χοροῖσι· φοινία δ' ἀνὰ
> πτόλιν βοὰ κατεῖχε Περ-
> γάμων ἕδρας· βρέφη δὲ φίλι-
> α περὶ πέπλους ἔβαλλε μα-
> τρὶ χεῖρας ἐπτοημένας·
> λόχου δ' ἐξέβαιν' Ἄρης,

I was singing and dancing in the palace in honour of the huntress daughter of Zeus, when suddenly a bloody shout possessed the city. Children clutched their mother's dresses with trembling hands. War had stalked from his hiding place.⁵⁵

The image of frightened children here anticipates the entrance of Andromache with Astyanax, in the next scene, while the scene of rape in the bedrooms which follows this passage and ends the ode, recalls the news of Polyxena's seizure by Achilles, and Cassandra's by Agamemnon.

> σφαγαὶ δ' ἀμφιβώμιοι
> Φρυγῶν, ἔν τε δεμνίοις
> καράτομος ἐρημία

νεανίδων στέφανον ἔφερεν
Ἑλλάδι κουροτρόφον,
Φρυγῶν πατρίδι πένθη.

Beside the altars, the Trojans
died in their blood. Desolate now,
men murdered, our sleeping rooms gave
up their bride's beauty to breed
sons for Greek men.[56]

By taking the Trojan war into the bedroom, Euripides is being consistent
in his theme of a sacked city as women see it. In this lay his original
contribution to the Trojan saga. It was a theme he had worked on in the
earlier *Hecuba*.[57] The earlier version is more purely pictorial, and has
some of the qualities of the quiet, domestic kind of interior scenes
represented on white lekythoi or on red-figure vases of the mid-fifth
century.[58] The mood of domestic intimacy into which the ensuing
Greek invasion seems all the more violent, is built up by a series of
ordinary actions pictorially conceived. The husband lies on the bed, his
spear hung up close-by on a peg, while his wife, dressed only in a shift,
brushes her hair in front of the mirror. Such visual detail, strikingly new
for tragedy, is a powerful way of presenting the horror of the Greek
attack, but it is doubtful in the *Hecuba* how far that attack is relevant to
the plot in hand. In the *Troades*, on the other hand, it is absolutely central.
The vitality of the women is coincidental with the existence of Troy itself.

A series of jarring pictorial juxtapositions reveal incidents in Troy's
history in the second *stasimon*. The city's walls have burnt before and
the chorus describe their destruction on an earlier occasion.

κανόνων δὲ τυκίσματα Φοίβου
. . πυρὸς φοίνικι πνοᾷ καθελὼν
Τροίας ἐπόρθησε χθόνα.
δὶς δὲ δυοῖν πιτύλοιν τείχη +περὶ+
Δαρδανίας ⟨φοινία⟩ κατέλυσεν ⟨αἰχμά.⟩

Lattimore's translation best captures the sensuous quality of these lines
with their bold use of colour and appeal to texture.

the scarlet wind of the flames swept over
the masonry straight hewn by the hands of Apollo.
This was a desolation of Troy
twice taken; twice in the welter of blood the walls Dardanian
went down before the red spear.[59]

The rare words κανόνων δὲ τυκίσματα draw attention to the chiselling marks made by Apollo's measuring line on the great walls.⁶⁰ Such stress is of much point here since it is from these walls, which have been destroyed and rebuilt several times over, that the child Astyanax is to be flung to his death. When his body is recovered, Hecuba in her lament comments upon the physical damage made on the child's body by these huge stones.⁶¹ A city's walls are also a tangible mark of its greatness and prosperity, and their destruction here and at the end of the play is stressed to indicate a spiritual as well as a physical collapse. The end of the walls means the end of a city's existence in all its aspects. The metaphor πυργόω 'to build towers' is reiterated during the play to reinforce this symbolism.⁶² Not only Greeks, but Gods, are responsible for the destruction of Troy. Laconically, with a minimum of moral comment, the chorus go on to draw two more visual pictures, which speak through their mere juxtaposition. In Heaven, Ganymede (a supposed divine benefactor of the city) picks his way delicately among the gold wine cups littered about Zeus' throne. Below on earth, the beaches of Troy are thronged with refugees. The pools where Ganymede used to bathe, and the fields where he exercised are gone. But his facial expression is unchanged. It is serene and full of youthful charm. The rare and striking epithet καλλιγάλανα suggests the unruffled surface of the sea on a fine day. Gods, is the implication, do not care, and the ode ends with another divine relative, white-winged Aurora, glancing down upon the tumbling city walls. The message implicit in all these juxtaposed images is that if the city is gone, the responsibility lies not in its citizens but in divine apathy. Betrayal is also the underlying theme of the last *stasimon* which presents the ceremonial aspects of city life pictorially, in terms of what has been lost.⁶³ The chorus recall in vivid sensuous terms the dawn sunlight striking Zeus' mountain, Ida, the altars laid out with barley cakes, and the inlay of gold gleaming on the statues. Only towards the end of the song does their imagination turn away from Troy to Greece to prepare the audience for their embarkation on Greek ships at the end of the play.

Throughout the choral odes of this play then, the city of Troy and all its associations are described in such a way as to store emotion cumulatively and make the audience sense the magnitude of its loss. Here, unlike the *Hecuba*, Euripides has enabled the chorus to achieve perfect balance between the general and the individual experience.

In the *Bacchae* the chorus are also protagonist. The imagery of their odes is less consistently prolonged than in the *Troades*, since philosophical reflection, ritual cries and cult elements all play a part in composition of considerable complexity. But the background of wild natural landscape so necessary to the Dionysiac reveller is never very far away. The women of Asia bring with them into the 'broad streets of Greece' associations of their own native Asia which permitted Bacchic rites, and offered the solitude in which the true devotee delights. The mountains of Phrygia and Lydia had been the scene of strange miracles which the chorus describe, among them the hunting of wild animals, the ritual eating of raw flesh and the appearance of wine, milk and honey springing from the earth.[64] The chorus wish for the natural surroundings of their worship to reappear in Thebes.

ὦ Σεμέλας τροφοὶ Θῆ-
βαι, στεφανοῦσθε κισσῷ·
βρύετε βρύετε χλοήρει
μίλακι καλλικάρπῳ
καὶ καταβακχιοῦσθε δρυὸς
ἢ ἐλάτας κλάδοισι,
στικτῶν τ' ἐνδυτὰ νεβρίδων
στέφετε λευκοτρίχων πλοκάμων
μαλλοῖς· ἀμφὶ δὲ νάρθηκας ὑβριστὰς
ὁσιοῦσθ'· αὐτίκα γᾶ πᾶσα χορεύσει –
Βρόμιος ὅστις ἄγῃ θιάσους –
εἰς ὄρος εἰς ὄρος, ἔνθα μένει
θηλυγενὴς ὄχλος
ἀφ' ἱστῶν παρὰ κερκίδων τ'
οἰστρηθεὶς Διονύσῳ.

O Thebes that cradled Semele,
Be ivy-garlanded, burst into flower
With wreaths of lush bright-berried bryony,
Bring sprays of fir, green branches torn from oaks,
Fill soul and flesh with Bacchus' mystic power;
Fringe and bedeck your dappled fawnskin cloaks
With woolly tufts and locks of purest white.
There's a brute wilderness in the fennel-wands –
Reverence it well. Soon the whole land will dance
When the god with ecstatic shout
Leads his companies out
To the mountain's mounting height
Swarming with riotous bands
Of Theban women leaving

Their spinning and their weaving
Stung with the maddening trance
Of Dionysus![65]

Part of the dramatic tension in the play consists in the way Euripides makes the free natural environment of the maenads come into contact and clash with the more restricted one of Greek city life. When their religion is restricted, the Asian maenads long for the places they have known 'empty of men'. They remember the lonely forests, river banks and green fields where like a playful fawn, they have run from the hostile pursuit of attackers. Places such as Cyprus, and the thickly wooded mountain slopes of Olympus, are associated in their imagination with the civilising qualities they see as an essential part of Dionysiac worship – love, peace, harmony and the subduing power of music over wild things. Because scenery is so closely associated with religious experience and strong emotion for the Bacchanals, visual description of the places frequented by them is integral to the dramatic action in a way that it is not, for instance, in a chorus in the *Phoenissae*, where the haunts of Dionysus' celebrants are quite extraneously introduced into the ode on the ground that they are the places now taken over by marshalling armies.

ὦ πολύμοχθος Ἄρης, τί ποθ' αἵματι
καὶ θανάτῳ κατέχῃ Βρομίου παράμουσος ἑορταῖς;
οὐκ ἐπὶ καλλιχόροις στεφάνοισι νεάνιδος ὥρας
βόστρυχον ἀμπετάσας λωτοῦ κατὰ πνεύματα μέλπῃ
    μοῦσαν, ἐν ᾇ χάριτες χοροποιοί,
ἀλλὰ σὺν ὁπλοφόροις στρατὸν Ἀργείων ἐπιπνεύσας
    αἵματι Θήβας
κῶμον ἀναυλότατον προχορεύεις.
οὐδ' ὑπὸ θυρσομανεῖ νεβρίδων μέτα δίνᾳ,
ἅρμασι καὶ ψαλίων τετραβάμοσι μωνυχοπώλων
    ἱππείαις ἐπὶ χεύμασι βαίνων
Ἰσμηνοῖο θοάζεις, Ἀργείοις ἐπιπνεύσας
    Σπαρτῶν γένναν,
ἀσπιδοφέρμονα θίασον ἐνόπλιον,
ἀντίπαλον κατὰ λάινα τείχεα
    χαλκῷ κοσμήσας.

Ares, fraught with trouble, why are you possessed by blood and death, out of harmony with Bacchic festivals? You do not, to

grace the beautiful dances of young girls in gay garlands, spreading
your hair loose to the blowing of the flute, sing a song in which the
dancing Graces take part, but having inspired the Argive army
and its warriors against the race of Thebes, you lead out a revel
quite unfit for flute accompaniment. You do not go, under the
influence of the thyrsus-maddened whirl of fawnskins, but you
proceed along the streams of the Ismenus with chariots and
bridles with the four-footed, single hoofed steeds, having incited
the race of sown men against the Argives, having decked with bronze
the spear-carrying, armed band ranged against the stone walls.[66]

Not only do the thirteen compound adjectives, most of four and five
syllables long, crammed into the space of nineteen lines, make Hermann's judgement of the style of this ode utterly intelligible (he called it
'tumidissimum inani verborum strepitu carmen'), but the use of Bacchic
place imagery here seems merely external, an extra rhetorical device
thrown in for good measure. This passage may serve as a contrast to
those where Euripides has so completely worked place imagery into the
texture of the plot that it cannot be isolated. Of course, he did not always
achieve or seek to achieve this degree of identification. It is most obvious
perhaps in plays where the chorus is protagonist, such as the *Bacchae* and
Trojan Women or in those where the place of action itself has strong
dramatic significance such as Delphi in the *Ion* or the rough barbarian
coasts of Tauris in the *Iphigeneia in Tauris* or the environs of Troy near
its time of destruction.

Sometimes however the emotional rhythm is deliberately broken for
the sake of a temporary effect, and the organic function of the choral
imagination served instead by a sharpening of the tragic crisis through
contrast. Such relief scenes may arise implicitly through built-in
exigencies of the plot, or from an overt and acknowledged impulse-wish
of the chorus to escape from the present by a deliberate indulgence of
their powers of imagination. In both kinds, one sees the emergence of
a new sort of poetic landscape, that of fantasy. Realism recedes into the
background as dreams are cast from idealised constructions which are
not encountered outside the imagination itself. This world is peopled with
the unthreatening creatures of fancy, Nereids, Graces, golden-haired
Harmony, Desire and heart-charming Loves.[67] It is inhabited only by
the more decorative of wild creatures, such as swans, kingfishers and
tawny-throated nightingales. Euripides has been much criticised for

writing the mythical-pastoral idylls which include such figures.[68] Does such 'sentimentalism' have a legitimate place in tragedy, even on the grounds of relief?

An early example comes in the famous chorus describing Athens in the *Medea*.

> Ἐρεχθεΐδαι τὸ παλαιὸν ὄλβιοι
> καὶ θεῶν παῖδες μακάρων, ἱερᾶς
> χώρας ἀπορθήτου τ᾽ ἄπο, φερβόμενοι
> κλεινοτάταν σοφίαν, αἰεὶ διὰ λαμπροτάτου
> βαίνοντες ἁβρῶς αἰθέρος, ἔνθα ποθ᾽ ἁγνὰς
> ἐννέα Πιερίδας Μούσας λέγουσι
> ξανθὰν Ἁρμονίαν φυτεῦσαι·
>
> τοῦ καλλινάου τ᾽ ἐπὶ Κηφισοῦ ῥοαῖς
> τὰν Κύπριν κλῄζουσιν ἀφυσσαμέναν
> χώρας καταπνεῦσαι μετρίας ἀνέμων
> ἡδυπνόους Αὔρας· αἰεὶ δ᾽ ἐπιβαλλομέναν
> χαίταισιν εὐώδη ῥοδέων πλόκον ἀνθέων
> τᾷ Σοφίᾳ παρέδρους πέμπειν Ἔρωτας,
> παντοίας ἀρετᾶς ξυνεργούς.

The descendants of Erechtheus fortunate over ages, children of the blessed Gods, come from a holy and unconquered land and feed on the wisdom for which it is renowned. They pass full of grace through the bright air where they say once golden-haired Harmony gave birth to the nine holy Muses of Pieria. By the waters of Cephisus, the fair-flowing river, they say that the mild sweet-scented breezes of the land breathed over Cypris as she drew water, while the Loves who sit beside Wisdom and share in the excellence of the arts, escorted her as she crowned her hair with a wreath of fragrant roses.[69]

The visual romanticism of this picture has much in common with paintings of the time which show Aphrodite in company with the Loves and nymphs who represent personified moral qualities, such as Harmonia or Eudaimonia. Its tone, like those of the prettily decorative Meidias vases, is light and graceful, and its function must surely be to provide relief, to bring, as Lattimore writes, 'a little desired sweetness to a play which will get none from any of its characters'.[70] No doubt it stirred the audience to hear of their city described in this way, and no doubt too, its idealised evocation does point to some extent, by contrast, the shocking 'reality' of Medea's plight to which the chorus return in the last stanzas. But like its counterpart in the *Hecuba*, it may still seem over-elaborate as preparation for events which properly lie beyond the end of the play. Aegeus, it is true, has offered Medea a refuge in Athens, but is the escape to it here by the chorus in imagination appropriate to the forthcoming miraculous flight there by a sorceress who is also a murderer? The contrast seems too sharp. So in the *Hecuba*, the scene of tapestry-making for the Panathenaeic festival seems inappropriate because too decorative as an appropriate imaginative exercise for desperate captives.

The long, static and decorative ode in the *Heracles* might from some points of view be classed as implicit escape from present action.[71] The chorus describe the labours of Heracles in terms of the far-away places he visited. Every scene is invested with a colourful glamour which appears to have little to do either with the grim confines of Lycus' palace, or with any serious strength or purpose on the part of Heracles himself. What the chorus depict is a pretty, idealised fairyland, whose descriptive strength consists almost exclusively in decorative adjectives. The golden apples glisten in the gardens of the Hesperides, silver rivers stretch out before him, even the animals Heracles kills are deprived of any menace by their enchanting appearance. The snake gracefully wound round a slender tree, the dappled hind with glistening gold horns are reminiscent of certain decorative treatments on vases where the painter has been more interested in making the setting look attractive, than in the violent exploits themselves.[72] The absence of verbs in this ode in comparison to adjectives, reduces action to a minimum, and gives the ode a static kind of pictorialism which in itself appears to make the myth seem merely trivially decorative. But in this case, there is a purpose for so presenting it. The chorus' ornamental embroidery is designed to contrast drastically with the astringent scepticism of Lycus who questions whether the labours ever took place at all. Indeed they can be construed as part justification for his view. Miracles such as the chorus embellish upon, in terms of exotic far-off scenes, seem to have little to do with any world which exists. And when Heracles himself appears, and is seen in a series of events which make of him a broken human being, the world the chorus had depicted seems remoter still. Here then the refuge by them to an idealised world of popular imagination is introduced into the drama precisely that it may be seen to be a mere refuge by others on the stage, and by the audience. Mythical mystique is replaced by a

4

secular interpretation of Heracles' saga, one which revitalised the legend by debunking some aspects of it and by humanising others.

There are escape motifs in the tragedies however which are openly acknowledged as such. Circumstances have robbed the sufferers of everything but an active imagination and a capacity for comforting illusions. This conception of the imagination itself as one of the last substantial pleasures left to the desperate, is more sophisticated than anything in Aeschylus or Sophocles. Here the imagery is as it were at two removes from reality. The audience are asked to contemplate not the chorus' 'actual' experience, but their imaginations.

> κἂν γὰρ ὀνείροισι συνεί –
> ην δόμοις πόλει τε πατρῴ –
> ᾳ τερπνῶν ὕπνων ἀπόλαυ –
> σιν κοινὰν χάριν ὄλβου.

Even in my dreamt imaginings I would like to be in my own home and city, because there is pleasure in the dreams pleasant sleep brings, and one is grateful for this source of richness which is open to everyone.[73]

Motivation of this kind lies behind much of the imagery of the 'elsewhere' (as Lattimore puts it), although there is considerable variation in style and in the ways in which it is related to the main theme. In the *Iphigeneia in Tauris*, for instance, the chorus are themselves Greeks and merely wish to return to their homeland. In the *Hecuba*, the Trojans wish for Athens merely as the best of many destinations over which they themselves have no control. The motif of wishing to escape by turning into a flying bird, is used, with differences, in the *Hippolytus* and *Helen*. In the *Hippolytus*, the chorus want to become a sea-bird which haunts precipitous cliffs that they might fly up and look down over a landscape outspread beneath them, over the waves that wash the Adriatic coast and the river Eridanus, where the daughters of Helios in pity for Phaethon weep tears which become shining drops of amber as they fall into the bright water.[74] The beguiling decorativeness of this picture need not obscure the relevance of Phaethon's fate to that of Hippolytus, since both scorned Aphrodite. As the chorus go on further with their imaginary journey, they come to the route which Phaedra herself once took from Crete to Troizen, and by the image of the white-sailed boat in which she came, they gently remind the audience of her Cretan ancestry and her own terrible recognition of it at 337 and 341.

The chorus of the *Helen* imagine themselves as a flock of migrant birds flying to escape the winter rains.

οἰωνοὶ στοχάδες
ὄμβρον λιποῦσαι χειμέριον
νίσονται πρεσβυτάτᾳ
σύριγγι πειθόμεναι
ποιμένος, ὃς ἄβροχα πεδία καρποφόρα τε γᾶς
ἐπιπετόμενος ἰαχεῖ.
Ὦ πταναὶ δολιχαύχενες,
σύννομοι νεφέων δρόμου,
βᾶτε Πλειάδας ὑπὸ μέσας
Ὠρίωνά τ' ἐννύχιον·
    καρύξατ' ἀγγελίαν,
Εὐρώταν ἐφεζόμεναι,
Μενέλεως ὅτι Δαρδάνου
    πόλιν ἑλὼν δόμον ἥξει.

Oh that we may fly high in the air
Winged high over Libya
where the lines of the migrant
birds, escaping the winter rain,
take their way, following
the authority of their leader's
whistle. And he flying into the rainless, the
    wheat-burdened flat
places, screams his clear call.
O flying birds with the long throats, who
share the course of the racing clouds,
go to the midmost Pleiades.
Go to Orion of the night,
cry like heralds your message
as you light down in Eurotas,
that Menelaus has taken the town
of Dardanus and will come home.[75]

Cast in the form of a *propemptikon* for Helen and Menelaus, the ode is an imaginative projection of the journey these two will make. The high tone of fantasy here, and the elaborate verbal and adjectival compounds, match the miraculousness of Helen's and Menelaus' escape from Egypt. In this sense, the wish of the chorus to fly upwards and look down over Egypt is only partly an escape motif. In that their wish is an imaginative accompaniment to the Greeks' journey, it is also a lyric way of forwarding dramatic action.

A double function is also served by the free play of pictorial daydreaming the Bacchic chorus allow themselves. Their colourful reconstructions of Cyprus and Egypt to which they would like from the mere pressure of events, to escape, are designed to seem both a paradise compared to Pentheus' drab world of prohibition, and an implicit condemnation of it. For the pictorial personifications the chorus choose here to associate with Dionysus and Aphrodite, are the same desirable and respectable ones which commonly appear in their company on vase paintings. That these gods should be associated with the Muses and with the Graces and with Harmony, compliments the new religion as highly as Pentheus has abused it.

> ἱκοίμαν ποτὶ Κύπρον,
> νᾶσον τᾶς Ἀφροδίτας,
> ἵν' οἱ θελξίφρονες νέμον-
> ται θνατοῖσιν Ἔρωτες,
> Πάφον θ' ἂν ἑκατόστομοι
> βαρβάρου ποταμοῦ ῥοαὶ
> καρπίζουσιν ἄνομβροι.
> οὗ δ' ἁ καλλιστευομένα
> Πιερία μούσειος ἕδρα,
> σεμνὰ κλιτὺς Ὀλύμπου,
> ἐκεῖσ' ἄγε με, Βρόμιε Βρόμιε,
> πρόβακχ' εὔιε δαῖμον.
> ἐκεῖ Χάριτες,
> ἐκεῖ δὲ Πόθος· ἐκεῖ δὲ βάκ-
> χαις θέμις ὀργιάζειν.

O to set foot on Aphrodite's island,
On Cyprus, haunted by the Loves, who enchant
Brief life with sweetness; or in that strange land
Whose fertile river carves a hundred channels
to enrich her rainless sand;
Or where the sacred pastures of Olympus slant
Down to Pieria, where the Muses dwell –
Take me, O Bromius, take me and inspire

Laughter and worship! There our holy spell
And ecstasy are welcome; there the gentle band
Of Graces have their home, and sweet Desire.[76]

As the *antistrophe* shows, this picture of the places where there is freedom
to revel undisturbed, is appropriate to a God who is most associated
with joy, χαίρει μὲν θαλίαισιν and peace, φιλεῖ δ' ὀλβοδότειραν
'Εἰρήναν and who is accessible to all.

> πλῆθος ὅτι
> τὸ φαυλότερον ἐνόμισε χρῆ-
> ταί τε, τόδ' ἄν δεχοίμαν.

What the majority of ordinary people consider and practise, that is
what is acceptable to me.[77]

These closing words come as if in confirmation of what has been an
appeal to the *popular* pictorial imagination. Personified human emotions
such as Love, Desire, Grace, and Peace, are the common visual accom-
paniments to the two Gods who alone can make all people equal,
Aphrodite and Dionysus.[78]

If it seems sentimental that Euripides' choruses should always be
wishing to escape to somewhere else, it should at least also seem appropriate to their own special situation. Euripides frequently chose dramatic
situations where the forcible separation from a particular environment
itself was the main source of emotional tension. Asians in Greece,
Greeks in Tauris or in Egypt, Cretans in Troizen, Trojans forcibly
transported to Greece. In such cases, there is point in recollecting or
anticipating the elsewhere, for this represents a past of lost experience or
hope for a future which by its very difference defines the present.

Place and the imagery describing it, have an importance in Euripides'
plays which arises from the particular situations the poet chooses to
depict in these plays. Descriptions both of the present scene, and of
invisible far-off ones, which can only be summoned in imagination, are
handled organically within the terms of the whole dramatic action.
The focus of emotion which such scenes provide, is a communal one by
the very nature of the chorus' function. Their visions cannot be appropriate only to them since the chorus must reflect what other actors on
the stage feel also. Through them, either by identification or contrast,
are registered the emotions proper to the total situation. It is true that to
describe a place does not have the immutable authority of a moral or

philosophical statement. Euripides' choruses were frequently in no position to make such statements, for to do so requires some degree of detachment from the main action. But they behave no less dramatically for sometimes lacking this philosophical dimension. The pictorial language the chorus use, conveys the world they and the other actors inhabit, as it has become immediately significant to them in imagination. Whether this is a city or the garden of the Hesperides, the Aegean sea or the mountains of Asia, what characterises the conveying of their experience is clear visual detail. 'Reality' is as it is present to the senses, and it is particularly the adjective in all its shapes and forms which communicates this.

Chapter III

Monody and Lyric Dialogue:
Subjective Landscapes

The language of actors' lyric must basically be the same as that of choral lyric since one is an extension of the other. Here too, elevated tone is achieved through the invention of new descriptive adjectives and these may occur as well in choral sections. Words for instance such as ἀργυροειδής, 'silvery', or μελάγχρως 'black-skinned', both apparently Euripides' own coinages, occur in monody as well as choral lyric.[1] The same pictorial motifs may also be used in both, as for instance scenes of escape, scenes of domestic tasks such as spinning and weaving, or scenes of festivity such as dancing and singing.[2] A variety of lyric metres is also common to both and the emotional range which they severally presuppose. Like that of choral lyric, the poetry of monody and lyric dialogue is by its conventions freed from the need to resemble ordinary conversations, and can in the combination of music and words, and through imagery, reflect the intensity of dramatic experience without its logical or narrative shell.

If there are resemblances, however, there are also differences. The form and function of monodies make enough different demands upon the imagination that it becomes a distortion to lump both these and chorus simply under one general heading of 'lyric'. The mere fact that actor's lyric is sung by one person makes a decisive difference. A poet cannot make a whole chorus mad or have them blaspheme en masse or die or fall excessively in love. The monody as Euripides saw it required extreme and various emotions and situations, and lyric dialogue was no longer restricted to mere lament as it once had been in the traditional *Kommos* form.[3] This extreme and varied emotion in fact was what marked the heroine as a heroine, or, less often in Euripides, the hero: it was what justified their lonely tragic roles. The imagery of monody and lyric dialogue therefore, while on the one hand more flexible because the areas of its expression could include greater extremes of emotion such as madness, love and total despair, was on the other restricted in its horizons because it must reflect the narrow obsessions of one character.

43

While therefore pictorial language in choral lyric consistently builds up background over the extended lengths of whole odes, setting a general atmosphere consonant with the total action, that of monody on the contrary represents foreground in points of high relief. As far as imagery is concerned, it is a difference not of basic means, but of disposition in relation to function.

Something of both likenesses and differences between choral ode and monody emerges in exaggerated and crude form in Aristophanes' parody of both in the *Frogs*.[4] The likenesses are clear in that details of language are not recognisably distinguishable in either. The long drawn out rhythm of εἱλίσσω (twir-ir-ir-ir-irl-ing as Way renders it) is parodied in both for instance.[5] Compounds in the parodied monody such as the colourful oxymoron κελαινοφαής, 'darkly shining', or the epithet δίπυρος 'twin flaming', are analogous to similar words in the choral odes such as μελαμφαής 'black shining' in an ode from the *Helen*, or ἀμφίπυρος 'double-flaming' also describing torches in the *Ion*.[6] That much loved verb of Euripides ἀναπέτομαι 'to fly up and away', which is parodied in the monody, appears in many places in the tragedies including a choral ode of the *Medea* and also the Phrygian's monody in the *Orestes*.[7] On the other hand, Aristophanes has grasped the differences in style between the two modes. Perhaps because he was a poet himself, he understood more thoroughly than any other ancient critic the sensuous nature of Euripidean imagery. We see it parodied to absurdity, in the pictorial elements flung together without purpose so that their incongruity merely makes a comic point; kingfishers dousing their wings in sea-spray, spiders spinning webs in dark corners, dolphins gambolling round blue ships' prows, the gloss on the grape clusters shining amid curling vine tendrils.[8] Aristophanes has a feeling for the colour and sensitivity to light and texture which appear in so many Euripidean lyric descriptions. But at the same time these parodies show a difference in handling of imagery between choral ode and aria. The ode is a general background scene which extends and changes its horizons: kingfishers flit across the sea, dolphins play, spiders creep into the eaves under the roof. It is nonsense, but it catches the panoramic and sometimes volatile vision of Euripides when he is writing choral odes. The monody on the other hand is more restricted in its imagery as befits the obsessive character of a dream. Words for gloom and darkness are repeated like a motif through it. The darkness of the Night is punctuated by intermittent gleams of light in its blackness (ὦ νυκτός κελαινοφαής / ὄρφνα).[9] The dream itself is conjured up from Hades' dim obscurity (ἐξ ἀφανοῦς / ᾽Αίδα πρόμολον).[10] It is a child of black Night (μελαίνας Νυκτός παῖδα)[11] and viewed as a frightful figure covered in black shrouds (φρικώδη δεινὰν ὄψιν, μελανονεκυείμονα).[12] This picture of gloom is relieved only by one implied colour contrast where the figure's bloody gaze is juxtaposed to its black shrouds, and by the mundane order finally to light the lamps.[13] All this too is nonsense on the level of logical meaning. But the comic poet has caught the flavour of Euripides' monodic style, the emotional extravagance, the narrow range of imagery indicating the heroine's obsessive dream, the violent contrast between the initial elevated and cosmic vision and more trivial concerns such as spinning and going shopping. It was no part of Aristophanes' purpose to relate form to function, or style to content. Indeed the comic point depends precisely upon the lack of correlation between these points. He is useful to us, therefore, in showing in exaggerated degree the style of monody, but not in the dramatic integration of that style.

Taken seriously, imagery in monody has an important and different dramatic function from that of the choral odes, and this is to reflect the individual obsessions or preoccupations of the singer of the monody. Imagery in this case may be the vehicle for the irrational or the unacknowledged. At least this is true in those plays where the singer of a monody is central to the tragic conflict. One has, of course, to be careful with the word 'obsession'. Private obsessions and idiosyncracies as we understand them do not exist even in Euripides. The area of imagination in Cassandra's delusion, for instance, is not one peculiar to someone named Cassandra: it is the kind of imaginative delusion which any woman in that situation might have. It defines situation even more than it characterises Cassandra. Nonetheless, the Euripidean monody does represent important advances in basic concepts of character and in the causation of human tragedy, and imagery plays an important part in making articulate such insights. This is particularly true of the plays belonging to the middle period of composition, that is, around 415 B.C., which include the *Ion*, *Troades*, *Electra* and *I.T.*

In the *Ion*, for instance, there are two monodies, one by Ion and one by Creousa.[14] They complement each other and the particular qualitative tone of each is conveyed through pictorial language of a selected and special kind. In Ion's song this consists basically of two motifs, pervasive imagery of light, and description of two objects of special significance to him, the broom with which he sweeps and the birds which wheel above the altar.

Metrically the song is divided into three stages.[15] The first is a transition from the previous iambics to lyric, for it is in ordinary marching anapaests and was probably not sung (the absence of Doric forms suggests this), but delivered in recitative. It serves as an introduction. In this part, Ion as he reaches the temple entrance is dazzled by the sight of the early morning sun as it touches the sights most familiar to him, the high peaks of Parnassus, the Castalian spring, the shrine of the Delphic prophetess and the smoke of incense drifting up to the temple roofs. He begins as follows:

> ἅρματα μὲν τάδε λαμπρὰ τεθρίππων
> Ἥλιος ἤδη λάμπει κατὰ γῆν,
> ἄστρα δὲ φεύγει πυρὶ τῷδ᾽ αἰθέρος
> ἐς νύχθ᾽ ἱεράν·
> Παρνησιάδες δ᾽ ἄβατοι κορυφαὶ
> καταλαμπόμεναι τὴν ἡμερίαν
> ἁψῖδα βροτοῖσι δέχονται.

Look, the sun's bright chariot is already lighting the earth, and with his flame drives the stars back into the sacred Night. The untrodden peaks of Mt. Parnassus blaze with light as they receive the wheel of day.[16]

To some extent such an opening description is literary cliché. Sunrise and sunset are described in numerous other places in terms of a personified figure with chariot and horses driving across the sky.[17] The opening lines of the *Phoenissae* provide a parallel to our passage in this respect.

> Ὦ τὴν ἐν ἄστροις οὐρανοῦ τέμνων ὁδὸν
> καὶ χρυσοκολλήτοισιν ἐμβεβὼς δίφροις
> Ἥλιε, θοαῖς ἵπποισιν εἱλίσσων φλόγα . . .

You who cut your way through heaven's stars, riding the chariot with its welded gold, Sun, with your swift mares whirling forth our light . . .[18]

Yet where these lines appear to be just a kind of decorative literary shorthand for saying it was morning when Cadmus first arrived in Thebes, the lines from the *Ion* suggest more than mere information. The contrast with the stars and with Night, together with the metaphor of driving to flight, suggests the suddenness with which the Dawn rises. The sun's gathering strength is conveyed in the repeated use with variations of the same root word to indicate brightness, λαμπρά ... λάμπει, and finally the more insistent compound καταλαμπόμεναι. Moreover, this language must be taken together with other words for light which Ion uses in the rest of the monody, to indicate the touch of sunlight upon external objects. The spring water has a silver shimmer to it, ἀργυροειδεῖς, the red claws of the swan gleam in the sun, φοινικοφαῆ, and the gold on the temple and the gold vessels of the God are similarly highlighted by epithets.[19] Such descriptive epithets suggest unobtrusively that Ion's horizons are marked by the Sun as it shines on the things he knows. They are a quiet reminder of Apollo's presence. Ion has never known anything else but this place and this view, and to him on this morning it seems as always, sunlit and secure. Ugliness, complication and hostility are not yet part of his experience, although they are waiting round the corner in the shape of his unknown relatives from Athens. It is not extravagant, I think, to suggest that the language of light here indirectly conveys to the audience not only Apollo's presence but also Ion's idealism and the vulnerability of his innocence, particularly since, as we shall see later, there are parallels in Creousa's aria for the calculated use of light imagery to indicate the attitude of the singer.[20]

In the central part of his monody Ion moves to a direct praise of Apollo which is marked by the shift to sung lyrics. This is the real heart of his aria and consists of two related elements, a three-lined refrain in paean form, and a work song as he sweeps the temple precincts.[21] In this work song he addresses and describes the broom he is holding, recognising it as an instrument of service which glorifies the God who is the subject of his praise. Because this common or garden object is associated with Apollo, it become transformed with sacred significance in Ion's eyes. He addresses it as if it were a person, and looks at the separate leaves which make it up. The epithet νεηθαλὲς 'fresh blossoming' is a new coinage,[22] and prominently placed as it is in the first line of this nine-line address to the laurel broom, draws attention to the object's significance in Apollo's service. It becomes the visual focus for a violent emotion, and as such shows first of all the depth of Ion's sense of reverence – that he can see praise of Apollo even in quite ordinary things he touches – and second the degree to which such an attitude has become second nature to him since he stresses repeatedly in these lines that this is a task he performs every day.[23] The broom thus has a symbolic role similar to that of the torch carried by Cassandra in her mad scene.[24]

It indicates reverential awe as her torch indicates blasphemous delusions of marriage. Both objects, 'obsessive objects' one might call them, acquire significance beyond their immediate use as stage props by the way their owners describe them.

In the last part of his aria which is in lyric anapaests, Ion describes the birds which constantly circle and threaten to desecrate the altar.[25] He cannot quite bring himself to shoot them. Wonderingly, he itemizes their separate features, the curved strong beak of the eagle, the red feet of the swan that shine in the sun and the nesting habits of the swallows.[26] In this last visual motif, Euripides is preparing for the incursion of outsiders into Ion's charmed existence.[27] As he looks up at them trying to swoop down, he is torn between a sympathy for their separate strangeness and a sense of threat. This seemingly trivial and decorative incident is a hint of the conflict which is to rage in Ion when he meets for the first time in his life the secular attacks of Creousa and Xuthos. Skilfully, Euripides makes the monody move from Ion's inner experience at the beginning and middle of the ode to the outer edge of it at the end, that is, to the beginning of a recognition of things beyond his own experience within the temple confines. Viewed in this way, the imagery throughout is itself dramatic texture and not as it has sometimes been called, merely 'fine description of the scenery of Delphi'. It is not an extra and external addition to the 'exciting plot . . . and the poignancy of the situations'.[28] It is an essential expression of both.

Creousa's monody is a complement to Ion's, as blasphemous towards Apollo as his is reverent.[29] Like his, it contains imagery of light which indicates not only Apollo's presence but a particular attitude of the singer, but unlike his, its pictorial language is both rarer and more condensed. Creousa's utterance has none of the even calm of Ion's gentle addresses, but bursts out in violent fits of oaths and accusations. The strongest of these occurs in the last stanza where Apollo is denounced as a malicious adulterer and fool. There is little pictorial description, but what there is, is concentrated, conspicuous, and dramatically significant. The song closes with a violent distortion of a familiar pictorial compliment to Apollo, giving new life to an old image. Delos, Creousa says, has come to hate (the word μισεῖ is given special prominence here by its position at the beginning of the line) both him and the things associated with him like the laurel and the delicate tracery of the palm trees which grow beside it on Delos, his birthplace.[30] The central and only other significant image occurs as Creousa is narrating the story of her rape by Apollo while she was picking flowers.

ἦλθές μοι χρυσῷ χαίταν
μαρμαίρων, εὖτ᾽ ἐς κόλπους
κρόκεα πέταλα φάρεσιν ἔδρεπον,
ἀνθίζειν χρυσανταυγῆ·
λευκοῖς δ᾽ ἐμφὺς καρποῖσιν
χειρῶν εἰς ἄντρου κοίτας
κραυγὰν ᾽Ω μᾶτέρ μ᾽ αὐδῶσαν
θεὸς ὁμευνέτας
ἆγες

You came to me, your hair flashing with gold as I gathered into
my dress, to use for dyeing, yellow crocuses that blazed with the
reflection of your golden light. Seizing then my pale wrists as
called upon the name of my mother, you led me to bed in a cave,
you a God and my lover.[31]

There is nothing traditional about the word χρυσανταυγῆ 'reflecting
back gold rays' or its context. This is the first time the word occurs, and
these lines are not a pleasant piece of local colour providing momentary
ornamental diversion from the main narrative. Their position at the
centre of Creousa's tirade, and the event they describe, are too important
for that. They do several things at once. The suddenness with which the
description is introduced is itself like the sudden appearance of the God
as he must have come upon Creousa like a flash of light. The precision
and emphatic concentration of the words suggesting brightness,
χρυσῷ / μαρμαίρων / κρόκεα / χρυσανταυγῆ, indicate Apollo's certain
presence, and would be pointless were Verrall right in assuming that the
only people on the scene were Creousa and a blond-haired delinquent
whom she mistook for Apollo.[32] The divine manifestation must have a
certain reality beyond Creousa's committed viewpoint.

As far as she herself is concerned however, the use of such pictorial
language has a certain ambivalence. As she tells the story from her own
experience the description must be strongly ironic, since the momentary
beauty of the image contrasts with the brutality of what follows and
with the terms of abuse she uses to describe it.[33] She curses Apollo for the
misery he has brought her.

On the other hand Wilamowitz may be right in saying that the image
contains a recognition of momentary susceptibility to Apollo's beauty.[34]
In this case her monody includes both a brief retrospective sense of awe
and a stronger present sense of passionate condemnation. In any case,
the pictorial language used significantly at this point in the monody has

implications for the whole play and not only this aria. Apollo must be not only as Creousa sees him, but as Ion sees him and the chorus sees him. To take only one of these views as the truth is like believing Ophelia's mad scene contains the only real clue to Hamlet's character. In Creousa's monody, as in Ion's, imagery of light is a constant reminder of the Sun God's presence as a force in the play and the source of bitterly conflicting emotions. It is a qualitative expression of these characters' own particular attitudes as well as a constant reminder of the independent presence of Apollo as the object of those attitudes.

Imagery in the monodies of the middle plays tends to work indirectly, and it is this which makes it all the easier for the parodist to detach it and apply it to the wrong things. There is some evidence that Euripides came to such stylistic uses only gradually. Since the monody form is not used much in the plays before 415 B.C.,[35] Hippolytus, an earlier prototype of Ion, whom he resembles in his young idealism and fanatical religious devotion, is given no monody. His attitudes are revealed by a multiplicity of different devices, part through his own direct statement in iambics and part through a prayer uttered by his companions.[36] Here the emotional force has to be split between different people and different modes, lyric and prayer formulae for the chorus, direct statement of his pious intentions in more prosaic language by Hippolytus himself. The monodies themselves show signs of gradual development in the indirect presentation of imagery. In that of the *Hecuba* and the *Trojan Women*, for instance, there is increasingly more indirect presentation in the later play.[37] It is the earlier monody in the *Hecuba* which Aristophanes parodies in terms of the imagery which illustrates her dream.[38]

Here Hecuba admits to being harried by an imaginative dream, and appeals to the forces of Night as being the generators of her dream.

> ὦ στεροπὰ Διός, ὦ σκοτία νύξ,
> τί ποτ᾽ αἴρομαι ἔννυχος οὕτω
> δείμασι, φάσμασιν; ὦ πότνια Χθών,
> μελανοπτερύγων μῆτερ ὀνείρων,
> ἀποπέμπομαι ἔννυχον ὄψιν,

I address the lightning flash of Zeus, and Night's blackness. Why am I haunted so at night by fearful imaginings? O Earth, mother of dark flying dreams, I exorcise this vision of the Night . . .[39]

The later Hecuba is in a similarly distraught state; like her prototype she refers to the fragility of her physical condition. Her back is stiff, her ribs ache and her temple throbs. But her language is so enigmatic at times as to prompt the chorus to ask her what she is talking about, as their words at 154 show, ποῖ λόγος ἥκει; She is in a nightmare state, half-dreaming, half-waking, but she nowhere openly admits to recognition of this. This is implicit in the nature of the imagery she uses, which reflects indirectly her innermost unvoiced fears. The source of these fears is the Greek ships which will take her off to some unknown destination in Greece. This she acknowledges in a much more rational passage later in the play[40] where she gives an explanation of the dread she feels. Here, however, they emerge only in the persistence with which the old Queen describes the Greek ships setting out for Troy, and in (what is rare for Euripides) a series of recurring nautical metaphors, sustained throughout her ode.[41] Hecuba is not on a ship nor in sight of one, yet she talks as if she were.

> δύστηνος ἐγὼ τῆς βαρυδαίμονος
> ἄρθρων κλίσεως, ὡς διάκειμαι,
> νῶτ' ἐν στερροῖς λέκτροισι ταθεῖσ'.
> οἴμοι κεφαλῆς, οἴμοι κροτάφων
> πλευρῶν θ', ὥς μοι πόθος εἱλίξαι
> καὶ διαδοῦναι νῶτον ἄκανθάν τ'
> εἰς ἀμφοτέρους τοίχους, μελέων
> ἐπὶ τοὺς αἰεὶ δακρύων ἐλέγους.

Unhappy and cursed I am in the cruel destiny which forces me to lie down here with my back stretched and cramped on this stiff bed. Oh my head aches and my temples throb, my side hurts and I want to rock from side to side, to both sides of the ship shifting the weight of my spine alternately to the accompaniment of endless laments of tearful song.[42]

The word τοίχους as it is used in this passage is ambiguous. It means the side of a ship.[43] Is it a metaphor? To Hecuba who is beyond fine distinctions between the waking world and the imagination, it may well not be. At the beginning of her song, the metaphors she used were quite obviously metaphors. 'Sail for the straits, sail as your destiny tells you to. Don't hold life's prow on course against the current, sailing as you do on waves of disaster.' But gradually, as if by natural association, she proceeds from this traditional figurative language to the literal belief that she is actually on a ship, rocking from side to side in imaginary movement with its rolling motion, an effect which the monotonous metrical rhythms and repetitions within the lines 102, 110, and 115 reinforces. There is a temptation in English, and most translators succumb to it, to convert the metaphor in Greek to a simile, 'as if I were on a ship', but the unusual force of the image is then lost. Several lines later, as if by natural transition, she moves to describing the actual Greek ships which crossed the sea to Troy before returning again to a nautical metaphor at 137.

In this combination of figurative and literal language restricted to the theme of ships, which puzzles the chorus, Euripides shows Hecuba's highly-wrought emotional state. The confines of her world have temporarily shrunk to the size of her own fears and the consistent ship imagery throughout her monody, as well as providing aesthetic unity to the song, defines the area of her fears in a way which is developed later in the play and borne out by the closing action itself.[44] This restriction of imagery designed to express indirectly the submerged emotions of the main character, is also at work in the *Hippolytus* in a lyric dialogue Phaedra has with the nurse.[45] To convey her delirium in wanting to be with Hippolytus although she dare not say so, Euripides gives her lines which describe in visual terms the scenes most associated with him. She dreams of lying under the black poplar trees in the grass of a meadow, and then of plunging into the pine forest where the hunt is in full cry. Since hunting is a wildly inappropriate occupation for a woman as delicate and luxuriously brought up as Phaedra, the Nurse is justly puzzled. Like Hecuba's chorus of companions, she has to ask for enlightenment 'why this sudden concern for hunting? Why do you want to go to the spring to drink when you can get water in the palace?' In this way Euripides indirectly through visual description explores the hallucinatory and semi-articulate nature of strong emotion, since Phaedra's reluctance to speak directly of her love also shows the poet's shrewd insight into psychology.[46]

Imagery then as it is used in actors' lyric tends to be restricted in its sphere, having one common theme, in order to reflect closely the constricting strength of the emotions which overwhelm the characters. It has also another characteristic. The poetic originality of the monodies often lies in the way they combine so as to seem dramatically natural, intense emotional and linguistic elevation being combined with ordinary physical actions such as sweeping and washing the floor, or lying down on the stage. The imagery is able to compass in the space of one ode both the detailed physical description of bodily aches which accompanies this action and the vision of ships crossing a purple sea – both the simple act of washing the step and the sensitivity to early dawn sunlight.

Aristophanes was accurate in seizing upon sharp juxtapositions between the pictorially elevated and the ordinary gesture as one of the significant stylistic characteristics of Euripidean monodies, although the absurdity he attributes to them is convincing only in comic parody. Viewed seriously, they do have a legitimate dramatic function, which is to convey by the use of such contrasts, several different moods and dimensions contained within the same situation. The monodies of Cassandra and Electra should perhaps be mentioned in this connection, as exemplifying variations of this close relation between elevated image and ordinary gesture.[47] Cassandra comes onto the stage carrying a torch. She holds it so shakily in fact that Hecuba attempts to take it from her in fear that she will set the whole place on fire.[48] This is an ordinary gesture on Hecuba's part and one which shows cognizance of the actual situation, namely that here is a girl whose mind is temporarily deranged and whose hands are too unsteady to keep a grip on anything. To Cassandra, this same torch and her holding of it appear quite different. She lavishes upon it terms describing its blazing brightness since to her it has a special importance.[49] It is the marriage torch to light her illusory wedding ceremony. It thus becomes in language and gesture the visual focus for her emotion, as Ion's laurel broom is for him.

In Electra's monody the combination of realistic gesture and imaginative language occurs in a slightly different way. The 'realistic' element is realised in the act of Electra's carrying water to Agamemnon's tomb and in her gestures of mourning. She has on her head a large water jar which she asks the servants to remove and set down for her.[50] As she laments for Agamemnon she tears her cheeks with her nails in characteristic Greek fashion, and holds her shorn head in her hands.

So much is commonplace enough to be classed as the stock gesture in this situation. But Electra does not stop here; she goes on with a simile in which she sees herself, more romantically, as a swan singing its last song on the river's edge in lament for another swan ensnared by hunters' nets.

αἲ αἲ, δρύπτε κάρα·
οἷα δέ τις κύκνος ἀχέτας
ποταμίοις παρὰ χεύμασιν
πατέρα φίλτατον καλεῖ,
ὀλόμενον δολίοις βρόχων

5

ἔρκεσιν, ὡς σὲ τὸν ἄθλιον,
πάτερ, ἐγὼ κατακλαίομαι,

Just as a swan by the river's edge sings its clear sounding notes in
lament for the parent bird it loved, and which has been destroyed
in treacherous hunters' nets, so I father mourn for your wretched
death . . .[51]

Swan similes are by no means unknown in such contexts,[52] but the
extended nature of the simile here in imitation of epic technique, gives it
uniqueness and prominence which not only brings out strongly the
contrast with what precedes, but also suggests perhaps a slightly self-
conscious note, a romantic posturing, on Electra's part which accords
with the things she says elsewhere. Euripides makes Electra's preoccupations as they reveal themselves in the lyrics she sings much more
self-concerned than those of Ion or Hecuba. Imagery is related almost
exclusively to her own appearance rather than to any outward object of
fear or veneration. This is evident not only in the monody itself, but also
in the extended lyric dialogue she holds with the chorus immediately
after the monody.

οὐκ ἐπ᾽ ἀγλαΐαις, φίλαι,
θυμὸν οὐδ᾽ ἐπὶ χρυσέοις
ὅρμοις ἐκπεπόταμαι
τάλαιν᾽, οὐδ᾽ ἱστᾶσα χοροὺς
Ἀργείαις ἅμα νύμφαις
εἱλικτὸν κρούσω πόδ᾽ ἐμόν.
δάκρυσι νυχεύ-
ω, δακρύων δέ μοι μέλει
δειλαίᾳ τὸ κατ᾽ ἦμαρ.
σκέψαι μου πιναρὰν κόμαν
καὶ τρύχη τάδ᾽ ἐμῶν πέπλων,
εἰ πρέπoντ᾽ Ἀγαμέμνονος
κούρᾳ ᾽σται βασιλείᾳ

The glitter of jewellery and gold necklaces can hold no excitement
for me, in my unhappiness. I am not leading the dance with
whirling feet beating the ground in the company of my friends in
Argos. I spend the night in tears: tears by night and tears by day:
they are my only concern. Look at my lank hair and these rags of
clothes and see if they suit the royal daughter of Agamemnon.[53]

The chorus gently point out in their lyric reply that Electra could put on fine clothes and jewellery if she wanted to. They are her friends and will lend her both. Their offer makes Electra's complaint at lack of friends seem what it is, mere posturing. The chorus and Electra's husband know that it is will, not abject poverty or cruelty which forces her to do menial tasks and wear squalid clothes.[54] The death of Agamemnon, and perhaps also her strange unconsummated marriage, have wrought in Electra an emotional unbalance which reveals itself not only here, but in the continuing persistence with which she harps on physical appearance. This lack of concentration on the ostensible object of her grief, Agamemnon's death, comes out also in the opulent picture she paints of Clytemnestra, sitting on a throne and surrounded by servants who are themselves draped in expensive Eastern linen and loaded down with the gold brooches of which she herself feels deprived.[55] Later still, she accuses Clytemnestra to her face of setting her hair in front of the mirror the minute her husband had left home and of working at her own beauty.[56] Seen in conjunction with these other references, Electra's words at the beginning of her lyric dialogue become more than a common rhetorical device to arouse pathos for her condition. They are also an indication of her twisted emotional attitude, of the envy and bitterness to which circumstances have reduced her.

It is mainly in the monodies of the middle plays that one sees the successful combination of different levels, and the different kinds of descriptive language. In those of the late plays, *Phoenissae, Orestes, Helen, I.A.*, such discrepancies as there are seem more genuine imbalance than calculated contrast. Often, the colourful elaboration of pictorial language seems out of all proportion to the emotion it purportedly illustrates.[57] This is particularly true in places where the monodist describes her appearance in detail. For instance, the language of Antigone and Jocasta in this connection, unlike that of Hecuba or of Electra, seems to have a decorative extravagance unrelated to the specific subject at hand. All Antigone does in the opening lines of her monody is to build up, by her statement that she is *not* wearing a veil, an elaborate picture of what she usually looks like when she does wear one.[58] The lavish description Jocasta paints of Polyneices' shining blue-black hair which falls over her cheek as he embraces her is in danger of eclipsing the instant happiness of the moment of reunion itself.[59] Many scholars have observed that in the monodies of the late plays the urgency of inner feeling somehow gets lost, or else is no longer given the same importance as it has in the plays of Euripides' middle period.[60]

Instead, their ornate style resembles a polished shell with the inside missing.

Before leaving monody, something should be said about actors' lyric in dialogue as distinct from actors' lyric delivered solo, since both have common characteristics which mark them off from choral lyric. The ascription of lyric lines to an actor in dialogue, as in monody, means a high emotional tone, and here they often contrast sharply with the more mundane trimeters which may be juxtaposed to them. As Masqueray has observed, 'Le trimètre n'a jamais été récité sur la scène des Grecs que par des personnages qui pouvaient encore maîtriser leurs émotions.'[61] One of Euripides' innovations was to increase and explore the possibilities of mixing trimeters and lyrics in dialogue.[62] The purpose of such mixed modes was to exploit the difference between emotional levels, which each metre pre-supposed, and thus to articulate through form specific emotional reactions. Imagery is not always integral to this form since dialogue must move more rapidly than monody and does not always allow for descriptive effects. But there are two scenes where it is very prominent and where its use also demonstrates strongly Euripides' dramatic imagination as it works through imagery. These scenes are the death of Alcestis and the *teichoskopia* in the *Phoenissae*.[63] The difference in stylistic treatment between the two scenes is in some measure the difference between Euripides' early and late style, the simple as opposed to the baroque, contentment with one compound adjective as opposed to a profusion of them. The dialogue in the *Phoenissae* however seems to me at least, to be dramatically more successful than the monodies in that play so that the contrast between early and late seems merely valid as a distinction between styles, and not between superior and inferior dramatic techniques.

In the *Alcestis*, Alcestis sees death approach in three brief impressionistic visions, each broken by a remark in iambics by Admetus. First she sees the rowing boat with two oars which takes the dead across the river and in it Charon, standing with his hand on the pole which propels the boat across its marshy borders. The three-and-a-half line description is economic: there are no decorative effects. She states her vision as a fact and accepts Charon's words to her as such. Second, she sees the winged figure of Hades himself looking out at her 'from underneath blue-black shining eyebrows' and feels him drag her away. It was the popular visual representation of Death, to give him wings, but the phrase ὑπ' ὀφρύσι κυαναυγέσι marks the image with Euripides' own inimitable eye for precise pictorial detail.[64] The audience saw the figure of Thanatos on stage in the prologue but this detail they could not have seen. Third, Alcestis describes the darkness of night already creeping over her eyes while Death stands there waiting. Then she faints. The lack of strict logical and temporal connection between the three images (they are alternatives, not causally related) illustrates Alcestis' gradually diminishing grip on the world about her as she sinks into an experience for which there are no adequately logical words – the revelation of Death. Her highly wrought state is emphasised also in the metre, the repetitions at 252, 259, 263, 266 and in the short sentences, 255–7, 259, 263 which suggest breathlessness. Her visions come and go uninvited and unwilled with the suddenness of spasms of pain. At no point do her words engage in reciprocal relation with those of Admetus who is wrapped up in his own platitudes and concern for his own grief.[65] The physical process of dying which the concrete imagery records in terms of sight for Alcestis who is undergoing it, does not impinge as reality upon Admetus. Only when Alcestis has fainted, and her conscious presence has disappeared, does he realise retrospectively his loss. Then his sudden outbreak into recitative anapaests at 273 (the most, one is tempted to think, of which he is capable) reflects this emotional change. It is the exploitation of the different metres here and the language permitted them which is itself a way of pointing the difference in situation and emotional level between the two main characters.

In the scene between Antigone and her tutor in the *Phoenissae*, the variation of metre and imagery to indicate emotional state is even more subtly controlled. The scene has its precedents in the *teichoskopia* of *Iliad* III and in a scene between Eteocles and the messenger in Aeschylus' *Septem*,[66] but the particular treatment demonstrates even more clearly by the difference in concept from these precedents, the originality of Euripides' own imagination. The Aeschylean scene is full of pictorial detail which serves to illustrate the character and emotions of the leaders on the battlefield rather than the viewpoint of the narrator. Each pictorial motif is a symbol. On Tydeus' shield, for instance, is painted a gleaming full moon; bronze bells are attached to it, shadowy plumes shake upon his helmet. But the device on the shield is to illustrate the hero's presumption, the bells are a source of fear to his enemies; it is anger which makes his helmet plume shake. As Euripides sees the scene, the heroes are important only insofar as they stand out visually as high points of relief in a much larger spectacle. Only what Antigone chooses to comment upon is interesting. It is through her prejudiced eyes Euripides chooses to communicate the scene: her attitude is what matters. As it is, she brings

before the audience a vision of the whole plain glittering with a light
which intermittently catches and illuminates the bronze and gold armour
of the warriors.

κατάχαλκον ἅπαν
πεδίον ἀστράπτει.

The whole plain plated with bronze flashes like lightning.[67]

The time seems to be that half-light in the very early dawn when the
moon has not yet disappeared from the sky and there is still a ground
mist, for Antigone several times addresses Selene and Hecate the moon
goddess.[68]

After her eyes have swept the battlefield, taking in in one rapid glance
the dazzling impression the massed armaments make, Antigone with the
Paidagogos' help begins to distinguish individuals by the colour of their
regalia. She spots Hippomedon, and as she watches him it seems to her
as though she is looking at a painting.

ἒ ἒ ὡς γαῦρος, ὡς φοβερὸς εἰσιδεῖν,
γίγαντι γηγενέτᾳ προσόμοιος
ἀστερωπὸς ἐν γραφαῖσιν, οὐχὶ πρόσφορος
ἀμερίῳ γέννᾳ.

Oh how boastful and fearful he looks, bright as a star like a giant
in painting, not like a human at all.[69]

The girl's imagination works by terms of reference known from art,
the only experience she has had of battle. The body of Hippomedon,
like the metal body of the giant Talos on the famous Krater, seems to
shine out in solitary relief.[70] Highlighting was a new discovery in the
painting of Euripides' day and it is not only these lines which suggest
that Euripides had in mind here the techniques of contemporary
painting.[71] The whole scene is seen by Antigone in terms of relief by
highlighting. The implication is that the light catches the glitter in
Parthenopaeus' eyes and brings out the colour of other heroes' equipment, namely the white plume of Hippomedon and his bronze shield,
the gold armour of Polyneices and the white chariot of Amphiaraus.[72]
Even Antigone's addresses to the Gods are made in pictorial terms almost
as if she were seeing them before her in a painting. Artemis has golden
curls, the Sun has a glittering belt and the Moon drives a set of horses.
All these are common motifs in art.[73]

Antigone cannot at first see Polyneices and she asks her Tutor where he is. He replies that the hero is standing near the tomb of the seven daughters of Niobe.

ὁρᾷς;   Αν. ὁρῶ δῆτ' οὐ σαφῶς, ὁρῶ δέ πως
μορφῆς τύπωμα στέρνα τ' ἐξηκασμένα.
ἀνεμώκεος εἴθε δρόμον νεφέλας ποσὶν ἐξανύσαιμι
    δι' αἰθέρος
πρὸς ἐμὸν ὁμογενέτορα, περὶ δ' ὠλένας
δέρᾳ φιλτάτᾳ βάλοιμ' ⟨ἐν⟩ χρόνῳ
    φυγάδα μέλεον. ὡς
ὅπλοισι χρυσέοισιν ἐκπρεπής, γέρον,
ἑῴοις ὅμοια φλεγέθων βολαῖς [ἀελίου.]

P. Do you see him?
A. Well, I do see him, but not clearly. I see somehow the moulded shape of his form and the outline of his breastplate. I wish I could run to my poor exiled brother through the air as swift as the hurrying clouds and at last fling my arms around his neck. But look how he stands out in his gold armour, as if blazing with the rays of the dawn.[74]

The difficulty with which Antigone discerns Polyneices enhances the effect of his sudden dazzling appearance when the mist clears at 167 and the sun suddenly shines full on him. At first he is obscured by shadow and she can see his outlined form only through a haze of clouds. It is an indistinct, impressionistic view and yet the outline promises more than she can actually see, for this is the implication of μορφῆς τύπωμα,[75] 'the moulded form of his shape'. The words too conjure up an idea of the great distance from which Antigone is viewing the scene, and the metre itself echoes the change the atmosphere makes over this distance. Trimeters express the effort Antigone makes to see properly, and they give way through a succession of resolved syllables of dochmiacs as Antigone impulsively expresses a wish to break through the clouds to get to him.[76]

Here too it seems as if the techniques of painting are in Euripides' mind. This preoccupation with light and shadow rendered by outline and by impressionistic use of colour was just what gave rise to the name σκιαγραφία, shadow-painting, for the new technique, as Parrhasios, Apollodorus and Zeuxis practised it. These lines recall other images already discussed, where a similar preoccupation with the play of light was observed, in the lines describing for instance Creousa's crocuses, the Delphic serpent, the eyes of the Cretan bull or the Sphinx in the tree.

When Antigone first climbs the ladder up to the battlements, the old man makes it clear that it is a special privilege for such a young girl to be allowed out of her private apartments. It is only because no-one else is about that this is possible, and because Polyneices is her brother, and it is natural she should want a glimpse of him. The image of light she uses, which wraps the grim battle scene in a soft golden glow, and the lyric metres which express it, in contrast to the old man's trimeter lines, suit her young age and her ill-concealed excitement, while the terms of reference from painting show the second-hand experience she has of battle. She sees the whole thing as a great romance, with Polyneices as its hero. This coloured view is a comment upon Antigone herself.[77] But it also prepares the audience for a sympathetic portrayal of Polyneices which, contrary to convention, he gets when he arrives on stage. Secondly it contrasts ironically with the *Realpolitik* as it is played out in debate between the two brothers. Antigone's romantic view is very far from 'reality' as others see it, and in particular Eteocles. Therein lies part of the tragedy.

These two examples of lyric used by an actor in mixed metrical dialogue may serve to show that some of the same kinds of pictorial technique are at work here as in monody and with similar aims. Thus, actors' lyric may be grouped together as something distinguishable from chorus' lyric. In spite of common stylistic elements which the two possess, such as descriptive compound adjectives and extensive use of visual motifs, the disposition and control of these elements are different in each as we have seen. The visual horizons of actors' lyric are deliberately more restricted and often more narrowly consistent within the space of one song, in keeping with the preoccupations of the singer. Certain objects acquire prominent and special significance as hidden recesses of subjective emotion are explored. Through imagery, the hidden or unacknowledged attitudes of character, the religious awe of Ion, the anger of Creousa, the fear of Hecuba, the overwhelming love of Phaedra, the warped bitterness of Electra, the misplaced idealism of Antigone. Many scholars have pointed out the frequency with which women rather than men are assigned monody and lyric dialogue in Euripides' plays.[78] The emotional extremes and highly subjective viewpoints are perhaps more suited to women or to the idealism of the very young.

Chapter IV

The Messenger Speech: Factual Landscapes

Where imagery in monody conveys the irrational and subjective attitudes which characterise the singer of that monody, that of the messenger must seem to convey a rational account of objective fact, the existence of which has nothing to do with him personally, except in the sense that he has happened to observe it. For the messenger is the one character in the play who is not caught up in the complicated entanglements of family dispute. He is an outsider in the sense that he is not of the same family or the same social class as the protagonists, and it is as a detached observer that he reports what he sees, as he comes upon it as it were cold, or by chance.[1] The pictorial language of the messenger speeches, accordingly, is suited to what is demanded of an eye-witness account of a crime, poetically conceived in the narrative mode. It is related to the way Euripides conceives of the messenger, the mode he must use, and the particular play in question. Stylistically it bears the same relation to lyric imagery as a black and white etching to a painting.[2]

Since the messenger is concerned with narrative of 'fact', there are no intuitive revelations for him, no visions through a haze of sunlit cloud, no incoherent passion. Both his persona and the narrative mode require that he keep to events in an ordered chronological sequence. The dilemma of the poet is to create through this narrative medium the illusion of undistorted information, while at the same time presenting this 'fictive fact' in such a persuasive way that it is accepted by the audience without question. For in Euripides one thing is certain. We must *believe* the messenger and not look beyond his account, as we might look beyond a monody, for a version which is different or less prejudiced. Euripides never allowed a messenger to lie: his description of the catastrophe, coming as it usually does at the highest point of tension in the play, is the definitive one.[3] There must therefore be conviction in his words without apparent distortion, drama viewed with enough detachment to be clearly communicated. Euripides solves this problem in several ways. One is to keep the character of the messenger unobtrusive. This he does by frequently ascribing to him merely the colourless generic name ἄγγελος,[4] by giving him moral platitudes at a point which will not interrupt the narrative,[5] and by allowing him only a narrow range of sympathetic adjectives, such as τλήμων, τάλας, δεινός, words which are so commonplace that they do not distract the listener as more subtly reactive comments would.[6] In this way the subjective element which is most likely to seem to distort, is kept at a minimum level. Another way the poet keeps the balance between apparent fact and colourful exaggeration is observable in his handling of certain formulaic devices which direct the listener's attention, but in such a predictable unobtrusive way that he is not distracted, but feels free to concentrate on the content of what is being said.[7] A third way is in the control of imagery. The descriptive passages in the narrative provide an area in which the skills of rendering a highly persuasive account, and at the same time an apparently detached one, may be carefully controlled.

Visual clarity is in itself a method of persuasion. In commenting upon a passage from the second messenger speech of the Bacchae, Mr Lattimore remarks 'We cannot believe it, but we can visualize it or most of it.'[8] Surely it is precisely because we can visualize it so clearly that we can believe it. The imagery of all Euripides' messenger speeches possesses an extraordinary etched clarity which gives the misleading impression of simplicity, but which in fact is so artfully constructed as to lead the listener into total acquiescence. Such aesthetic controls which help one through the long narrative sequences, consist for instance of setting the scene, arranging people in groups against a background, changing the perspective of certain points, varying the pace by controlling the density of verbs and constructing images in terms of contrast.

Like most good storytellers,[9] Euripides begins these messenger speeches with a brief indication of time and place.

> λαμπρὰ μὲν ἀκτὶς ἡλίου, κανὼν σαφής,
> ἔβαλλε γαῖαν· ἀμφὶ δ' Ἠλέκτρας πύλας
> ἔστην θεατὴς πύργον εὐαγῆ λαβών.
> ὁρῶ δὲ . . .

A brilliant ray of sunlight, straight and clear,
Was striking the ground as I stood by Electra's gate,
Where a watchtower gave a sweeping view. I saw . . .[10]

> ἐπεὶ τὸν ἐσρέοντα διὰ Συμπληγάδων
> βοῦς ὑλοφορβοὺς πόντου εἰσεβάλλομεν,
> ἦν τις διαρρὼξ κυμάτων πολλῷ σάλῳ

κοιλωπὸς ἀγμός, πορφυρευτικαὶ στέγαι.
ἐνταῦθα . . .

Just as we drove our cattle from the woods
To that long hollow where the curving tide
Has cut away the cliff, where the beach-men rest
From purple-fishing, one of us . . .[11]

ἐπεὶ μελάθρων τῶνδ' ἀπήραμεν πόδα,
ἐσβάντες ἦμεν δίκροτον εἰς ἁμαξιτὸν
ἔνθ' . . .

When we rose from your cottage and walked down the hill
We came across a beaten double wagon-truck,
And there . . .[12]

Such opening scenes orientate the listener and make sure that the action
is properly led up to. Euripides' messengers never plunge 'in medias res',
as, for instance, does the Paidagogos who acts as a messenger in Sophocles' *Electra*.[13] Setting documents the event by measuring it against an
inanimate, impersonal background; at the same time, it is a persuasive
way of enabling one to picture the action more easily.

Euripides maintains a strong sense of spatial relations throughout the
speeches, so that it is almost possible to approach the action diagram-
matically as one might move groups of chequers on a board. The first
position is usually a static one, where a still figure or groups of figures are
related to the background scene. Troops, for instance, are massed in
three positions on different terrain;[14] children are clustered in a circle
round the altar gazing fixedly at the central figure, Heracles;[15] a girl in a
new dress points her feet out straight and glances at the fall of the hem-
line;[16] Hippolytus stands poised at the chariot rail ready to drive off.[17]
Such clearly conceived poses are a way of gauging the full effects of the
violence which then disturbs them. The troops are soon thrown into
imbalance, the cavalry advancing, the left wing retreating; the children
are scattered in disorder around the colonnades; the girl over-balances
and falls sideways onto a chair. Pictorial contrast here as elsewhere is a
means of rendering action exciting.

The perspective frequently alternates between a wide-angled view of
the whole scene and close-ups of particular details. Extreme examples of
this occur in the *Ion* and the *Helen*. The servant in the *Ion* moves from a
general description of a crowded banquet scene to one tiny detail, the
relaxed claws of the dying bird which has drunk the poison meant for Ion.

This detail is made vivid by the one single visual epithet φοινικοσκελεῖς, 'scarlet-clawed' which draws attention to the bird's red feet. It is one of the very few compounds and one of the few significant words for colour in the speeches.[18]

Another example verging on the gratuitously ornamental occurs in the *Helen*, where the messenger proceeds from giving a general description of preparations on the ship to a close-up view of Helen's beautiful feet protruding through the rungs of a rope-ladder.[19] Here the single ornamental epithet εὐσφύρου, 'pretty-ankled', highlights this detail. There are various ways of shifting the perspective of vision. Sometimes, as in both speeches of the *Bacchae*, the messenger will go from detailed presentation to an impressionistic view of the whole scene.[20] Or he will sum up by a comment on the general human reaction as in the remark in the *Medea* that everyone was afraid to touch the body.[21] This follows a particularly minute and harrowing itemisation of the physical symptoms of disintegrating flesh. More rarely, he will suddenly switch from general comment to his own personal reaction, as for instance at that point in the *Supplices* where the messenger says that he responded to a particularly definitive action in the battle by shouting out, dancing up and down, and clapping his hands.[22] Frequent alteration between different groups keeps the interest alive, as in the description in the *Andromache* of the fight between the lone Neoptolemus and his numerous attackers who are concealed behind the laurel bushes growing in front of the shrine.

χὠ μὲν κατ' ὄμμα στὰς προσεύχεται θεῷ·
οἳ δ' ὀξυθήκτοις φασγάνοις ὡπλισμένοι
κεντοῦσ' ἀτευχῆ παῖδ' Ἀχιλλέως λάθρᾳ.
χωρεῖ δὲ πρύμναν· οὐ γὰρ εἰς καιρὸν τυπεὶς
ἐτύγχαν'· ἐξέλκει δὲ καὶ παραστάδος
κρεμαστὰ τεύχη πασσάλων καθαρπάσας
ἔστη 'πὶ βωμοῦ γοργὸς ὁπλίτης ἰδεῖν,
βοᾷ δὲ Δελφῶν παῖδας ἱστορῶν τάδε·
Τίνος μ' ἕκατι κτείνετ' εὐσεβεῖς ὁδοὺς
ἥκοντα; ποίας ὄλλυμαι πρὸς αἰτίας; –
τῶν δ' οὐδὲν οὐδεὶς μυρίων ὄντων πέλας
ἐφθέγξατ', ἀλλ' ἔβαλλον ἐκ χερῶν πέτροις.
πυκνῇ δὲ νιφάδι πάντοθεν σποδούμενος
προὔτεινε τεύχη κἀφυλάσσετ' ἐμβολὰς
ἐκεῖσε κἀκεῖσ' ἀσπίδ' ἐκτείνων χερί.

ἀλλ' οὐδὲν ἦνεν· ἀλλὰ πόλλ' ὁμοῦ βέλη,
οἰστοί, μεσάγκυλ' ἔκλυτοί τ' ἀμφώβολοι,
σφαγῆς ἐχώρουν βουπόροι ποδῶν πάρος.
δεινὰς δ' ἂν εἶδες πυρρίχας φρουρουμένου
βέλεμνα παιδός. ὡς δέ νιν περισταδὸν
κύκλῳ κατεῖχον οὐ διδόντες ἀμπνοάς,

So Neoptolemus stood there facing the God and made a prayer.
They armed to the hilt with new-sharpened blades and seeing that
he wore no corselet, lunged at him treacherously. He reeled back,
not fatally stabbed, snatched from the hooks some armour hanging
in the front colonnade, and leapt onto the altar, eyes glittering.
He challenged the Delphians in a loud voice. 'Why murder me
when I have come on a pilgrimage? What have I done to deserve
death?' Not one man there of the many spoke a word, but they
began to pelt him with stones. He was battered on all sides with a
constant volleying. He tried to hold out his weapons [for protection],
and to fend off their attacks by putting his shield arm out straight and
covering himself at the separate points where they struck, but he
could not do it. Too many weapons came at once: arrows, javelins,
unfastened spits and meat cleavers came flying to his feet. Then you
would have seen a terrible dance as the boy tried to dodge the
weapons. The men were edging round him in a circle giving him
no time for breath. . . .[23]

In this short piece of narrative, not only is variety maintained by natural
shifts in subject from Neoptolemus to his opponents, and from them to
an impersonal description of the many weapons coming at him, but as
the narration moves to its climax, there is also a very dramatic and
unexpected change from the third to the second person, as the messenger
appeals to Peleus who is on-stage and can only imagine the scene through
the messenger's eyes.[24]

The combined qualities of setting, grouping, and perspective-change
which thus make the narrative clearly visible, and as such, convincing,
are exemplified in the first messenger's speech from the *Bacchae*. The
scene is set in the opening lines.

ἀγελαῖα μὲν βοσκήματ' ἄρτι πρὸς λέπας
μόσχων ὑπεξήκριζον, ἡνίχ' ἥλιος
ἀκτῖνας ἐξίησι θερμαίνων χθόνα . . .

The pasturing herds of cattle had just begun to climb the steep
mountain ridge, at that hour when the sun was beginning to send
out its rays to warm the earth, when I . . .[25]

The steepness of the terrain is indicated in the word λέπας and the rare
double verbal compound ὑπεξήκριζον.[26] Against this background, the
maenads are first visualised in three groups in repose, some sitting with
their backs leaning against a fir tree, others lying down with their heads
resting on a bed of oak leaves. As they hear the sound of the approaching
cattle they begin to stir. ἀνῆξαν ὀρθαί indicates instant movement in
contrast with the previous σώμασιν παρειμέναι.

> αἳ δ᾽ ἀποβαλοῦσαι θαλερὸν ὀμμάτων ὕπνον
> ἀνῇξαν ὀρθαί, θαῦμ᾽ ἰδεῖν εὐκοσμίας,
> νέαι παλαιαὶ παρθένοι τ᾽ ἔτ᾽ ἄζυγες.
> καὶ πρῶτα μὲν καθεῖσαν εἰς ὤμους κόμας
> νεβρίδας τ᾽ ἀνεστείλανθ᾽ ὅσαισιν ἀμμάτων
> σύνδεσμ᾽ ἐλέλυτο, καὶ καταστίκτους δορὰς
> ὄφεσι κατεζώσαντο λιχμῶσιν γένυν.
> αἳ δ᾽ ἀγκάλαισι δορκάδ᾽ ἢ σκύμνους λύκων
> ἀγρίους ἔχουσαι λευκὸν ἐδίδοσαν γάλα,
> ὅσαις νεοτόκοις μαστὸς ἦν σπαργῶν ἔτι
> βρέφη λιπούσαις· ἐπὶ δ᾽ ἔθεντο κισσίνους
> στεφάνους δρυός τε μίλακός τ᾽ ἀνθεσφόρου.
> θύρσον δέ τις λαβοῦσ᾽ ἔπαισεν ἐς πέτραν,
> ὅθεν δροσώδης ὕδατος ἐκπηδᾷ νοτίς·
> ἄλλη δὲ νάρθηκ᾽ ἐς πέδον καθῆκε γῆς,
> καὶ τῇδε κρήνην ἐξανῆκ᾽ οἴνου θεός·
> ὅσαις δὲ λευκοῦ πώματος πόθος παρῆν,
> ἄκροισι δακτύλοισι διαμῶσαι χθόνα
> γάλακτος ἑσμοὺς εἶχον· ἐκ δὲ κισσίνων
> θύρσων γλυκεῖαι μέλιτος ἔσταζον ῥοαί.

>   rubbing the bloom of soft sleep
> from their eyes, they rose up lightly and straight –
> a lovely sight to see; all as one,
> the old women and the young and the unmarried girls.
> First, they let their hair fall loose, down
> over their shoulders, and those whose straps had slipped
> fastened their skins of fawn with writhing snakes

that licked their cheeks. Breasts swollen with milk,
new mothers who had left their babies behind at home
nestled gazelles and young wolves in their arms,
suckling them. Then they crowned their hair with leaves,
ivy and oak and flowering bryony. One woman
struck her thyrsus against a rock and a fountain
of cool water came bubbling up. Another drove
her fennel in the ground and where it struck the earth,
at the touch of a god, a spring of wine poured out.
Those who wanted milk scratched at the soil
with bare fingers and the white milk came welling up.
Pure honey spurted, streaming from their wands.[27]

From here the viewpoint shifts to the messenger's own companions who
form a rival group hidden in the bushes to observe the women. After
their conversation the messenger reverts to the women moving in a
mass movement, and then to the whole scene which he attempts to sum
up in the words which form a focal point of his speech.

$$\pi\hat{\alpha}\nu \ \delta\grave{\epsilon} \ \sigma\upsilon\nu\epsilon\beta\acute{\alpha}\kappa\chi\epsilon\upsilon' \ \acute{o}\rho\sigma\varsigma$$
$$\kappa\alpha\grave{\iota} \ \theta\hat{\eta}\rho\epsilon\varsigma, \ o\grave{\upsilon}\delta\grave{\epsilon}\nu \ \delta' \ \hat{\eta}\nu \ \grave{\alpha}\kappa\acute{\iota}\nu\eta\tau\sigma\nu \ \delta\rho\acute{o}\mu\omega.$$

Suddenly the whole mountain and all the animate life on it were
stirred by the spirit of Dionysus and there was nothing that did not
move.[28]

These artfully simple words[29] represent a turning point, a moment of
equilibrium before the separate acts of violence become distinguishable,
and the quiet static beginning is transformed into one of wild energetic
movement. The *sparagmos* of the cattle follows in which the women are
again seen in groups which match the grouping of the earlier description,
and then again brought together in one mass movement in which they
are compared to a flock of birds moving in on a field of corn.

What is remarkable is that at no point does one lose *sight* of the action.
The sequences change pictorially as they might change in a sequence of
film. Of course there are infinitely more devices at work besides those
which evoke the purely visual. To name only a few, *anaphora* and
repetition underline important moments,[30] verbs are used two and three
in a line to indicate concentration of action,[31] rare words are used for
emphasis.[32]

And all these devices are in a sense empathetic ones. A measure of the art and aesthetic persuasion that exists through them, may be illustrated by a contrast with one of Euripides' imitators, Philostratos. In his *Imagines*, this author produces descriptive renderings of mythological subjects from paintings, based in some cases as he himself acknowledges, on Euripides' messenger speeches. The *Heracles Mainomenos* is one such attempt.[33] He describes here the scene of desolation at the altar when it has been overturned by Heracles' violence.

> κανᾶ δὲ καὶ χέρνιβα
> καὶ ὀυλαὶ καὶ σχίζαι κὰι κρατήρ, τὰ
> τοῦ Ἑρκείου, λελάκτισται πάντα καὶ ὁ μὲν
> ταῦρος ἕστηκεν, ἱερεῖα δὲ προσέρριπται
> τῷ βωμῷ τὰ γένη καί τῇ λεοντῇ.

The basket and the basins and the barley-corn and the wood-shavings and the mixing bowl were all kicked aside, and the bull stood there while the sacred objects were hurled on top of the altar, and the children on top of the lionskin.

This is essentially an undigested list to which the children seem to be appended in inverse order to their importance. Whether Philostratos intended this or not, the focus, by its position and the strong active verb accompanying it, is the bull who stands doggedly on in the scene of chaos all round him. This and much else in Philostratos' account show the difference (even allowing for that between prose and verse) between catalogue and ordered narrative, second hand topography and real imagination.

Nonetheless, however exciting and well-told the messenger's story as it is expressed in iambic verse may seem to be, he must not appear to stray beyond 'fact'. It is not for him to wander from this path by stray visual associations of his own, or by an over-indulgence in colourful side-lights. His business is essentially to present to the characters on-stage and to the audience, evidence of a crime which has been committed, and one which is to require some sort of judgement and analysis. Only the messenger's account can provide the basis for this analysis. This, I think, accounts for the graphic but also calculatedly austere landscapes and descriptions these speeches contain. How austere they are may be illustrated by two pertinent parallels from less successful messenger speeches containing similar subject matter by other tragedians.

The first is from Chaeremon, who in part of a messenger speech which survives from the *Oeneus* describes a Bacchic revel.³⁴ His maenads, far from the simplicity of plain oak leaves, are idling in soft fields luxuriant with dew-drenched marjoram. They lie on beds of calamint, violets and crocuses whose colours make patterns of light and dark reflection on their clothes. Their dresses are torn revealing breasts, thighs and arms (carefully itemised in succeeding couplets) which gleam in the moonlight. One 'naked before the watching sky' looks 'like a living painting'; another 'bears the mark of love without hopes in the smiling flower of youth'. The language and style of the pictorial imagery here are like Euripides in another mode, that of lyric, or perhaps even a speech attributed to Pentheus, since there is a sense of the gloating observer which would fit his dramatic character.

> ἔκειτο δ' ἡ μὲν λευκὸν εἰς σεληνόφως
> φαίνουσα μαστὸν λελυμένης ἐπωμίδος,
> τῆς δ' αὖ χορεία λαγόνα τὴν ἀριστερὰν
> ἔλυσε· γυμνὴ δ' αἰθέρος θεάμασιν
> ζῶσαν γραφὴν ἔφαινε, χρῶμα δ' ὄμμασιν
> λευκὸν μελαίνης ἔργον ἀντηύγει σκιᾶς.
> ἄλλη δ' ἐγύμνου καλλίχειρας ὠλένας,
> ἄλλης προσαμπέχουσα θῆλυν αὐχένα.
> ἡ δὲ ῥαγέντων χλανιδίων ὑπὸ πτυχαῖς
> ἔφαινε μηρόν, κἀξεπεσφραγίζετο
> ὥρας γελώσης χωρὶς ἐλπίδων ἔρως.
> ὑπνωμέναι δ' ἔπιπτον ἐλενίων ἔπι,
> ἴων τε μελανόφυλλα συγκλῶσαι πτερὰ
> κρόκον θ', ὃς ἡλιῶδες εἰς ὑφάσματα
> πέπλων σκιᾶς εἴδωλον ἐξωμόργνυτο,
> [ἔρση δὲ θαλερὸς ἐκτραφεὶς ἀμάρακος]
> λειμῶσι μαλακοῖς ἐξέτεινον αὐχένας.

One was lying there in the moonlight, her shoulder strap loosed to reveal her breast shining white; another's left flank was exposed as she danced, and naked before the watching sky she looked like a living painting, and the whiteness of her skin made a bright contrasting radiance to the dark shadows. Another had bared her arms and with her pretty hands was encircling the neck of one of her girl companions. This one showed through the folds of her torn tunic glimpses of her thigh, and the mark of love without hope in the smiling flower of youth. They fell asleep upon beds of calamint

6

and crushed the petals of dark-hued violets, and the crocus which imprinted upon their clothes an impression of brightly shining shadow [and delicate marjoram nourished by the dew] and they stretched out their necks in these soft meadows.[35]

How close this description is in basic subject matter to that of the herdsman's account in the *Bacchae* is obvious. The women are sleeping in relaxed fashion on the ground and have accordingly unfastened their tunics and let their hair fall loose. Even the grammatical structure is similar in both passages, dependent as it is upon the distributive ἡ μὲν . . . ἡ δὲ . . . or αἱ μὲν . . . αἱ δὲ.[36]. Both vocabulary and style in the Chaeremon passage are reminiscent of Euripides, in particular the simile from painting, the strong contrasts of light and dark and the use of the metaphors κἀξεπεσφραγίζετο and ἐξωμόργνυτο.[37] But this is not the Euripides of the messenger speeches. While the subject matter resembles the messenger's narrative in the *Bacchae*, the style with its extravagant colouring and dallying descriptive effects which impede action almost entirely, is much more like Euripidean lyric. It may have been a *tour de force* on Chaeremon's part to incorporate the concentrated but static pictorialism of lyric into the messenger's normally more descriptively restrained iambics, but if so, it seems to remain exactly this and no more, since intensity of colour alone does not ensure artistic success. The simple monotony of the anatomical catalogue, combined with the over-blown pictorial elaboration in iambics, seems to get the worst of both worlds.[38] It is perhaps unfair to judge from only part of a speech, but Croiset's judgement still seems to me apt: 'C'est le language d'une précieuse, qui est bien près quelquefois de devenir ridicule.'[39]

The messenger speech from Seneca's *Phaedra* provides a second viewpoint from which to judge Euripides' handling of imagery in a narrative passage, since both authors cover the same ground in describing the wrecking of the chariot by the bull from the sea. Euripides leaves much about the bull to the imagination. It emerges from a tidal wave and is first sensed by the horses.

> ἐπεὶ δ' ἔρημον χῶρον εἰσεβάλλομεν,
> ἀκτή τις ἔστι τοὐπέκεινα τῆσδε γῆς
> πρὸς πόντον ἤδη κειμένη Σαρωνικόν.
> ἔνθεν τις ἠχὼ χθόνιος ὡς βροντὴ Διὸς
> βαρὺν βρόμον μεθῆκε, φρικώδη κλύειν·
> ὀρθὸν δὲ κρᾶτ' ἔστησαν οὖς τ' ἐς οὐρανὸν

ἵπποι· παρ' ἡμῖν δ' ἦν φόβος νεανικὸς
πόθεν ποτ' εἴη φθόγγος. ἐς δ' ἁλιρρόθους
ἀκτὰς ἀποβλέψαντες ἱερὸν εἴδομεν
κῦμ' οὐρανῷ στηρίζον, ὥστ' ἀφῃρέθη
Σκίρωνος ἀκτὰς ὄμμα τοὐμὸν εἰσορᾶν·
ἔκρυπτε δ' Ἰσθμὸν καὶ πέτραν Ἀσκληπιοῦ.
κἄπειτ' ἀνοιδῆσάν τε καὶ πέριξ ἀφρὸν
πολὺν καχλάζον ποντίῳ φυσήματι
χωρεῖ πρὸς ἀκτάς, οὗ τέθριππος ἦν ὄχος.
αὐτῷ δὲ σὺν κλύδωνι καὶ τρικυμίᾳ
κῦμ' ἐξέθηκε ταῦρον, ἄγριον τέρας·
οὗ πᾶσα μὲν χθὼν φθέγματος πληρουμένη
φρικῶδες ἀντεφθέγγετ', εἰσορῶσι δὲ
κρεῖσσου θέαμα δεργμάτων ἐφαίνετο.
εὐθὺς δὲ πώλοις δεινὸς ἐμπίπτει φόβος.

When we were entering the lonely country
the other side of the border, where the shore
goes down to the Saronic Gulf, a rumbling
deep in the earth, terrible to hear,
growled like the thunder of Father Zeus.
The horses raised their heads, pricked up their ears,
and gusty fear was on us all to know,
whence came the sound. As we looked toward the shore,
where the waves were beating, we saw a wave appear,
a miracle wave, lifting its crest to the sky,
so high that Sciron's coast was blotted out
from my eye's vision. And it hid the Isthmus
and the Asclepius Rock. To the shore it came,
swelling, boiling, crashing, casting its surf around,
to where the chariot stood.
But at the very moment when it broke,
the wave threw up a monstrous savage bull.
Its bellowing filled the land, and the land echoed it,
with shuddering emphasis. And sudden panic
fell on the horses in the car.[40]

Euripides' narrative has, throughout, visual appeal, but he does not
judge it expedient to describe the bull at such length that it will either
slow down the action, or appear to distort fact. If he concentrates upon

the wave, this is perhaps partly because an inanimate phenomenon is less liable to seem ridiculous in description than a monster, and partly because by concentrating upon the sea and the seashore rather than the bull, he could also integrate the whole scene neatly and economically into descriptive imagery as it is used significantly in the play as a whole.[41] Seneca is neither so economic, nor so restrained in his description of the same event.

> quis habitus ille corporis vasti fuit!
> caerulea taurus colla sublimis gerens
> erexit altam fronte viridanti iubam;
> stant hispidae auris, cornibus varius color,
> et quem feri dominator habuisset gregis
> et quem sub undis natus: hinc flammam vomunt
> oculi, hinc relucent caerula insignes nota;
> opima cervix arduos tollit toros
> naresque hiulcis haustibus patulae fremunt;
> musco tenaci pectus ac palear viret,
> longum rubente spargitur fuco latus;
> tum pone tergus ultima in monstrum coit
> facies et ingens belua immensam trahit
> squamosa partem. talis extremo mari
> pistrix citatas sorbet aut frangit rates.
> tremuere terrae, fugit attonitum pecus
> passim per agros, nec suos pastor sequi
> meminit iuvencos; omnis e saltu fera
> diffugit, omnis frigido exsanguis metu
> venator horret.

What an extraordinary sight that monstrous body was! It was a gigantic bull with a blue-black neck and its head was green and had a long mane protruding from it. Its shaggy ears stood out and its horns were of various colours, one reminding me of the colour the leader of the fierce herd had, the other the colour we see on the native sea-cow. Its eyes began to belch out flames at one moment, and at another to glow conspicuously with a clear blue gleam: its splendid neck supported great muscles: its wide-spreading nostrils puffed as it drew its breath in and out: its chest and dewlap were green with clinging sea-weed and its long side was spotted here and there with reddish streaks. Then the rear part following its back completed the monster and this creature covered in scales dragged along its own huge structure. It was just like that marine phenomenon of the outer ocean, the pistrix which swallows or breaks ships as they proceed in full course. The earth trembled, the cattle fled in astonishment over the fields and the herdsmen forgot to go after the heifers. Every animal fled from its wooded haunt, every huntsman turned pale and went stiff with cold fright.[42]

This messenger begins with a vague judgement of his own, which the ensuing description in any case makes redundant. The profusion of coloured and ornamental detail leads away from the action rather than towards it (the presence of sea-weed for instance does not affect the way the bull destroys Hippolytus), while the comparisons with various marine phenomena reduce the animal to a mere museum curiosity. Such extended and lavish treatment undermines both credibility and imagination, and this passage, and others further on,[43] make this messenger's account seem like verbose rhetorical pomposity, whereas the leanness and economy of Euripides' narrative aid both the progress of the action and the illusion of an objective factual report. Austerity itself seems a guarantee of integrity.

Taking Euripides' narrative speeches as a whole, there are few purely ornamental adjectives,[44] and few details of scenic description which are not germane in some way to the event itself. If the sun is just coming up, that is to tell us what time of day it was when the reported events took place. In the case of Bacchic revels for instance, this is also significant because it contradicts Pentheus' expectation that all orgies must necessarily take place in the dark.[45] If cattle are mentioned early in the speech, this is to prepare for their reappearance as victims later on. Pine trees are props for Pentheus' death and the rock-strewn terrain a source of weapons. Hippolytus drives his chariot by the sea-shore because it is from the sea Poseidon will send the bull. The horses are mentioned early in the speech because they later become the main agents in the wreck. Description is thus determinative and restricted in such a way as to keep the illusion of a strictly factual report. Even the similes have the function of facilitating a more *precise* view of the event itself, and while in many ways resembling those of Homer, they are (partly because they are shorter) more disciplined to the main action they describe.[46] The maenads move like birds over a cornfield, or like colts just released from the yoke. Men attack like wild boars sharpening their teeth, or like a whirlwind. Heracles brings down the club onto his child's head like a blacksmith smiting bronze. Blood oozes from flesh like tears bled from pine bark.[47]

In these, the concern is not one of communicating ideas, nor as in Seneca is it to reveal encyclopedic reminiscences of the messenger himself. Clarity in picturing the event is all.

Since crime and not sin is the main business of the objective witness, the determinative element in the descriptions of Euripidean messengers is (at its lowest level) not unlike a poetical version of clues in ashtrays, car-numbers noted or pistol shots counted. But then one wants to ask whether there are not within this factual landscape degrees of factual depth. Are there varieties of level at which the necessary environment is dramatically handled? In the *Medea* for instance, the princess is poisoned inside the palace. The poet mentions certain items of furniture, notably a chair, to make her death imaginatively credible and realistic. The context is thus related to the happening of the crime but not to its fundamental nature or motivation. Medea is far away and the event when it happens could equally have been set outside the palace, in the grounds or on the street. In other plays like the *Heracleidae*, *Supplices* or *Phoenissae* a battlefield scene is required. It is indispensable to the action again, but one battlefield is much like another and the particular location carries no significance beyond the minimum plot requirement. This is all quite satisfactory. One looks for no more. Nonetheless, there are plays where the setting is more than this, and where it takes on what is, for dramatic purposes at least, almost sociological significance. Take the *Electra*. Aegisthus, the messenger specifically says, was murdered in a garden, where he welcomed Orestes as a guest and a fellow worshipper.

> κυρεῖ δὲ κήποις ἐν καταρρύτοις βεβώς,
> δρέπων τερείνης μυρσίνης κάρᾳ πλόκους·
> ἰδών τ᾽ αὐτεῖ· χαίρετ᾽, ὦ ξένοι·

He happened to be walking in the gardens by the river, cutting glossy myrtle shoots to put on his hair. He saw us and called out 'You are most welcome, my guests'.[48]

This fleeting piece of imagery establishes a new context for the traditional crime, not just to arouse pathos, but also to enable an audience to understand intellectually the peculiarly obsessive nature of Orestes' act of murder. Unlike Hamlet with Claudius he has no scruples, but disregards claims both of hospitality and sacred ground and cuts Aegisthus down in the middle of a sacrifice. Even here the garden seems to be introduced rather suddenly to provide an environment which will suitably relate to the nature of the event. There are two plays, however, where the environment the messenger describes seems to grow out of the wider setting of the play itself and where the link to the catastrophe is so close as to be almost inseparable from it. These are the *Heracles* and the *Bacchae*. In the *Heracles*, Euripides so handles setting in the messenger speech that the hero's madness actually manifests itself in the way he interprets his surroundings. Looking at the place long familiar to him, with its altar and colonnades, he suddenly imagines it to be somewhere else. He gets into an imaginary chariot and makes an imaginary journey.

> ὁ δ' εἷρπ' ἄνω τε καὶ κάτω κατὰ στέγας,
> μέσον δ' ἐς ἀνδρῶν' ἐσπεσὼν Νίσου πόλιν
> ἥκειν ἔφασκε· δωμάτων τ' ἔσω βεβώς,
> κλιθεὶς ἐς οὖδας, ὡς ἔχει, σκευάζεται
> θοίνην. . .

Up and down through the house he drove, and riding through the great hall, claimed it was Nisus' city, though it was, in fact, his house. He threw himself to the floor, and acted out a feast . . .[49]

Heracles' madness thus emerges through a description of the phantom journey he makes in his mind only. The messenger recreates it through a series of sensuous visual images calculated to strike home the urgency of the physical facts. Heracles is described in a succession of poses each caught and held in one brief image. He takes up the imaginary reins of a non-existent chariot. He prepares for a banquet. He joins in an imaginary athletic contest, stripping himself of his buckles and wrestling with the empty air. He circles round the columns of his own palace, thinking they are those of Eurystheus, and backs his own child up against a stone buttress and runs him through. He finds another crouching at the base of an altar and clubs him on the head. He kills a third under the impression that he is uprooting the Cyclopean walls at Mycenae where he thinks he is. The creation here of a double landscape and a double level of action is quite brilliantly done, and one feels that only an independent witness in this case could properly convey, as Euripides' messenger has done, the full discrepancy between 'illusion' and 'reality', enabling the audience to hold both in balance at the same time within the terms of reference of this narrative. Through his quite factual description of setting, the messenger nonetheless shows how in madness the hallucinatory world in which Heracles has moved for much of his life, and the 'real world' in which superhuman violence has no place, may meet. The palace at Thebes which is to him successively the city of Nisus, the wooded valley of the Isthmus, Eurystheus' palace and the battlements at Mycenae, is recreated in all these guises by the messenger, and provides the area within which Heracles' madness is defined. This is therefore more than the mere setting of a crime: it is also a kind of sociological documentation of its nature, recorded through objective observation.

Another play in which the setting is related to the nature as well as to the happening of the event is the *Bacchae*, where the wild and lonely mountain-side is an essential condition for the maenads' behaviour. It would have been inconceivable that the attack on the cattle or upon Pentheus should have taken place in the city. The emotions of the women are released only by the sense of solitude and peace which is found in open spaces and in an inanimate but non-human environment. Their anger is aroused by the interruption of that sense. The man from the city πλάνης κατ' ἄστυ who hunts them down is lacking this sensitivity. The women's feeling for nature is no romantic or sentimental one, but a primary instinctive recognition of the roots of their own being. This recognition is communicated through the pictorial language of both messengers. The only terms which seem appropriate to them to describe the women's movements are ones of animal life.[50] They sleep, wake suddenly, and are startled into flight with the quickness of animals. They move like birds in full flight or like colts frisking. They are hunted as if they were animals, and they call each other by animal names. There is a reciprocal relationship too between them and the wild-life around them, since young animals freely allow themselves to be nursed by the women, and snakes lick their cheeks. Such factual notations by the messenger show that the distinctions between civilised living and the jungle are momentarily obliterated. The women treat this lonely mountain landscape as if it were their natural home. They lie on the ground, eat and drink by scratching the earth, and run over rocks and boulders barefoot as easily as if they were carpeted. This one-ness with environment is stressed to some extent through the use of the prefix συν – in such words as συνεβάκχευ' 'joined in revelry together' or συγκεραυνοῦσαι 'hurled their weapons together', or in the compound nouns Agave uses to describe Dionysus, as him who hunted and worked *together* with her, τὸν ξυγκύναγον, τὸν ξυνεργάτην ἄγρας.[51] This identification of the women with their environment, as the messenger describes it in concrete terms, is in sharp contrast to the awkwardness with which his own party hide in the bushes, or the slow care with which Pentheus is conspicuously planted in a tree to spy. Neither the city-men nor Pentheus belong to this place, and as hunters they become hunted in turn, just as ordinary hunters may be savaged by the animals upon whom they intrude.

What the messengers present in their factual observations of this mountain-side scene is documentary material for the analysis of a particular kind of behaviour, in this case Bacchic ecstasy. From these basic sense data, the audience are free to make a judgement.

'If I choose to see *Richard III*', says Brecht, 'I don't want to feel myself to be Richard III but to glimpse this phenomenon in all its strangeness and incomprehensibility.'[52] The advantage of the messenger as he is conceived in Euripidean tragedy is that he can seem to achieve this distance of view. The austere and determinative quality of the pictorial language operates within the narrative form to maintain an illusion of factual objective reporting. It must be an illusion because the 'facts' themselves are imaginative, in the sense that they do not occur visibly on-stage and the presentation of them must be done with enough art to persuade one of their credibility. But the irrefutable circumstantial evidence which is the substance of these speeches provides a basis for judgement of a crime, not merely an emotional reaction to the horror of its commitment. Unlike monody, or lyric, the messenger speech is not primarily a mode of feeling. The full impact of pity and fear at Medea's or Heracles' act, or Hippolytus' accident, or Agave's murder of her son, cannot be felt until these characters appear and speak themselves. The messenger's report which precedes their appearance permits first a factual assessment which contributes to the understanding of the nature of these acts. The full emotional impact of them is not released until the pitiable appearance of the survivors complements this preceding account. It is not only the narrative mode, but the skilful and controlled handling of pictorial language within this mode which makes this possible.

Euripides is thus responsible for two innovations in this mode, the first was to give the messenger's role an importance it did not have with the other tragedians. This is shown as we saw at the beginning by the sheer number of lines attributed to this character, to the fact that there may be several reported speeches in one play, and to the practice also of allowing the messenger to communicate only objective truth, whereas his Sophoclean counterpart may be allowed to lie, or present news in a way which particularly suits his own persona. The second was to develop in it a kind of descriptive imagery which achieves this end. 'Ars est celare artem' is particularly true of the messenger speeches in Euripides; this becomes even clearer when they are compared with the messenger speeches of such imitators as Chaeremon, Philostratos and Seneca. And it is largely owing to the control of imagery that one must attribute to these speeches a uniformity of excellence unequalled in any other part of the drama.

Chapter V

Rhesis and Iambic Dialogue:
Imagery of Physical Appearance

Descriptive images are not one of the commonest means of expression in iambic dialogue and *rhesis*. The urgency of a case to plead, or an argument to debate, or immediate information to communicate, on the whole precludes the luxurious adjectival dwelling upon other environments or other times, as in lyric, or upon the detailed pictorial presentation of a series of past events as in the messenger speeches. The elsewhere, the invisible, and the off-stage, are not primarily the concern of *rhesis* and iambic dialogue, both of which must concentrate upon the present action and place as it is *visibly* revealed *on*-stage. Here of course the audience have the visual aids of costume, and some scenery: the characters are themselves present to act out their conflicts through self-deliberation or argument. They are not consistently objects of others' accounts as they are in the choruses' imaginative constructions or the messengers' 'accurate' reporting. In general references to the scene are passing ones, no more than is required for a natural allusion to what is observably around one and relevant to the action, as for instance Orestes' and Pylades' startled comments upon the blood stains visible on the edge of the altar, and on the weapons they see nailed to the temple *triglyphs* at the beginning of the *Iphigeneia in Tauris*.[1]

None the less, there is one kind of description that Euripides uses as a means of dramatic expression more commonly than either of his predecessors in tragedy, and that is comment upon the personal appearance of characters. With the exception of his two latest plays, the *Philoctetes* and the *Oedipus at Colonus*, which may owe something to Euripides' influence, physical characteristics play very little dramatic part in Sophocles.[2] His Electra, for instance, is obviously in pretty poor shape physically. She is dressed shabbily and looks haggard, but her shabbiness and bad state are alluded to as facts without being elaborated at length.[3] Neither she nor the other characters describe her appearance in minute detail. In Euripides the situation is different. Details of personal appearance are made to acquire dramatic significance as part of the whole

79

concept of a character's role. Such things belong to the new realism which
Euripides introduced into tragedy. Physical condition as well as material
environment become significant as dramatic factors, and this new
emphasis appears in two ways. First the traditional expectations about
costume were changed. The unorthodox dress of Euripidean heroes is
the common butt of Aristophanes' jokes.[4] And with some factual
justification. The royal Telephus appears in rags. Menelaus comes
onstage wrapped solely in an old piece of sail cloth. Hecuba the old
Trojan Queen lies down on an old straw mattress.[5] It is not certain how
far conventions of the theatre went in abandoning the old stately costume, and representing these new guises. But the concept is so radically
new, and the situations so extreme, as to suggest that some physical
adaptation in the theatre convention was necessary.[6] Second, where
convention itself fell short, Euripides went beyond it by making significant and subtle verbal and poetic use of the smallest physical detail.
Masks and costume were designed on the grand scale: they could not
show (nor would they be observed beyond the first few rows) nuances
of expression, or small alterations in appearance such as the trace of
blood on a sleeve or the marks of tears on a face. One dramatic use of
such description is to heighten emotional tension at selected critical
points. It is just such effects which Euripides puts to dramatic use through
the poetry in iambic *rhesis* and dialogue. In the *Andromache*, for instance,
Peleus refers to the chafing marks which the binding ropes have made
on Andromache's hands.[7] Menelaus and his henchmen have tied her up
as if she were an ox or a lion. The significance of this small visual
observation, impossible to communicate to an audience except through
language, is that it brings out the gentleness of Peleus and the violence
of Menelaus' faction in a way that the cruder plain stage enactment could
not. In the *Trojan Women*, Hecuba looks at the shield of Hector which is
to carry the body of her grandchild to his grave. As she looks at it closely
she observes the ring of sweat which has marked its circumference.

> ὦ καλλίπηχυν Ἕκτορος βραχίονα
> σῴζουσ᾽, ἄριστον φύλακ᾽ ἀπώλεσας σέθεν.
> ὡς ἡδὺς ἐν πόρπακι σῷ κεῖται τύπος
> ἴτυός τ᾽ ἐν εὐτόρνοισι περιδρόμοις ἱδρώς,
> ὃν ἐκ μετώπου πολλάκις πόνους ἔχων
> ἔσταζεν Ἕκτωρ προστιθεὶς γενειάδι.

You are the shield that guarded the broad arm of Hector, and you
have lost him although he looked after you so well. The imprint of

his arm on your strap is pleasant to my sense, and on the circular
rim, the stain of sweat that fell from Hector's brow as he leaned
his cheek against you in the course of many combats.[8]

The sensuous and visual evocations of this picture convey the sharp almost detached vision of someone under severe emotional stress. Hecuba's
grief is throughout rooted in realistic observation. That she describes,
for instance, the grazes on the child's head made by the stones,[9] the
disarranged hair and the tiny hands which suddenly strike her as being a
replica of Hector's, makes her heroic acceptance of horror and violence
seem greater. Perhaps Euripides saw physical reality as being the strongest hold still over human beings. As Medea nerves herself to relinquish her
children for ever, it is the visual features of their faces which haunt her.
As the blind Oedipus senses beside him the outstretched bodies of his
sons slain in battle by each other's hands, he strokes their faces in a final
parting gesture.[10]

Another use of verbal description of appearance is to establish a type
of character, particularly in minor cases. In the Orestes, for instance,
Electra gets the measure of Helen and conveys this impression to the
audience by describing in a few significant words the way she cuts her
hair. In the traditional observance of the dead, she has been careful to
cut off snippets from the very ends of the hair only so as not to damage
the total effect.[11] A suggestion of honest poverty characterising the old
countryman in the Electra is depicted in a series of descriptive observations which range from the old cloak he wears over his bent spine and
sagging knees to the fresh cheeses he carries in his basket.[12]

By far the most significant use, however, of language descriptive of
personal appearance in rhesis and dialogue affects major characters, and
the establishment of 'permanent' (for the purposes of the play) attitudes
of character in them. Beyond the resources of costume and mask, such
language may be a clue to the degree of emotional damage a character is
suffering, or on the contrary may stress the gap there can be between
external show and inward reality, or again may tell the audience certain
otherwise unacknowledged traits about the person to whom the description is attributed. In all these functions descriptive language itself has
differing degrees of dramatic weight, and tends to be more prominent
also in the later than the earlier plays.

This is apparent for instance if one looks at the places where the main
characters' appearance seems to be a clue to their emotional disturbance.

Clearly the wasted frames of Medea and Phaedra are intended to be such clues. Yet comments upon their looks do not amount to very much more than allusions. Medea's nurse tells us that Medea rolls her eyes so wildly as to look dangerously threatening, that her body is given over completely to grief which is expressed by almost total motionlessness. Only occasionally will she turn her head.[13] The chorus in iambic dialogue with the Nurse in the *Hippolytus* alludes to Phaedra's physical deterioration, κατέξανται δέμας, 'Her body is wasted away.' Surely her husband can tell she is ill by merely looking at her face.[14] The establishment of physical illness is important, since it is only this the Nurse can grasp and act upon. In the *Hippolytus*, tragedy lies partly in the fact that the Nurse, while perceiving that physical ailment may be a clue to a mental one, does not understand that the treatment of each requires different degrees of complexity. But establishment of illness depends here on all kinds of dramatic devices (the direct appearance of Phaedra lying on the *ekkyklema* for example, and what Phaedra herself says in her hallucinatory lyrics) and not merely on descriptions by other characters.

In two later plays, however, the *Electra* and the *Orestes*, the link between appearance and mental condition is expressed less through spectacle and abstract statement than through descriptive observation which supplements what the audience can already see. Electra draws attention not only to her dilapidated home-spun clothes but also to the withered texture of her skin (ξηρὸν δέμας) and to her shorn hair.[15] Orestes when he first sees her, mistakes her for a servant. Orestes in the *Orestes* is so far gone in physical deterioration that Menelaus at first glance takes him for dead. When Orestes then speaks, he cannot resist attempting to put into words the appalling sight that confronts him. Orestes' hair is matted and greasy. The eyes are shrunken. The effect of disfigurement is overwhelming to Menelaus who is seeing it for the first time.

> Με. ὦ θεοί, τί λεύσσω; τίνα δέδορκα νερτέρων;
> Ορ. εὖ γ᾽ εἶπας· οὐ γὰρ ζῶ κακοῖς, φάος δ᾽ ὁρῶ.
> Με. ὡς ἠγρίωσαι πλόκαμον αὐχμηρόν, τάλας.
> Ορ. οὐχ ἡ πρόσοψίς μ᾽, ἀλλὰ τἄργ᾽ αἰκίζεται.
> Με. δεινὸν δὲ λεύσσεις ὀμμάτων ξηραῖς κόραις.
> Ορ. τὸ σῶμα φροῦδον. τὸ δ᾽ ὄνομ᾽ οὐ λέλοιπέ μοι.
> Με. ὦ παρὰ λόγον μοι σὴ φαεῖσ᾽ ἀμορφία.

> MEN.   Gods in heaven,
>   Is this some corpse I see?

OR.   More dead than living,
          I admit, but dead of my despair.
MEN.   And that wild, matted hair – how horrible you look!
OR.   It is my crimes, not my looks, that torture me.
MEN.   That awful stare – and those dry, cold eyes . . .
OR.   My body is dead. I am the name it had.
MEN.   But I did not expect this – alteration.[16]

Electra, on the other hand, has been living with it and in the opening
of the play, the symptoms of madness are described as something
familiar to them both in such remarks as: 'Wipe the clotted froth from
my poor mouth and eyes' (ἐκ δ'ὅμορξον ἀθλίου στόματος ἀφρώδη
πέλανον ὀμμάτων τ' ἐμῶν.), or 'Brush this lank hair from my face'
(καὐχμώδη κόμην ἄφελε προσώπου.).[17] Realism comes out in the textural and visual quality of the words throughout the opening scene between them. πέλανον describes clotted liquids, such as blood, or the thick
mixture of oil, honey, and barley meal used in sacrifices. As a medical
term it can refer also (as well as to foaming at the mouth, as here) to the
secretion at the corner of the eyes.[18] ἀφρώδη describes the frothy texture
of the dribbling at the mouth. Again, it seems to be a medical term, also
sometimes used of blood.[19] πινῶδες, applied to Orestes' hair, refers to its
greasy sheen. The word appears in other contexts to characterize natural
grease in wool.[20] Electra uses a related adjective πιναρὰν κόμαν to
describe her own greasy hair near the beginning of the Electra. αὐχμώδη
κόμην suggests the grubby appearance which comes from not washing
enough. αὐχμηρὸς, a similar adjective, is used of a dirty floor in the
Alcestis.[21] λεπτὰ in the phrase λεπτὰ λεύσσω κόραις at 224, describes the
fading vision of Orestes in which objects seem to him dim. A mask could
have shown none of these things adequately. Yet they are necessary to
Euripides' dramatic protrayal both of Orestes' physical and mental
disintegration, and as a measure of Electra's devotion in tending him
despite the repugnance of his illness.

Beauty or repugnance of appearance is also sometimes given weight
through descriptive imagery in the iambic sections, simply because it
is *not* a clue to the inner man or woman. Tension then comes from the
separation between external appearance and inner reality, a separation
which the discerning perceive and the others do not. The idea of this gap
is expressed also by direct abstract statement in several plays and frag-
ments; this from the *Chrysippus* for instance.

γνώμης σόφισμα καὶ χέρ' ἀνδρείαν ἔχων
δύσμορφος εἴην μᾶλλον ἢ καλὸς κακός.

I would rather have discerning judgement and courage with ugliness
than be of bad character but good looking.[22]

Or this from the *Oedipus*:

νοῦν χρὴ θεᾶσθαι, νοῦν· τί τῆς εὐμορφίας
ὄφελος, ὅταν τις μὴ φρένας καλὰς ἔχῃ;

The mind, it is the mind one must look to. For what use is beauty
when the mind is disfigured?[23]

Medea and Hippolytus complain with feeling that there is no external
visible mark like the stamp on a coin whereby one can tell from the
outside what people are really like, and Electra remarks that Orestes is
looking at her like a man looking at the stamp of a new silver coin.[24]

Such notions overturn the old Homeric assumptions that physical
ugliness and moral inferiority go together, as do nobility and aristocratic
good looks.[25] In the *Iliad* Thersites' physical repugnance is a concomi-
tant of his character, loud-mouthed, a rabble rouser and at heart a
coward. The physical description of him underlines his moral weakness.

αἴσχιστος δὲ ἀνὴρ ὑπὸ Ἴλιον ἦλθε·
φολκὸς ἔην, χωλὸς δ' ἕτερον πόδα· τὼ δέ οἱ ὤμω
κυρτώ, ἐπὶ στῆθος συνοχωκότε. αὐτὰρ ὕπερθε
φοξὸς ἔην κεφαλήν, ψεδνὴ δ' ἐπενήνοθε λάχνη.
ἔχθιστος δ' Ἀχιλῆϊ μάλιστ' ἦν ἠδ' Ὀδυσῆϊ·

He was the ugliest man that had come to Ilium. He had a game
foot and was bandy legged. His rounded shoulders almost met
across his chest; and above them rose an egg-shaped head, which
sprouted a few short hairs. Nobody loathed the man more heartily
than Achilles and Odysseus.[26]

Helen's beauty exempts her from blame. She is aristocratic and beautiful
and therefore beyond reproach from others.

"οὐ νέμεσις Τρῶας καὶ ἐϋκνήμιδας Ἀχαιοὺς
τοιῇδ' ἀμφὶ γυναικὶ πολὺν χρόνον ἄλγεα πάσχειν·
αἰνῶς ἀθανάτῃσι θεῇς εἰς ὦπα ἔοικεν·

Who on earth could blame the Trojan and Achaean men-at-arms for suffering so long for such a woman's sake? Indeed she is the very image of an immortal goddess.[27]

Euripides' separation of appearance and character also overturns the old idea that murderers and madmen should be publicly shunned, a view of which he allows only the old-fashioned Tyndareus to be the exponent in the *Orestes*. This old man sees Orestes' disfigurement as divine punishment 'Our ancestors were right to ban murderers from public sight.' Initially he does not think of him in human terms at all but as a feverishly glittering snake coiled at the door.[28] Electra's devotion is intended to refute his view.

The stress on Orestes' repugnant visual aspect enhances acceptance of him as a human being in desperate need of help. The same is true even more markedly of Heracles. Throughout, every visible stage of his madness has been charted. Lyssa describes his rolling eyeballs, his twisting head and gasps for breath. The messenger draws attention to the swollen veins and frothing mouth.[29] As he finally regains sanity, his physical distress is still harped upon. He is so confused that he thinks he is in Hades. He is rooted to the spot and rigid with fear. He can hardly pick up his bows and arrows, imagining that if he does they will knock against his ribs in such a way that every touch seems like an accusation. He has blood on his clothes and is afraid it will rub off on Theseus.[30] His head is covered up because of his abject shame. The purpose of emphasizing such details of appearance is not only to show the hero's distress, but also to reveal the humanity of Theseus in disregarding it for the suffering man underneath. He rips away the cloak from Heracles' head.

> Ἡρ. τί δῆτά μου κρᾶτ' ἀνεκάλυψας ἡλίῳ;
> Θη. τί δ'; οὐ μιαίνεις θνητὸς ὢν τὰ τῶν θεῶν.
> Ἡρ. φεῦγ', ὦ ταλαίπωρ', ἀνόσιον μίασμ' ἐμόν.
> Θη. οὐδεὶς ἀλάστωρ τοῖς φίλοις ἐκ τῶν φίλων.

> H. How could you then uncloak me to the sun?
> T. No mortal man can stain what is divine.
> H. Away, rash friend! Flee my foul pollution.
> T. Where there is love, contagion cannot come.[31]

Theseus' penetration of the outer layers is a triumphant rebuttal of the old views of morality.

7

A different relation between outer layer and inner truth is explored in the *Andromache*. When Hermione first comes onstage she describes the splendour of her own appearance.

> κόσμον μὲν ἀμφὶ κρατὶ χρυσέας χλιδῆς
> στολμόν τε χρωτὸς τόνδε ποικίλων πέπλων
> οὐ τῶν ’Αχιλλέως οὐδὲ Πηλέως ἄπο
> δόμων ἀπαρχὰς δεῦρ’ ἔχουσ’ ἀφικόμην,
> ἀλλ’ ἐκ Λακαίνης Σπαρτιάτιδος χθονὸς
> Μενέλαος ἡμῖν ταῦτα δωρεῖται πατὴρ
> πολλοῖς σὺν ἕδνοις, ὥστ’ ἐλευθεροστομεῖν.

This pure gold coronet I'm wearing and the fine cut of these richly embroidered clothes I put on to come here are not gifts from Achilles or Peleus, but wedding presents from my father Menelaus. They come from Sparta among many other gifts. They give me independence.[32]

The audience are thus first made to observe Hermione through her looks. The language, in particular the words χρυσέας χλιδῆς and ποικίλων πέπλων, reinforces the doubtless flaunting sight of Hermione's actual costume. It is important that the audience should take this in, because the psychological development of the action depends upon the ruthless but accurate penetration of this façade by Andromache who is on the contrary poorly dressed, older and much less beautiful. Hermione's desperate self-advertisement in fact masks a certain barrenness of body and soul. She is unable to keep Neoptolemus' love on any level and the reason, Andromache suggests, is that her sense of values is wrong. 'It's not beauty that keeps a husband's love but moral integrity.'[33] Hermione's miscalculation about herself is not unlike Helen's of Paris. In the *Trojan Women* Hecuba not only draws attention to the discrepancy between Helen's appearance and character by alluding to her clothes,[34] but she also accuses Helen of totally miscalculating Paris. He looked so dazzling that Helen's senses were overwhelmed.

> ἦν οὑμὸς υἱὸς κάλλος ἐκπρεπέστατος,
> ὁ σὸς δ’ ἰδών νιν νοῦς ἐποιήθη Κύπρις·
> τὰ μῶρα γὰρ πάντ’ ἐστὶν ’Αφροδίτη βροτοῖς,
> καὶ τοὔνομ’ ὀρθῶς ἀφροσύνης ἄρχει θεᾶς·
> ὃν εἰσιδοῦσα βαρβάροις ἐσθήμασι
> χρυσῷ τε λαμπρὸν ἐξεμαργώθης φρένας.

ἐν μὲν γὰρ "Αργει μίκρ' ἔχουσ' ἀνεστρέφου.
Σπάρτης δ' ἀπαλλαχθεῖσα τὴν Φρυγῶν πόλιν
χρυσῷ ῥέουσαν ἤλπισας κατακλύσειν
δαπάναισιν· οὐδ' ἦν ἱκανά σοι τὰ Μενέλεω
μέλαθρα ταῖς σαῖς ἐγκαθυβρίζειν τρυφαῖς.

You saw him scintillating with gold in the barbaric splendour of
Eastern dress and you went out of your mind. With such poverty
in Argos you were attracted to him and hoped that with Sparta
behind you, you could swamp Troy a city overflowing with gold,
with your own extravagance. Evidently Menelaus' palace was not
enough for your luxurious taste to run riot in.[35]

The gold of Paris' dress is echoed in the phrase χρυσῷ ῥέουσαν of Troy
where χρυσῷ occupies the same place in the line. The impression of
violent extravagance is forcefully brought out in the three rare compound verbs ἐκμαργόομαι 'to go raving mad', κατακλύζω 'to deluge' or
'swamp', and ἐγκαθυβρίζω 'to riot in', all of which imply excessive
behaviour.[36]

Here, in Hecuba's view, the long disastrous war is seen to have its
beginnings not as Helen pleads, in divine command, but in the osten-
tatious way in which one oriental wore his clothes.[37]

Dionysus presents the paradox of appearance and reality in another
way. Much attention is given to the way he looks, in iambic dialogue and
rhesis. He is youthful and delicate of complexion. He has long hair which
falls over his cheek in soft curls.[38] Who would suppose, and certainly
Pentheus does not, that a figure of such apparent languid effeminacy as
this stranger, could possess also relentless energy and an unmatchable
power of will? Pentheus is not among the discerning, and he dies for his
miscalculation.

The dramatist however must show in the character not only miscalculation in an objective sense, but subjective depths of self-delusion
also. Hermione deceives herself: she is not merely the catalyst for
Andromache's accuracy. Hecuba, perhaps, reveals unacknowledged
envy when she describes Helen's beauty. The instance of Pentheus,
particularly, raises the question as to the weight which should be
attached to the actual choice of words a character uses in describing
another or himself. Is such language 'objective', or coloured to show up
the speaker in revealing ways he would not himself openly acknowledge?
The answer in his case is both. Dionysus does look as Pentheus says he

looks. There are plenty of precedents in art and literature for the youthful delicate looking god, among them a parody in the *Thesmophoriazusae* of a passage from Aeschylus' *Lycurgus* tetralogy in which the God's effeminacy is the subject of some comment.[39] Not even this passage, however, seems to justify Pentheus' language as totally disinterested and mere traditional description of the God's arrival. Pentheus' language, not merely here but throughout his speeches, has a consistent quality peculiar to him. One might characterize this style as an apparently gratuitous sensuousness which is appropriate to his own suppressed nature. This sensuousness is significant to him in a way that other descriptive passages are not to their authors. Both Electra and Menelaus, for instance, use the same descriptive terms of Orestes' symptoms of illness, although their attitudes to it are very different. Euripides there uses description more objectively, bringing out their differing responses to the same fact by other devices, such as exclamation, direct statement or moral reflection. Here, however, the descriptive language itself seems to be the medium for conveying a basic attitude. There are four iambic passages which most clearly illustrate this; only two are exclusively devoted to Dionysus' physical appearance, but the other two are necessary to establish their context and the continuity of quality in Pentheus' language.

> κλύω δὲ νεοχμὰ τήνδ' ἀνὰ πτόλιν κακά,
> γυναῖκας ἡμῖν δώματ' ἐκλελοιπέναι
> πλασταῖσι βακχείαισιν, ἐν δὲ δασκίοις
> ὄρεσι θοάζειν, τὸν νεωστὶ δαίμονα
> Διόνυσον, ὅστις ἔστι, τιμώσας χοροῖς·
> πλήρεις δὲ θιάσοις ἐν μέσοισιν ἑστάναι
> κρατῆρας, ἄλλην δ' ἄλλοσ' εἰς ἐρημίαν
> πτώσσουσαν εὐναῖς ἀρσένων ὑπηρετεῖν,
> πρόφασιν μὲν ὡς δὴ μαινάδας θυοσκόους,
> τὴν δ' Ἀφροδίτην πρόσθ' ἄγειν τοῦ Βακχίου.

There are new vices, I hear about the city. Women have left their homes for fake Bacchic celebrations and are gadding about in the dark mountain woods to dance for this latest God Dionysus, whoever he is. Wine bowls overflow in their midst, while one woman after another skulks off to some lonely spot or other to serve male lust. They make the excuse that they are maenad priestesses so as to put Aphrodite before Dionysus.[40]

λέγουσι δ' ὥς τις εἰσελήλυθε ξένος,
γόης ἐπῳδὸς Λυδίας ἀπὸ χθονός,
ξανθοῖσι βοστρύχοισιν εὐοσμῶν κόμην,
οἰνῶπος ὄσσοις χάριτας Ἀφροδίτης ἔχων,
ὃς ἡμέρας τε κεὐφρόνας συγγίγνεται
τελετὰς προτείνων εὐίους νεάνισιν.
εἰ δ' αὐτὸν εἴσω τῆσδε λήψομαι στέγης,
παύσω κτυποῦντα θύρσον ἀνασείοντά τε
κόμας, τράχηλον σώματος χωρὶς τεμών.

A strange man has come, so they tell me, a charlatan charmer from
Lydia. He has blond hair that reeks of perfume, a blushing complexion and all love's blandishments in the eyes. He keeps company
day and night with young girls, dangling before them his mysteries
of joy. I'll stop his thyrsus ringing and his hair tossing if I catch
him in this house. I'll sever his neck from his body.[41]

οὐ μὴ προσοίσεις χεῖρα. βακχεύσεις δ' ἰών,
μηδ' ἐξομόρξῃ μωρίαν τὴν σὴν ἐμοί;
τῆς σῆς ⟨δ'⟩ ἀνοίας τόνδε τὸν διδάσκαλον
δίκην μέτειμι. στειχέτω τις ὡς τάχος,
ἐλθὼν δὲ θάκους τοῦδ' ἵν' οἰωνοσκοπεῖ
μοχλοῖς τριαίνου κἀνάτρεψον ἔμπαλιν,
ἄνω κάτω τὰ πάντα συγχέας ὁμοῦ,
καὶ στέμματ' ἀνέμοις καὶ θυέλλαισιν μέθες.
μάλιστα γάρ νιν δήξομαι δράσας τάδε.
οἳ δ' ἀνὰ πόλιν στείχοντες ἐξιχνεύσατε
τὸν θηλύμορφον ξένον, ὃς ἐσφέρει νόσον
καινὴν γυναιξὶ καὶ λέχη λυμαίνεται.

Keep your hands off me won't you? Go to your Bacchic rites and
don't wipe off your demented emotions on me. I shall punish the
man who has taught you this idiocy. Let someone go to the place
where Teiresias practises augury, smash it with crowbars, turn
everything upside down all over everywhere. Throw his wreaths
to the winds and storms. I shall hurt him most by doing this. The
rest of you go and track down this effeminate foreigner who is
introducing our women to a new disease and fouling their beds.[42]

ἀτὰρ τὸ μὲν σῶμ' οὐκ ἄμορφος εἶ, ξένε,
ὡς ἐς γυναῖκας, ἐφ' ὅπερ ἐς Θήβας πάρει·
πλόκαμός τε γάρ σου ταναός, οὐ πάλης ὕπο,

γένυν παρ' αὐτὴν κεχυμένος, πόθου πλέως.
λευκὴν δὲ χροιὰν ἐκ παρασκευῆς ἔχεις,
οὐχ ἡλίου βολαῖσιν, ἀλλ' ὑπὸ σκιᾶς,
τὴν Ἀφροδίτην καλλονῇ θηρώμενος.
πρῶτον μὲν οὖν μοι λέξον ὅστις εἶ γένος.

Well now, you are not unshapely, my friend, as far as attracting
women is concerned, which is why you've come to Thebes. How
long your hair is – you're no wrestler evidently – it pours down
your cheeks positively dripping desire. How carefully white your
skin is too: you don't walk in the sun – shade is what your loveliness needs to seek out love in. But tell me, what nationality are
you?[43]

On the surface this last description seems very like the archetype which
must lie behind Aristophanes' parody.

καί σ' ὦ νεανίσχ' ὅστις εἶ, κατ' Αἰσχύλον
ἐκ τῆς Λυκουργείας ἐρέσθαι βούλομαι.
ποδαπὸς ὁ γύννις; τίς πάτρα; τίς ἡ στολή;
τίς ἡ τάραξις τοῦ βίου; τί βάρβιτος
λαλεῖ κροκωτῷ; τί δὲ λύρα κεκρυφάλῳ;
τί λήκυθος καὶ στρόφιον; ὡς οὐ ξύμφορον.
τίς δαὶ κατόπτρου καὶ ξίφους κοινωνία;
τίς δ' αὐτὸς ὣς παῖ; πότερον ὡς ἀνὴρ τρέφει;
καὶ ποῦ πέος; ποῦ χλαῖνα; ποῦ Λακωνικαί;
ἀλλ' ὡς γυνὴ δῆτ'· εἶτα ποῦ τὰ τιτθία;
τί φῄς; τί σιγᾷς;

And now my dear young man, whoever you are, I want to question
you in words from Aeschylus' Lycurgus trilogy. Where does
this effeminate stranger come from then? What nationality?
What fashion is this? What is all this commotion? Why a lute and
a priest's costume? a lyre and a hair-net? an oil bottle and a girdle?
That's not a very appropriate combination. What's this sword
doing beside a looking glass? What are you? Is that what a man
wears? Where's your virility? Have you a cloak? Red shoes?
Well perhaps you are a woman, but if so, where are your breasts?
What do you say? You're silent.[44]

Only one line (136) is certainly Aeschylus' own. The rest must be
radically extended and adapted from the original, possibly in a way that
keeps the question form but alters the content. As in the *Bacchae*, one

must suppose that Dionysus' extraordinarily un-Greek appearance caused considerable surprise and comment upon details. But the parody at least suggests that the mood remained one of surprise, and detached curiosity. The questions are direct, designed to get an answer, the kind of questions Greeks still ask strangers today. Euripides does not cast Pentheus' speech in question form at all, until the very end. The description is presented as a sort of digression which is marked by the introductory ἀτὰρ and is recalled suddenly by the belated πρῶτον μὲν. . . which begins the last line, as if Pentheus were suddenly pulling himself up to ask the usual polite questions. The descriptive digression itself is structured in a series of phrases which begin as adjectival admiration of some physical attribute, and end in a hasty critical qualification, that is, οὐκ ἄμορφος is qualified by ὡς, πλόκαμος ταναός by οὐ, and λευκὴν χροιὰν by οὐχ. The scornfully explosive alliteration at the end of 456 also acts as a brake to the first part of the phrase which describes Dionysus' hair tumbling over the cheek. Details of vocabulary and structure thus suggest that Pentheus is attracted to the sight of Dionysus in spite of himself. The added negatives are an attempt at self control. The second passage which also describes Dionysus supports this interpretation. Pentheus begins almost gloatingly with a lingering description of the stranger's physical charms: scented hair, flushed face, alluring eyes. Then suddenly, seemingly out of keeping with this almost trivially decorative picture, he ends with the extraordinarily violent but still physically oriented phrase: 'I shall sever his head from his body.' Such a phrase shows Pentheus' suppressed violence which is the extreme counterpart to his attraction for Dionysus' appearance.

The language of the other passages also suggests the suppressed imagination at work. As Professor Winnington-Ingram has written of Pentheus, 'Devoid of sense he may be; devoid of imagination he is not.'[45] The first passage is his vision of maenads out on the mountain. The tone of it comes out in the strong assonance of πλασταῖσι βακχείαισιν again suggesting scorn, and in epithets and verbs. The mountains are dark, wine-bowls have to be full to overflowing and the women skulk or slink off to lonely places. πτώσσω is a word used by Pindar of skulking in an alley, and by Tyrtaeus of hiding or crouching beneath a shield.[46] It suggests awkward secrecy – in fact the very opposite of what we hear elsewhere of the Maenads. For Pentheus, Maenads, sex, drinking and the dark are natural associations.

Characteristic of all these descriptions is a strong physical susceptibility in Pentheus which the sensuous, physically slanted language conveys.

In the third passage, he sees Bacchic worship as a corrupting disease spreading through his people. As Dodds says, he speaks of it 'as if it were a physical infection transmissible by contact. His violent horror of such contact is a fine psychological stroke: something in him knows already the fascination and the mortal peril which the new rites hold for him.'⁴⁷

Not just here, however, but consistently, Pentheus' visual and textural descriptions, often seemingly gratuitous for one who holds Dionysus in such contempt, are designed by Euripides to express his real attitude, his attraction for the figure he scorns. He is condemned by his own words and his death merely makes overt the inner dependence, as it reveals, also contrary to appearance in the God's case, Dionysus' real power.

A similar consistently significant use of descriptive language in iambic dialogue and *rhesis* characterizes Electra in the *Electra*. It is exaggeration which reveals her inner weakness. And this shows particularly in the verbs by which she describes her own physical state, and the contrasting ones of Clytemnestra and Aegisthus which follow.

> ἄγγελλ' Ὀρέστῃ τἀμὰ καὶ κείνου κακά,
> πρῶτον μὲν οἵοις ἐν πέπλοις αὐλίζομαι,
> πίνῳ θ' ὅσῳ βέβριθ', ὑπὸ στέγαισί τε
> οἵαισι ναίω βασιλικῶν ἐκ δωμάτων,
> αὐτὴ μὲν ἐκμοχθοῦσα κερκίσιν πέπλους,
> ἢ γυμνὸν ἕξω σῶμα κἀστερήσομαι,
> αὐτὴ δὲ πηγὰς ποταμίους φορουμένη,
> ἀνέορτος ἱερῶν καὶ χορῶν τητωμένη.
> ἀναίνομαι γυναῖκας οὖσα παρθένος,
> ἀναίνομαι δὲ Κάστορ', ᾧ πρὶν ἐς θεοὺς
> ἐλθεῖν ἔμ' ἐμνήστευον, οὖσαν ἐγγενῆ.
> μήτηρ δ' ἐμὴ Φρυγίοισιν ἐν σκυλεύμασιν
> θρόνῳ κάθηται, πρὸς δ' ἕδραισιν Ἀσίδες
> δμωαὶ στατίζουσ', ἃς ἔπερσ' ἐμὸς πατήρ,
> Ἰδαῖα φάρη χρυσέαις ἐζευγμέναι
> πόρπαισιν.   αἷμα δ' ἔτι πατρὸς κατὰ στέγας
> μέλαν σέσηπεν, ὃς δ' ἐκεῖνον ἔκτανεν,
> ἐς ταὐτὰ βαίνων ἅρματ' ἐκφοιτᾷ πατρί,
> καὶ σκῆπτρ' ἐν οἷς Ἕλλησιν ἐστρατηλάτει
> μιαιφόνοισι χερσὶ γαυροῦται λαβών.
> Ἀγαμέμνονος δὲ τύμβος ἠτιμασμένος
> οὔπω χοάς ποτ' οὐδὲ κλῶνα μυρσίνης

ἔλαβε, πυρὰ δὲ χέρσος ἀγλαϊσμάτων.
μέθῃ δὲ βρεχθεὶς τῆς ἐμῆς μητρὸς πόσις
ὁ κλεινός, ὡς λέγουσιν, ἐνθρῴσκει τάφῳ
πέτροις τε λεύει μνῆμα λάινον πατρός,

Tell Orestes of our troubles, his and mine, first the clothes I'm
stalled in, and the filth that clutters me, and the house I must live
in after a royal palace. I must make my own clothes at the loom or
else go naked in deprivation, and draw water myself from the well.
I am unfit to join in religious functions or dances, since I have to
reject wives' company being still a virgin, and also the thought of
the company of Castor who courted me once as his fellow countryman, before he went to join the heavenly gods. As for my mother,
she sits on a throne surrounded by loot from the East: the Asiatic
servants standing beside her are the ones my father enslaved. Even
they are dressed in Trojan finery and yoked up with priceless gold
jewellery. Meanwhile my father's dark blood has rotted and still
goes on rotting while his murderer drives a chariot over the grave
and arrogantly brandishes in blood-stained hands the very sceptre
with which he fought amongst the Greeks. Agamemnon's tomb
is dishonoured; he has taken no libations or myrtle branches to it,
the altar for sacrifices is bare of decoration. My mother's eminent
lover, they tell me, gets drunk and dances over the tomb, hurling
rocks to damage its stone facing.[48]

This is an active imagination which gains power as one picture
prompts another. Of the three portraits, Electra, Clytemnestra and
Aegsithus, the last is the most extreme. That Aegisthus should brandish
a sceptre, drive a chariot over the grave, throw stones at it in a drunken
frenzy, and dance, is highly improbable, the more so when we hear from
the messenger of his calmly walking in a garden and cutting myrtle
shoots. All the life of the images is in the verbs, some of which are
strongly metaphorical. Both αὐλίζομαι 'to stall' and ζεύγνυμι 'to yoke',
in their literal senses naturally refer to animals. The extension, not only
to human beings but also to human clothing, is a bold one. The dirt, the
rotting blood in the grave, the bloody hands, all render the dark brooding visions of this isolated and embittered woman. That the brooding has
warped her is suggested by the way in which other characters undercut
the posturing of her opening image. Fetching water is unnecessary as
her husband has told her. Going naked if she does not weave her own

clothes is not strictly true since the chorus offer to lend her theirs, at least for the festive occasion they attend. She is also included in their invitation to dance. The preoccupation here with her own physical appearance is a theme which also characterizes Electra's lyrics, although there it is presented with more linguistic elevation as befits the different mode. At the end of the play in the confrontation with Clytemnestra, Electra taunts her mother to her face with *her* concern for beauty. She made this a conscious aim, working at her hair and face while Agamemnon was away, to attract Aegisthus.[49] As Clytemnestra goes into the house to her death, Electra sardonically expresses concern that her mother's gown may get blackened by smoke from the sacrificial fire.[50] Through such detail Electra's anger and warped envy are revealed. Euripides surely intends that her imagination should seem oppressive: like that of Pentheus, it has an independent life of its own which goes far beyond what would be required by facts alone. Quite apart from the arguments she puts up in her defence, the reputedly fierce Clytemnestra's language seems almost gentle beside Electra's. There is a realistic tenderness, for instance, in the line in which she alludes to Iphigeneia's death:

> ἔνθ' ὑπερτείνας πυρᾶς
> λευκὴν διήμησ' Ἰφιγόνης παρηίδα.

> stretching her high above the fire,
> like pale field grass he splashed Iphigeneia's throat.[51]

The style of the Greek is hard to reproduce accurately in translation and the calculated word order impossible. The form Ἰφιγόνη is unique here as a variant for Ἰφιγένεια and may have the force of a diminutive. The verb διήμησ' is a metaphor from cutting grass or corn and is in sharp contrast to the λευκὴν . . . παρηίδα a phrase which it bisects by position as well as sense. λευκὴν 'pale', suggests the delicacy of the cheek and also pale corn being cut down before it is ripe.[52] It is a visual image very different from the dark haunting ones of Electra, although the subject matter, a murder, is as gruesome as any death (Agamemnon's for instance) that Electra might describe.

Here, as in the *Bacchae*, it is a question of the descriptive language as well as the argument being appropriate to characters. Through the imagery of appearance, Euripides expresses unacknowledged attitudes of the speaker: in Pentheus suppressed Puritanism, in Electra warped envy.

The language of personal appearance is fundamental to Euripides' dramatic ideas and concepts of character. It cannot be adequately explained as a mere supplement to stage spectacle, nor as superfluously following a current popular trend in art, although both these elements may come in. Attic stage conventions, it is true, were hampering to realism in the theatre. And among their many other functions, Euripides' descriptions may also serve as stage directions. But this is a minor function compared with what they do for theme and character in depth. As far as art is concerned, realistic portraiture and paradoxical treatment of subject were new developments of late fifth-century painting. They are not peculiar to Euripidean drama. A new individualism comes into the treatment of facial expression, hair and dress for instance. Painters attempted difficult subjects in new ways.[53] Parrhasios' Theseus looked as if he had been 'fed on roses, not beef'.[54] His portrait of the Demos combined many fickle traits within one expression.[55] His Centaur family, Lucian said, managed to combine expressions both of tenderness and untamed wildness.[56] Such comments suggest that painters of the time too were trying to break away from the old conventions in art, and to capture in their paintings complexity rather than the old fixed smile. Centaurs need not be savage all through. Theseus could be a hero and still not have to look like a superman. Parrhasios, like Euripides, may have been trying to drive a wedge between appearance and inner nature. Euripides' imagination may here as elsewhere show a close rapport with that of art. But the fact remains that drama can go far beyond art in the expression of psychological realism; the complexity of Euripides' Pentheus, or Electra, or Hermione, or Hecuba, or Theseus and Heracles is more than the complexity of Parrhasios' Theseus or his Centaurs because of the inter-action of characters one with another, and because of the many levels at which language may be taken simultaneously.

To sum up then, although iambic dialogue does not at first sight seem the most likely place in which to find extensive imagery because of its rapid pace and development of argument, the one significant exception to this is description of external personal appearance. Euripides saw in details of clothing and facial expression an importance which some of his contemporaries, such as Aristophanes, either considered absurd, or wilfully misunderstood for the purposes of comedy. In Euripides' hands, however, they become a utilized source of dramatic energy, a way of exploring in terms of convincing psychological realism the attitude of a character towards himself or the reaction of one character to another.

Chapter VI

Simile and Metaphor
as supporting imagery

So far it is evident that in Euripides' case it is possible to discuss imagery without necessarily including simile and metaphor. It is pictorial language of a sensuously descriptive kind which commonly serves dramatic function, and this, organically used, may act symbolically, even though simile and metaphor are not conspicuously present. Ion's language of light, choral descriptions of sea or city, the messenger's handling of palace or mountain scenery are instances already dealt with. This is not to say that Euripides never used simile or metaphor, merely that it does not seem to be his most natural element. However, now that some investigation of other types of imagery used by him has been made, it seems to make sense to look again at simile and metaphor, not as the sole and single criterion of his genius, but from the point of view of a supporting role, 'supporting', that is, in the purely empirical sense that a case for imagery has first been made without it. To what degree is descriptive language reinforced by these other modes of imagery? Metaphor, in that it is not much conditioned by mode, is particularly suitable as linking imagery which may appear in different parts of a play. Viewed in this light, for the part it plays in the context of other imaginative language, metaphor may appear to have an important function, though not the lonely one which has hitherto been the despair of scholars and which has caused them to deny Euripides any serious claim to poetic inspiration.

Before considering this function however, it is worth looking briefly at the accusations of metaphorical poverty on their own ground. Without wishing for a moment to elevate this kind of imagery to a central place in Euripides' work, a place it would be false to suggest it deserves, one cannot help asking whether the metaphorical cupboard is quite as bare as it has been made out to be.

The charges of poverty are clearly there. Breitenbach accuses the poet of absence of poetic inspiration, and then goes on to specify. Metaphors are usually short, unoriginal, too few, and carelessly repeated to the point of cliché.[1] Delulle likewise speaks of lack of exuberance, lack of impetuous movement, hasty composition and formulaic elements.[2] Altum, in his discussion of similes, finds Euripides 'minus excellentem' than the other tragedians, and blames him for being un-Ionian, by which he seems to mean the most remote and most alien to the spirit of Homer.[3] Pauer allows Euripides some invention and boldness, but complains that he adds simile and metaphor for additional ornament rather than using it organically as Aeschylus and Sophocles do.[4]

This general conclusion of bleak uninspiration seems to have been arrived at from an averaging-out of all recorded instances of either device, whether they are dead or new, emphatic or non-emphatic; that is, it is based on an assumption of even distribution. Second, it is an assessment based on content of images, and not on use of that content.[5] It is relatively easy to find out from such studies what areas Euripides draws his metaphors from, what the range of vocabulary is in these areas, and how many similes and metaphors drawn from them occur in each play. But this is to ignore the contextual difference between plays, and the variable relative density of individual passages: it takes no account of spacing in relation to function, and the way this is controlled by total context.

In fact, neither counting numbers of metaphors, nor cataloguing by content is a reliable guide to Euripides' skill in handling language, for quite apart from natural differences in context, the distribution between different plays, not to mention different passages within plays, varies enormously. Looking at the *Heracleidae* or the *Alcestis*, one might doubt whether the poet had much capacity for metaphor at all. After reading the *Medea*, one might recognize the facility for it, but regret the conventional flavour, particularly as it appears in a strong preference for nautical terms. On the other hand, the *Hippolytus* or the *Heracles* or the *Bacchae* might convince one that Euripides' feeling for metaphor was impressive and far from conventional. A closer look at the *Medea* and the *Hippolytus* should serve to illustrate this, since the difference in the handling of metaphor seems to bear no relation to the natural difference of subject matter in the two plays, and one is forced to conclude that from this point of view at least, the *Hippolytus* is just better written.

The nautical metaphors and similes in the *Medea* obtrude upon one's notice because many of them are extended beyond one word, and because several characters use them.[6] Medea talks of her enemies 'letting out all the rope and leaving her no landing place' and describes Aegeus as a harbour to which she can attach the stern cables of her ship.[7] Jason speaks of himself somewhat elaborately as like a helmsman who must run out from beneath Medea's verbiage with his sails closely reefed.[8] The Nurse speaks of new troubles being added to the old in terms of new water pouring in before all the boat's bilge-water has been drained.[9] Even the messenger, as well as Medea, uses the word commonly applied to ships labouring in heavy seas, of himself and the servants.[10] Such language however is not uncommon. Words such as κάμνω, κάλως λιμὴν ἐξαντλέω and κλύδων are metaphorically used by Euripides on many occasions, and it is well known that the general area of sea and ships is one from which he consistently quarries similes and metaphors.[11] Ships' cables are metaphorically let out in other plays besides this.[12] Other characters besides Aegeus appear to their interlocutors as a harbour or land to weary sailors.[13] Figurative bilge-water is drained in other contexts besides this one.[14] This need not necessarily matter if the poetic clichés were justified by some special dramatic exigency which made the nautical terms appropriate. But there seems to be no such exigency in the *Medea*. It may be natural that Medea in her insecurity should speak of having no haven of refuge to which to turn, and no landing place, and that Aegeus when he appears, should in an extension of these metaphors appear to provide her with anchorage and mooring ropes. But this does not explain the penchant of the other characters for mariners' terms. Ships are not immediately relevant to character and situation in the same way that they are for instance in the *Troades*,[15] and for this reason the metaphorical language here seems both tame and inorganic. In marked contrast is the *Hippolytus*, written within only three years of the *Medea*. This too has a number of metaphors immediately apparent, because conspicuously placed. But these are both more original, and more closely illustrative of the play's dramatic themes, in a way which includes appropriateness to the character uttering them. Take for instance certain figurative expressions of three strongly contrasting roles, Hippolytus, the Nurse and the chorus. Hippolytus' first spoken words onstage include a sustained and elaborate metaphor, that of Reverence as the gardener of the meadow from which he picks flowers to honour Artemis. This is no random decoration, but carefully suited to his attitude of awe before Artemis, and his desire (ironic as it turns out), to live a life untouched by evil.

Ιπ. σοὶ τόνδε πλεκτὸν στέφανον ἐξ ἀκηράτου
λειμῶνος, ὦ δέσποινα, κοσμήσας φέρω,
ἔνθ' οὔτε ποιμὴν ἀξιοῖ φέρβειν βοτὰ

οὔτ' ἦλθέ πω σίδαρος, ἀλλ' ἀκήρατον
μέλισσα λειμῶν' ἠρινὴ διέρχεται,
Αἰδὼς δὲ ποταμίαισι κηπεύει δρόσοις.
ὅσοις διδακτὸν μηδέν, ἀλλ' ἐν τῇ φύσει
τὸ σωφρονεῖν εἴληχεν ἐς τὰ πάνθ' ὁμῶς,
τούτοις δρέπεσθαι, τοῖς κακοῖσι δ' οὐ θέμις.

For you, my lady, I bring this woven garland I have put together
from an untouched field where no shepherd presumes to graze his
sheep, and no plough has yet come: untouched it is, and the bee
passes through it in spring and Reverence tends it with river water
like a garden. Its flowers are to be picked by those to whom nothing
comes by teaching, but in those whose essential nature goodness
has been assigned her place. The evil have no right to it.[16]

The metaphor which involves the personification of 'Αἰδὼς is at the
heart of these lines, forming a transition, as it does, between the 'straight'
description of the meadow and its full symbolic significance. It characterizes an attitude of rare unchanging reverence, which is to remain with
Hippolytus throughout the play in spite of severe trials.[17] It is in this
sense an apt tribute to him. But the lines which precede and follow it,
make it plain that it is also a double-edged compliment. The untouched
field which allows nothing but Reverence to tend it is analogous to the
enclosed religious attitude of Hippolytus, who will admit only blind
faith, and refuse to acknowledge any other point of view but his own.
He too is untouched, but the exclusive untouchability is in another
sense against nature. Sheep and ploughs are after all normal. And why
should only the untaught few be allowed to pick the flowers? It is such
questions that these lines suggest, with their extraordinary economy,
their strong central metaphor led up to by a figurative description
which gives special stress through placing and repetition to the adjective
ἀκήρατος 'untouched',[18] and a following moral explanation, which still
preserves the image of picking flowers, this time in the metaphor of
δρέπεσθαι. With neatness and great irony, they summarize Hippolytus'
devotion, vulnerability and also arrogance.

Very different are the metaphorical expressions of the Nurse. These
illustrate her easy home-spun philosophizing, and the rapidity with
which the clichés change is here perhaps an indication of the confused
indiscipline of her thinking.

Φ. κρύπτε· . . . .
. . . .

Τρ. κρύπτω· τὸ δ' ἐμὸν πότε δὴ θάνατος
σῶμα καλύψει;
πολλὰ διδάσκει μ' ὁ πολὺς βίοτος.
χρῆν γὰρ μετρίας εἰς ἀλλήλους
φιλίας θνητοὺς ἀνακίρνασθαι
καὶ μὴ πρὸς ἄκρον μυελὸν ψυχῆς,
εὔλυτα δ' εἶναι στέργηθρα φρενῶν
ἀπό τ' ὤσασθαι καὶ ξυντεῖναι.
τὸ δ' ὑπὲρ δισσῶν μίαν ὠδίνειν
ψυχὴν χαλεπὸν βάρος, ὡς κἀγὼ
τῆσδ' ὑπεραλγῶ.
βιότου δ' ἀτρεκεῖς ἐπιτηδεύσεις
φασὶ σφάλλειν πλέον ἢ τέρπειν
τῇ θ' ὑγιείᾳ μᾶλλον πολεμεῖν.
οὕτω τὸ λίαν ἧσσον ἐπαινῶ
τοῦ μηδὲν ἄγαν·
καὶ ξυμφήσουσι σοφοί μοι.

Ph. Cover me up . . .
N. I cover you then. But when will death cover my body? A long
life has taught me a great deal. The love people feel for one
another should be moderate in its mixture and not reach the
extreme marrow of the soul. The heart's affections should be
easy to undo, easy both to release and to tighten. It's a heavy
burden that one soul should labour for two, as I feel pain for
her. They say that it is the single-minded behaviour in life that
trips one up more often than it brings happiness, and it is more
likely to be the enemy of good health. So I praise extremes less
than I praise moderation in everything and the wise will agree
with me.[19]

Nine metaphors within the space of seventeen lines, and most of them
commonplace.[20] Yet they exactly suit the kind of talk one would expect
from a character such as this. Complexity is beyond the comprehension
of the Nurse, and these metaphors suit her somewhat casual view of love
as something to be remedied by a little adjustment of strings or by drinking the right potion. It is dramatically right that one should miss here
the taut tension which comes from, say, certain rare and single metaphors

other characters use at strained moments. There is nothing of cliché about Phaedra's bitter description of the Nurse as a 'procuress of wrong',[21] nor of Theseus' description of Justice acting like the crushing mechanism in an animal trap.[22] Their brevity is not indicative of a lack of tension, any more than the Nurses' long metaphorical sortie is indicative of profundity or strain.

All these examples are again different from the metaphorical language the chorus use when they describe love. The vein is lighter here to provide relief from the grimness of the stage-action, but the content is central to the play's main theme. Love is powerful, all pervasive and capricious. Such themes come across in decorative personifications of Cypris and Eros which are given special prominence in the first stasimon. The metaphors, some traditional, some not, are indicative of that double-edged quality of love which at that very moment in stage time is working its will upon Phaedra. Aphrodite's key-keeper

$$τὸν τᾶς Ἀφροδίτας$$
$$φιλτάτων θαλάμων κλῃδοῦχον^{23}$$

sounds harmless enough, but this key-keeper is also a tyrant (the metaphor is ambiguous) with the power to destroy.[24] The same ambivalence occurs in the opening image of an Eros who brings 'bewitching grace into the souls of those he is campaigning against'.

$$εἰσάγων γλυκεῖαν$$
$$ψυχᾷ χάριν οὓς ἐπιστρατεύσῃ^{25}$$

Love's power is measured in terms of a comparison with the beams of light.

$$οὔτε γὰρ πυρὸς οὔτ' ἄστρων ὑπέρτερον βέλος,$$
$$οἶον τὸ τᾶς Ἀφροδίτας$$
$$ἵησιν ἐκ χερῶν$$
$$Ἔρως, ὁ Διὸς παῖς.$$

The shafts neither of fire nor of the stars surpass that of Aphrodite launched from the hands of Eros.[26]

The decorative element, and that almost frivolous note upon which the ode ends, where Aphrodite is compared to a bee on the wing, may seem at first sight incongruous with the seriousness of Phaedra's real predicament. But in fact its tone exactly suits the Nurse's superficial appeal

8

to Cypris immediately before the chorus begins, and the two-edged metaphors enable the poet to keep in mind both the Nurse's popular attitude to Love, and the more serious implications which underlie the traditional concepts, and which of course are realized in the scene which follows this when Phaedra realizes she has been destroyed.

The example of both these plays will have shown that context must be the determining factor in estimating metaphorical skill. There are no uniform laws of distribution, or rules for correct content or density. And the same goes for individual passages. The mere presence of a metaphor need not necessarily indicate anything dramatically arresting. Many images are so common as to be hardly deserving of the term 'metaphor' any longer. Words such as νοσέω, δάκνω, κάμνω, κνίζω, phrases with βάρος or κλύδων, are as dead as some English equivalents, such as 'cut to the quick', 'labour in distress', 'weight of sorrow' or 'sea of troubles'.[27] It is doubtful whether taken singly they should be counted at all in any assessment of positive poetic weight, for it is not usually the high points of action they exemplify. It is by the conspicuous rare word, or the single image prominently placed, or numbers of images concentrated into a short space that the important moments are most likely to be marked.

It is more arresting, for instance, when Hecuba asks that her grief be contemplated as a painting might be contemplated, when the artist stands back from his canvas to get the full perspective,[28] than it would be if she were merely to say that she felt the weight of her suffering, using the cliché βάρος κακῶν 'weight of troubles'. The unique simile marks a grief so overwhelming that it requires an effort of vision and concentration for anyone else to measure it fully.

An example of what one might call emphasis by architectural spacing is the epic simile. Its extended nature makes it particularly easy to spot, as for instance the one in Electra's monody.

> αἲ αἲ, δρύπτε κάρα·
> οἷα δέ τις κύκνος ἀχέτας
> ποταμίοις παρὰ χεύμασιν
> πατέρα φίλτατον καλεῖ,
> ὀλόμενον δολίοις βρόχων
> ἔρκεσιν, ὧς σὲ τὸν ἄθλιον,
> πάτερ, ἐγὼ κατακλαίομαι,

Like a swan calling the beloved parent bird at the river water's edge, when it has been fatally trapped in the treacherous meshes of net, so I, father, mourn you for your wretched death.[29]

There are two points of apt comparison here. Not only does the en-
meshed swan resemble Agamemnon's death in the net Clytemnestra
used before she stabbed him, but Electra thinks of herself as a swan; this
is appropriate because she is singing a mourning dirge as swans reputedly
do, and it also surely has a touch of ironic pathos about it. Electra, a
hag-ridden and squalid sight, can nonetheless still think of herself as such
a graceful creature. Conventional though the image is,[30] it is also in
keeping with Electra's somewhat self-conscious preoccupation with
appearance. Whatever she tells us elsewhere of how she actually looks,
there is no doubt that she would *like* to be beautiful. The isolation of this
extended simile makes it stand out as a high point of the monody.
Parallel to the epic simile is the sustained metaphor or allegory, which
occurs in both lyric and *rhesis*. The prolonged image at the beginning of
the *Iphigeneia in Tauris*, of Orestes as the last surviving pillar of a col-
lapsed house, is an instance of this,[31] as in lyric is the elaborate view of
Time as a race-course upon which Order, Lawlessness and Happiness
exercise their competing chariots until that of Happiness is wrecked.[32]
In this class too are figurative treatments of the cosmic elements, Night,
Sun, Moon, and Stars. These are metaphorical in the sense that no-one
any longer seriously believed that Night drove a chariot or stars danced,
but this was a convenient poetic device for setting a desired mood. Thus
Andromeda addresses the Night as charioteer at the beginning of her
monody,

> O sacred Night, how vast is the ride you take in your chariot across
> the starry back of holy heaven . . .

> Ὦ νὺξ ἱερὰ
> ὡς μακρὸν ἵππευμα διώκεις
> ἀστεροειδέα νῶτα διφρεύουσ'
> αἰθέρος ἱερος. . . [33]

and Ion describes the sun and chariot at the beginning of his.[34]

The reverse of such leisurely spacing occurs in the bunching together
of different short similes or metaphors, to create a sense of urgency or
speed. Lyssa's speech as she moves in upon Heracles to infect him with
madness has this effect.

> τάχος ἐπιρροίβδην θ' ὁμαρτεῖν ὡς κυνηγέτῃ κύνας,
> εἰμί γ'· οὔτε πόντος οὕτως κύμασιν στένων λάβρως
> οὔτε γῆς σεισμὸς κεραυνοῦ τ' οἶστρος ὠδῖνας πνέων,
> οἷ' ἐγὼ στάδια δραμοῦμαι στέρνον εἰς Ἡρακλέους.

I shall move in on him swiftly in full cry, like the hounds that bay the huntsman. Neither the sea's furious breakers, nor earthquake, not the hurting stroke of Thunder shall rival me when I rush into the heart of Heracles.[35]

So has Ion's outburst when he discovers Creousa's intent to murder him.

οἵαν ἔχιδναν τήνδ' ἔφυσας ἢ πυρὸς
δράκοντ' ἀναβλέποντα φοινίαν φλόγα,
ᾗ τόλμα πᾶσ' ἔνεστιν, οὐδ' ἥσσων ἔφυ
Γοργοῦς σταλαγμῶν, οἷς ἔμελλέ με κτενεῖν.
λάζυσθ', ἵν' αὐτῆς τοὺς ἀκηράτους πλόκους.
κόμης καταξήνωσι Παρνασοῦ πλάκες
ὅθεν πετραῖον ἅλμα δισκηθήσεται.

What serpent is this you have sired, or dragon with bloody fire in his looks in this woman who will balk at nothing, match for the Gorgon's bloody drops with which she tried to poison me. Take hold of her, and let Parnassus' surface comb out her unshorn hair as she is hurled like a discus in a death dive onto the rocks.[36]

Yet it would be a mistake even from this to conclude that numbers of images are necessarily a guarantee of intensity. Anger is expressed differently in the same play by one short and simple metaphor emphatically placed in the middle of Creousa's monody.

ψυχὴ δ' ἀλγεῖ κακοβουλευθεῖσ'
ἔκ τ' ἀνθρώπων ἔκ τ' ἀθανάτων.

Gods and men have conspired against my soul and it is in pain.[37]

The weighty personification here picks up the opening words of the monody which Creousa addresses to her soul.

These examples should suffice to show that mere counting of images and classification according to content are not enough to determine poetic effectiveness. Context is what matters. Consideration of these instances in their context should also have gone some way to answering Pauer's charge that Euripides' images are mere functionless ornament. It is worth questioning two more charges before finally proceeding to a consideration of metaphor and simile in a co-operative role with other imagery; one is that shortness of image means lack of inspiration and the other is that repetition is in itself weak.

Shortness in itself is not an inevitable sign of inferiority. Although Breitenbach complains that so many of Euripides' metaphors are insignificant one word affairs which do not stay in the mind,[38] some of the shortest are the most original and psychologically penetrating. Among these are those used by characters in a near delirium. When Agave refers to Pentheus in the tree as a 'climbing beast', τὸν ἀμβάτην/θῆρ' it is one of those instances where metaphor and realistic portrayal of delusion meet.[39] Agave's language is metaphorical to all but herself. There is a similar instance when Hecuba in the *Troades* uses the word for 'ship's bunks' τοίχους and, at the end of the play, the chorus refer to the approaching men carrying the firebrands which are to burn down the city as 'rowing with flaming torches' φλογέας δαλοῖσι χέρας/διερέσσοντας her delusion, like Agave's, and the womens' suppressed fears, are expressed in terms which are metaphors to everyone but them.[40] Moments of horror may be captured in one striking word: the blood that in a gaping wound 'laughs out between the torn bones', ἐκγελᾷ / ὀστέων ῥαγέντων φόνος, or as it is hurled to its death from the citadel summit, the light-weight body of a child which is a 'quoit-throw' from the walls, πύργων δίσκημα[41], a maenad 'playing ball' διεσφαίριζε with dismembered limbs, or 'decapitating' devastation, καράτομος ἐρημία, ranging the palace bedrooms.[42] Such metaphors, new in conception, may seem less elevated than those other tragedians use, but they are alive with the force of physical realism. They make the moment of horror impossible to gloss over, or ignore, or soften, with an abstract or comfortably vague circumlocution.

What about repetition? It is undeniable that Euripides both repeats images of his own and takes over traditional ones. This is sometimes tedious. It is doubtful, as we have seen, how much dramatic advantage there is in the recurrence of fairly stereotyped nautical metaphors in the *Medea*. Delulle has done a study of the random way Euripides repeats some imagery;[43] the particularly common example he cites is the motif of the mother bird protecting her young. This occurs over and over again, with slight variations, both in separate plays and within the same one. And one has to admit that this theme does wear a little thin if one performs the somewhat unnatural feat of contemplating all the scattered instances together and out of context. One must concede that there is no such frequent pattern of repeating a favourite image, at least in different plays, in either Aeschylus or Sophocles. On the other hand neither repetition in itself, nor traditional usage, necessarily mean lack of imagination in context. To take the latter first, there may be explanations other than a policy of desperation or sheer carelessness, for employing the traditionally commonplace. It seems likely that the Homeric similes and metaphors used in the messenger's narratives of the *Phoenissae*, for example, are deliberate evocations. To an audience brought up on epic recitations, to hear of 'warriors biting the dust', or attacking 'like whirlwinds' or 'boars sharpening their teeth', or tumbling from their chariots 'like divers', might have given the special pleasure which comes from recognizing the familiar in an unfamiliar place.[44] This is the same sort of pleasure, presumably, as that which comes from recognizing in Euripides' *Electra* variations on the *Choephoroe*, or of noticing that, when in the *Orestes* Electra speaks of the 'yoke of necessity', Euripides is using the same image as Aeschylus in the *Agamemnon*.[45] But what if the poet repeats his own images? Is this cliché rather than traditionalism? It need not be. Quite apart from conscious recollection which is something else, the same metaphor may appear so different in different contexts that it hardly seems the same word. Take the Greek word for 'dog' κύων as applied to human beings. When Helen is called a κύων by Peleus it is abusive in tone, like the term 'bitch'.[46] But when the maenads call each other κύνες it is in a spirit of inspired comradeship such as is felt by a pack of hunting hounds with a common instinct.[47] But the word is the same, and both are metaphors.

Conscious repetition may be assumed when the recurrence of certain images effectively underlines a central dramatic idea, as for example the metaphor of stitching or weaving plots underlines the theme of vicious intrigue in the *Andromache*. Here ῥάπτω and πλέκω occur several times in a metaphorical sense in conjunction with μηχανή or alone. Although both verbs, which in their literal senses mean to weave and to plait respectively, are commonly employed in the figurative sense of 'plot' or 'contrive', special prominence is given to them here, partly through repetition, and partly through the form of the combination as it appears, for instance, in the compound μηχανορράφος used once by Andromache to describe the Spartans in a passage full of forceful abuse, and later by the messenger to describe Orestes.[48] The commonness of an image, or the frequency with which it is repeated does not always mean weakness. Yoking metaphors are very common indeed to express close relationships between people,[49] but in a play where the dependence of people upon one another is the mainspring of the action, they seem a natural and effective way of communicating that idea although they are not in themselves original. Variations of the metaphor ζεῦγος and ζεύγνυμι occur throughout the *Heracles*. Megara thinks of herself and her children as corpses ignominiously yoked together

ἀγόμεθα ζεῦγος οὐ καλὸν νεκρῶν
ὁμοῦ γέροντες καὶ νέοι καὶ μητέρες. [50]

Heracles after the murder of his wife and children feels as if he has been forcibly unyoked from them

κἀποζεύγνυμαι
τέκνων γυναικός τ'. [51]

On the other hand he recognizes in his friendship with Theseus a new relationship which he expresses again in the same metaphor ζεῦγός γε φίλιον[52] at the end of the play. Here then traditional imagery is suitable. But it is also part of a whole cluster of images which express this same idea of necessary dependence upon family and friends, and cannot properly be considered in isolation. Allied to this is the picture of Megara's children dragging round her feet like horses on a tracing rein

ἄλοχόν τε φίλην ὑπὸ σειραίοις
ποσὶν ἕλκουσαν τέκνα. [53]

But there are other quite different images still related to these because they express the same idea of dependence. The former security of Megara's family life is described in terms of the firm anchoring cables which moor a ship.[54] The dependence of Heracles' children is characterized in a striking new simile, which is then repeated in metaphor form.[55] As Heracles, early in the play, confidently allays his family's terror, he looks affectionately at his children who are clinging to his clothes and won't let go. The introductory ἆ outside the regular metrical line gives the moment some importance.

ἆ,
οἵδ' οὐκ ἀφιᾶσ', ἀλλ' ἀνάπτονται πέπλων
τοσῷδε μᾶλλον· ὧδ' ἔβητ' ἐπὶ ξυροῦ;
ἄξω λαβών γε τούσδ' ἐφολκίδας χεροῖν,
ναῦς δ' ὡς ἐφέλξω· καὶ γὰρ οὐκ ἀναίνομαι
θεράπευμα τέκνων.

Ah, just look at these children: they won't let go, but cling to my clothes even more. Were you so much on a knife edge? Well I'll take them with me, leading them by the hand like little boats on tow. I can't refuse my children.[56]

After the terrible attack of madness which leads him to kill the very children he loves, Heracles uses the image of ἐφολκίς again. A crushed man now, in abject despair, he realizes his own dependence on Theseus, the one friend left to him, and he applies the word to himself.

> ἡμεῖς δ᾽ ἀναλώσαντες αἰσχύναις δόμον,
> Θησεῖ πανώλεις ἑψόμεσθ᾽ ἐφολκίδες.

I have destroyed my own house and family in shame and I must now follow Theseus as absolutely as small boats follow the tow-rope.[57]

The whole *peripeteia* of the action, and the reflective implications which follow from it, that dependence is necessary even for the greatest of heroes, is thus built up in a series of more or less common metaphors and similes, and characterized in the emphatic repetition of this one unusual visual image. As if in confirmation come Heracles' last words, 'Whoever wants to acquire money or physical strength in preference to reliable friendship is a fool.'[58]

Other ideas in this tragedy are similarly served by clusters of simile and metaphor, repeated for emphasis. The powerlessness of old age is one expressed by the recurring comparison the chorus make of themselves to a swan singing its death dirge.[59] The transitory nature of happiness and the merciless action of Time is another which is developed in a set of related figurative images.[60] In assessing such imagery, neither repetition nor traditional language are sufficient criteria in themselves to condemn the poet out of hand. It is use and the degree of integration with other contexts which count.

It is doubtful then whether the criticisms of Euripidean simile and metaphor are quite as justified as has sometimes been supposed. It is true that Euripides' universe basically is a human and not a divine one, and his imagery does not have the soaring faith in obscure but ultimate divine justice which inspires some of Aeschylus' most striking language. I shall return to this point in the last chapter.[61] On the other hand, neither did Homer's, and here Pauer's charge that Euripides is un-Ionian seems to me particularly inappropriate. Euripides' language shows a clear grasp of things as they are, and his figurative imagery is also cast in the form of concrete and tangible things. Imagine Homer's descriptive techniques applied to domestic detail, and one might not be so far from Euripidean style. Yet that same clarity which is a virtue in Homer, must it seems be a vice in Euripides.

Nonetheless, it makes most sense to look at metaphorical language not as an independent but as a strengthening role. Previous chapters have established the poet's inclination towards, as well as the extent and character of, his pictorial visualization in different modes. A case could have been made for his poetic skill on this alone, without the consideration of metaphor in its strict sense. But this would have been too limited, since as we have just seen, some simile and metaphor does occur. It is necessary now to consider the two types of imagery in relation to one another in passages where both exist. There are particularly clear cases of examples in all modes in the messenger speeches. We have already seen that there is a consistent pictorial presentation in these, which builds up from a quiet setting at the beginning to the violent climax of action in the later part. Although such visual conceptions do not depend upon imagery of a metaphorical kind, occasional similes or short metaphors contribute sharpness to this pictorial narrative without in any way disturbing the predominant style. In fact by increasing the visual precision, they continue it. The similes themselves contain description of the same kind as that which is outside them and the metaphors do not carry one off into abstract realms of ideas where the visual is not important, but require imagination with the eyes alone. They are concerned like the rest of the speech with *how* an action happened, not why. As in Homer, the material for such imagery is frequently derived from common sights in Greece, both natural phenomena, storms, clouds, whirlwinds, snow and so on, and familiar occupations such as harvesting, diving, wrestling, racing, forging metal or playing games.[62] They enrich the texture of the main description, not by a complex ambivalence which is not required in this mode, but by a sharpening focus which emerges from explicit or implicit comparison.

λαβὼν γὰρ ἐλάτης οὐράνιον ἄκρον κλάδον
κατῆγεν, ἦγεν, ἦγεν ἐς μέλαν πέδον·
κυκλοῦτο δ᾽ ὥστε τόξον ἢ κυρτὸς τροχὸς
τόρνῳ γραφόμενος περιφορὰν ἕλκει δρόμον·

Taking the topmost skyward branch of a pine-tree he bent, bent, bent it down to the dark ground. He made a circle out of it like a bow, or the way the curved circumference of a wheel-rim is slowly traced round with a pair of compasses.[63]

In this simile from the *Bacchae*, the feeling for shape in the attention to detail which emerges in the circular tracing of the wheel is similar to the precision of description outside the simile, when the messenger describes the straightening of the branch for instance, or when he describes the hurling of branches from a particular rock.⁶⁴ The general uniformity of style is not broken by this simile. One action is merely made more imaginable by the precise visual conjuring of another. Had the messenger used a different sort of analogy: had he said, for instance, that the bending of the tree was accomplished with such strength as only the Gods possess, this uniformity of style would not have been preserved, for the poet would then have directed the attention away from mere visual observation to more metaphysical estimations of divine power. How much strength do Gods possess? And such questions. The same point is neatly illustrated, this time by metaphor, in another messenger speech. In the *Supplices*, in the middle of his battle narrative, the messenger describes Theseus as whirling his club as if it were a sling, and 'harvesting' a row of helmets.

> αὐτός θ' ὅπλισμα τοὐπιδάυριον λαβὼν
> δεινῆς κορύνης διαφέρων ἐσφενδόνα
> ὁμοῦ τραχήλους κἀπικείμενον κάρα,
> κυνέας θερίζων κἀποκαυλίζων ξύλῳ.

Theseus himself picking up his Epidaurian club, that terrible weapon, swung it in all directions like a sling, harvesting with his club a row of necks and covered helmeted heads, snapping them off like stalks.⁶⁵

The two metaphors of cutting corn, together with the one of the sling, facilitate a precise vision of the quick decapitating movement of Theseus within the short space of three lines. The speed and force of the act is enhanced by the placing together first of the object-nouns 'necks' and 'covered heads', then of the two cutting metaphors next to each other in the centre of the next line, so that there seems to be an instant's hesitation before the club makes its devastating impact. All concentration is, as in the last passage, on the mechanism of the action, not at this moment its significance in the whole battle, or its cause, or its potential danger, or indeed anything which would stray beyond the seeing of the act itself.

In iambic *rhesis* too, a few well chosen metaphors heighten but are not indispensable to the symbolic meaning of descriptive language. The attitudes of Electra, Pentheus and Hecuba, as indicated earlier, are characterized by the way they describe certain scenes and actions, and metaphor plays some part in this description.⁶⁶ In Electra's *rhesis*, the

two metaphors of animal life contribute to the sense of degradation
created by the graphic and sensuous description which is the predominat-
ing style of her speech. In the *Bacchae* too, the metaphors Pentheus uses
reinforce the lurid pictorial imagination of his speeches. He frequently
uses the language of animal tracking and hunting, words such as θηράω,
ἐξιχνεύω, ἐν ἄρκυσιν, ἐν ἕρκεσιν, showing that he regards the maenads
in bestial terms.[67] The physically centred language shows in metaphors
as well as straight description, some of which have already been quoted.
Dionysus' ringlets are 'full of sexual desire' and his eyes of 'Aphrodite's
allure'.[68] He is thought of as 'defiling women's beds' and in danger of
'wiping off' his folly on Pentheus himself.[69] When Pentheus pictures the
maenads, he imagines himself as surprising them in the act of love,
caught like birds in the bushes.

> καὶ μὴν δοκῶ σφᾶς ἐν λόχμαις ὄρνιθας ὡς
> λέκτρων ἔχεσθαι φιλτάτοις ἐν ἕρκεσιν

> Think,
> I can see them already, there among the bushes,
> mating like birds caught in the toils of love.[70]

He calls their activities σαθρὸν 'diseased' or 'rotten', a word Hippo-
crates uses literally of the decaying human body.[71] Once again, such
imagery heightens the effect of the sensuous descriptions already
discussed without altering their tone.

Numerous examples could be cited from lyric also. At the opening of
a pictorial ode in the *Hecuba*, several metaphors help set the general
scene before the chorus move to more specific detail of the scene in the
palace apartments on the night Troy falls. They begin by addressing the
city personally in a series of metaphors.

> τοῖον Ἑλλάνων νέφος ἀμφὶ σε κρύπτει.

> Such is the cloud of Greeks that covers you.[72]

> ἀπὸ δὲ στεφάναν κέκαρ-
> σαι πύργων

> You have had your crown of towers shorn away.[73]

> κατὰ δ' αἰθάλου
> κηλῖδ' οἰκτροτάταν κεχρω-
> σαι.

> You are pitifully blackened with smoke stains.[74]

The metaphorical element is not very strong here in the sense that it is not startling or original. To describe Troy as a person, or one's enemies as a cloud, or the Trojan towers as the city's crown, is language characteristic both of Euripides elsewhere and of other poets.[75] The main strength is in the three parallel compound verbs to which the *tmesis* in each case draws special attention. But these apt metaphors adequately introduce the more detailed picture which is to follow without detracting from it. At the same time, continuity of style is preserved in the sensuous content both of the metaphors and of the descriptive passages which come after them.

Sometimes the mere suggestion of metaphor enhances the quality of lyric description without disturbing its overall non-figurative quality. Thus when the chorus in the *Iphigeneia in Aulis* describe the scene for the wedding of Peleus and Thetis, the slight metaphor contained in the words 'goblets' golden hollows'

$$\chi\rho\upsilon\sigma\acute{\epsilon}\omicron\iota\sigma\iota\nu \ldots$$
$$\acute{\epsilon}\nu \ \kappa\rho\alpha\tau\acute{\eta}\rho\omega\nu \ \gamma\upsilon\acute{\alpha}\lambda\omicron\iota\varsigma \ldots^{76}$$

preserves the dazzling impressions made by other kinds of description in the passage, such as the shining expanses of white sand conveyed in the adjective λευκοφαῆ with ψάμαθον and the flash of gold-sandalled feet suggested by χρυσεοσάνδαλον qualifying ἴχνος as the Muses strike the ground in the movements of the dance. In the same way, when Electra in the *Orestes* describes the pursuit of Myrtilus across the raging sea, the one apt metaphorical word 'flying' applied to the chase, adds to the sense of swift urgent movement without claiming exclusive attention.[77] Or when Antigone in the *Phoenissae* refers to her 'clustered cheeks' this is only one small element in a longer pictorial description of her own physical appearance.[78] The role of metaphor in such cases may be humbler than that ascribed to it by many other poets, but it is useful, and contributes satisfactorily to the harmony of a much larger whole.

This harmony of an intensely visual style served by different kinds of image is most clearly illustrated by that ode in the *Bacchae* where the chorus compare themselves to a fawn in flight.

$$\mathring{\alpha}\rho' \ \acute{\epsilon}\nu \ \pi\alpha\nu\nu\upsilon\chi\acute{\iota}\omicron\iota\varsigma \ \chi\omicron\rho\omicron\hat{\iota}\varsigma$$
$$\theta\acute{\eta}\sigma\omega \ \pi\omicron\tau\grave{\epsilon} \ \lambda\epsilon\upsilon\kappa\grave{\omicron}\nu$$
$$\pi\acute{\omicron}\delta' \ \mathring{\alpha}\nu\alpha\beta\alpha\kappa\chi\epsilon\acute{\upsilon}\omicron\upsilon\sigma\alpha, \ \delta\acute{\epsilon}\rho\alpha\nu$$

εἰς αἰθέρα δροσερὸν ῥίπτουσ᾽,
ὡς νεβρὸς χλοεραῖς ἐμπαί-
ζουσα λείμακος ἡδοναῖς,
ἡνίκ᾽ ἂν φοβερὰν φύγῃ
    θήραν ἔξω φυλακᾶς
εὐπλέκτων ὑπὲρ ἀρκύων,
θωΰσσων δὲ κυναγέτας
συντείνῃ δράμημα κυνῶν·

Shall I ever again dance bare-foot in night-long Bacchic ecstasy, throwing my head back in the dew-drenched air, playing in the green joys of a meadow like a fawn does when it has fled from the fearful hunt away from its watchers and beyond the meshed nets, while the huntsman shouts and drives on his dogs in pursuit. It bounds along storm-swift beside the river bank, running with hard exertion, taking pleasure in the places empty of men and in the luxuriant foliage of the shadowy forest.[79]

The sensuous quality consistently maintained in these lines is observable in descriptive epithets, simile and metaphor alike. In fact the separate pictorial devices are hardly distinguishable since their end is the same. Adjectives strongly evoking of sight and texture, 'bare white feet', 'dewy air', 'close-meshed nets', 'shadowy forest', occur not only inside as well as outside the simile, but also in the metaphors contained within the simile itself, 'green joys of a meadow'[80] and 'storm-swift leaps',[81] all stimulating a visual imagination into which, for the moment, no abstract idea is allowed to intrude. And yet this imagination as it is concretely expressed here is so closely connected to the rest of the play that it is organically part of a whole complex of ideas which ultimately express the philosophy of Bacchic worship: the need for escape, the hedonistic pleasure in nature, the feeling of persecution and the closeness to the instinctive life of animals.[82]

It is this connection of individual passages to the whole, and the relation of one image to others in the play which ultimately make all classifications into image-type seem merely artificial. Similes and metaphors are in the end only a part of that whole network of language which makes one total articulate shape. As part of that shape they may stand in their own right, serving a temporary purpose by single occurrence, or they may, as in the examples just discussed, help to add to the density of texture in a particular description, or they may by repetition establish cross-links which underline a key theme in the drama. The simile and metaphors in the ode in the *Bacchae* just quoted do all these things. The 'green joys' metaphor is unique, and makes its own point which would stand were there nothing else around it. But as it happens there is, and so it also strengthens the description of the maenad dancing like a fawn in the forest adding to it the note of visually appreciative pleasure. The fawn simile both stands in its own right, strengthens the existing description, and recalls animal similes elsewhere in the play. To do full justice to the strengthening and linking function of simile and metaphor in the context of other imagery, one would have to take each play on its own merits, and this would require a far more extensive study than the scope of this book permits. But a brief look at one play, the *Trojan Women*, may show how this multiple function is consistently maintained throughout.

There are metaphors and similes in this drama which occur only once, and then not in the context of descriptive imagery. The similes are particularly prominent, the comparison of fortune to an impulsive man for instance

$$\text{τοῖς τρόποις γὰρ αἱ τύχαι}$$
$$\text{ἔμπληκτος ὡς ἄνθρωπος, ἄλλοτ’ ἄλλοσε}$$
$$\text{πηδῶσι.}$$

Fortune like an impulsive man changes the direction of its ways from one moment to the next.[83]

or of Hecuba herself to a drone or a dim shadow

$$\textit{Εκ. φεῦ φεῦ.}$$
$$\text{τῷ δ’ ἀ τλάμων}$$
$$\text{ποῦ πᾷ γαίας δουλεύσω γραῦς,}$$
$$\text{ὡς κηφήν, ἀ δειλαία,}$$
$$\text{νεκροῦ μορφά,}$$
$$\text{νεκύων ἀμενηνὸν ἄγαλμα,}$$
$$\text{αἰαῖ}$$
$$\text{τὰν παρὰ προθύροις φυλακὰν κατέχουσ’}$$
$$\text{ἢ παίδων θρέπτειρ’, ἀ Τροίας}$$
$$\text{ἀρχαγοὺς εἶχον τιμάς;}$$

And I,
whose wretched slave
shall I be? Where in my gray age,
a faint drone,

poor image of a corpse,
weak shining among dead men? Shall
I stand and keep guard at their doors,
shall I nurse their children, I who in Troy
held state as a princess?[84]

These similes underline an idea, the capriciousness of fortune, the debility of Hecuba and the demands of labour to be made on her. This is also the function of certain recurring metaphors which are not specifically linked to descriptive imagery. The image of the garland of victory is repeatedly used ironically to stress the illusory nature of success.[85] Destruction is personified several times as a reminder of its live force among both sides.[86] Madness is continuously described in Bacchic metaphors which most accurately explain its irrational nature.[87]

But apart from this use of independent figurative language there is the important role which simile and metaphor consistently play in giving support to other imagery, either in the same passage or by recalling descriptions located elsewhere. We have already seen how the choral odes of this play are presented in language of great visual brilliance. In these, the concrete pictorial style is largely unbroken by moral comment or discursive reflections, and when it is strengthened by an occasional metaphor or simile these too are as sensuous as the rest of the description of which they form a part. Thus forty lines of straight description of the scene on the night the Greeks invade Troy are concluded by several metaphors which continue in visual terms the picture of violence the chorus are trying to recreate. 'A blood-red shout' may not be entirely logical, but the synaesthesia captures not only the sound but the vision of blood which assailed the women at this time.[88] Similarly war itself is personified as the figure of Ares stalking out from his place of ambush,[89] and devastation is glimpsed as the figure which rampages the bedrooms decapitating Trojan men in their beds.[90] In the second *stasimon*, several metaphors centrally placed give point and contrast to the much longer descriptive context of which they are a part. But their appeal is still to the senses of sound and sight.

μάταν ἄρ᾽, ὦ χρυσέαις ἐν οἰνοχόαις ἁβρὰ βαίνων,
    Λαομεδόντιε παῖ,
Ζηνὸς ἔχεις κυλίκων πλήρωμα, καλλίσταν λατρείαν·
ἁ δέ σε γειναμένα πυρὶ δαίεται·
    ἠιόνες δ᾽ ἅλιαι
    ἴακχον οἰωνὸς οἷ-

ὸν τεκέων ὕπερ βοᾷ,
ᾇ μὲν εὐνάτορας, ᾇ δὲ παῖδας,
ᾇ δὲ ματέρας γεραιάς.
τὰ δὲ σὰ δροσόεντα λουτρὰ
γυμνασίων τε δρόμοι
βεβᾶσι, σὺ δὲ πρόσωπα νεα-
ρὰ χάρισι παρὰ Διὸς θρόνοις
καλλιγάλανα τρέφεις· Πριάμοιο δὲ γαῖαν
Ἑλλὰς ὤλεσ᾽ αἰχμά.

All for nothing then, child of Laomedon, do you hold your honoured service in filling Zeus' cups, stepping your way daintily among the gold wine ladles. The land that bore you is eaten by fire. The beaches cry out as a mother bird screams for her lost young; in one place it is for a husband, in another for a child, in another for an old mother. The pools where you bathed, and the courses where you exercised are gone, but you in your position by Zeus' throne still look beautifully serene, and youthful in your charm. Priam's land has been destroyed by the Greek spear.[91]

The sight of suffering which the metaphors of groaning beaches and children looking like lost fledglings underline, makes a strong contrast to the initially decorative picture of Ganymede who is a classic example of frivolous and heedless divine behaviour.

In both these cases, the total density of description is increased by the skilled use of metaphor. And there are other instances outside lyric, as for example when Hecuba's harrowing account of the appearance of her grandson's mangled body is made more horrific by the one metaphor ἐκγελᾷ.

δύστηνε, κρατὸς ὥς σ᾽ ἔκειρεν ἀθλίως
τείχη πατρῷα, Λοξίου πυργώματα,
ὃν πόλλ᾽ ἐκήπευσ᾽ ἡ τεκοῦσα βόστρυχον
φιλήμασίν τ᾽ ἔδωκεν, ἔνθεν ἐκγελᾷ
ὀστέων ῥαγέντων φόνος,

How wickedly, poor boy, your father's walls, Apollo's handiwork, have crushed your pitiful head tended and trimmed to ringlets by your mother's hand, and the face she kissed once, where the brightness now is blood shining through the torn bones.[92]

Lattimore's translation of ἐκγελᾷ as 'shining' does not quite catch the other associations this word has in Greek. It also means to laugh, and it is probable that the word has connotations here of sound as well as sight. The blood not only shines, but gurgles like the noise of laughter, as it gushes out from the gaping wound.[93]

Metaphors also work with description in another way. They may be extended beyond the area of description but designed to recall it. Thus the city's walls, or the Greek ships literally described in one place, may be metaphorically recalled in another. For instance the construction of the rough hewn stones of the battlements is carefully alluded to in several places, in the prologue, in the second *stasimon* by Hecuba several times, and at the end of the play. The fact that they are part of the stage set, that they are the physical embodiment of the Trojan community and that they are the object both of Astyanax' execution and the Greek demolition squads, makes it appropriate that their importance is brought out in descriptive passages. These cumulatively demonstrate by implication that Troy's rise and fall is synonymous with the presence or absence of her walls. But this symbolic significance is also underlined in metaphor which recalls the descriptions of the building of Troy's towers. Twice the word πυργόω is used in abstract context as if the physical building of the city is appropriate to other things too.

ὡς τότε μὲν μεγάλως Τροίαν ἐπύργωσας, θεοῖσι
κῆδος ἀναψάμενος.

'How mightily you built Troy up then' sing the chorus to Eros, 'promoting its divine connections'.[94] They refer here not merely to the physical construction of the city but also to the favour shown in general by the Gods to Troy, a favour which they have now withdrawn. Hecuba has earlier used the same metaphor.

ὁρῶ τὰ τῶν θεῶν, ὡς τὰ μὲν πυργοῦσ' ἄνω
τὸ μηδὲν ὄντα, τὰ δὲ δοκοῦντ' ἀπώλεσαν.

I see the work of gods, who pile tower-high the pride of those who were nothing, and dash present grandeur down.[95]

Here descriptive imagery and metaphor work co-operatively to stress the symbolic significance of Troy's city battlements, but they do not work in the same geographical area.

The same is true, as was suggested in an earlier chapter, of the way in which nautical metaphors extend the literal description of ships so that both indicate the fearful preoccupation of the Trojan women with what

9

is an unfamiliar threat to them.[96] Not only do the captives keep alluding to the Greek ships and describing them, but they begin using nautical language. There are several instances, other than Hecuba's monody, of such nautical metaphors. The women speak of being wrecked. The wooden horse takes on the appearance of a dark ship, a suitably sinister thing with which to compare it.[97] The line between the literal and the metaphorical is often hard to draw. When the women speak of wreck, the audience know that a real wreck has been prophesied by Poseidon for the journey home. This hovering between the real and the imaginary is clearly illustrated in a speech Hecuba makes in the middle of the play giving expression to her fears.

> Εκ. αὐτὴ μὲν οὔπω ναὸς εἰσέβην σκάφος,
> γραφῇ δ᾽ ἰδοῦσα καὶ κλύουσ᾽ ἐπίσταμαι.
> ναύταις γὰρ ἦν μὲν μέτριος ᾖ χειμὼν φέρειν,
> προθυμίαν ἔχουσι σωθῆναι πόνων,
> ὁ μὲν παρ᾽ οἴαχ᾽, ὁ δ᾽ ἐπὶ λαίφεσιν βεβώς,
> ὁ δ᾽ ἄντλον εἴργων ναός· ἢν δ᾽ ὑπερβάλῃ
> πολὺς ταραχθεὶς πόντος, ἐνδόντες τύχῃ
> παρεῖσαν αὑτοὺς κυμάτων δρομήμασιν.
> οὕτω δὲ κἀγὼ πόλλ᾽ ἔχουσα πήματα
> ἄφθογγός εἰμι καὶ παρεῖσ᾽ ἐῶ στόμα·
> νικᾷ γὰρ οὐκ θεῶν με δύστηνος κλύδων.

I myself have never been on a ship, but I have seen paintings and I know about them from hearing people talk. If the weather is calm the crew are all eagerness to secure their own safety; one man takes the rudder, another watches over the sails, another pumps out the bilge-water. But if the sea is very heavy, then they give in to haphazardness and let themselves go with the running swell of the tide. It's like that with me. I have so many toubles that I don't have any words to say; I am inarticulate, so powerful are the waves the Gods have sent.[98]

The first two lines state clearly that Hecuba's terror of ships lies in sheer unfamiliarity with the sea. The Trojans were a land people and in any case the women would have no cause in normal circumstances to leave the walled city. Like Hippolytus' knowledge of sex, her only information is derived from pictures.[99] What follows is an imaginative attempt on the Queen's part to work out what actually happens on a ship at sea. It thus follows naturally from the reference to the information she has gleaned, and stresses the imaginative effort she is making to come to grips with the unknown. On the other hand it is also a straight simile designed to illustrate her own condition in terms familiar to the audience; 'Just as there are storms at sea so bad that sailors are overwhelmed by them, so am I overwhelmed by what has hit me.' At the same time the simile is not merely a random one: the reference to a storm also serves to remind the audience of the real storm which will overtake the ships on their voyage back to Greece. Therefore irony is also at work here. Hecuba is unaware how true her figurative words are to prove.

This transition between the literal and the symbolic was perhaps more common in the imagery of the ancient Greeks than in that of modern authors. One could find other instances in this play, such as the theme of dancing which is both literally present in Cassandra's performance and symbolic of former happiness; or in the descriptions of gold objects which acquire symbolic significance through repeated description and are used in simile.[100] Such transitions are significant because they show the ways in which simile and metaphor co-operate with descriptive imagery to give the play depth and richness of texture. For this purpose it is meaningless to take into consideration one kind of imagery only. Euripides used both for a common dramatic purpose, and ultimately the successful stylistic texture of a play depends not only upon the cross-links between one kind of image and another, but also on the relation of these to other kinds of stylistic device and theme as it is expressed in the language.

Chapter VII

Conclusion

It has been the aim of the last six chapters to build up a sufficient body of experience of imagery to show that it is an essential, and not merely an extraneous ornamental part of Euripides' dramatic constructions. There is a predominance, as we have seen, of descriptive imagery which is controlled to a large extent by mode. But simile and metaphor which cut across mode, are also important in the role they assume in the context of other imagery. Both kinds work to the same end, and both to some extent have the same nature. Symbolism, for instance, may be achieved by either kind or both in any given context. Emotional texture, elucidation of character, enlargement of mood, clarification of action, underlining of certain themes – all these may be conveyed by straight description, simile or metaphor, or a combination of these working together. The poet's imagination (in a sense which includes the active working of all these stylistic devices) finds expression primarily through appeal to the sense of sight, and in such a way that the impact of an image tends initially to be sensuously perceptual rather than intellectual. War, for instance, is first of all seen in its external visual manifestation, as a figure stalking out from an ambush, or in such observed effects as smoke rising from burning buildings or children clinging to their mothers' skirts.[1] Its function may then be assessed not from the single economic metaphor, but from a correlation of different observable phenomena. Euripides' descriptions, and also his similes and metaphors, as we have seen, show the considerable degree to which he was sensitive to colour, shapes, effects of light, movement and texture. Repeatedly, the words he uses convey a sense of the physical components of substances, often in contrast one with another, fire against stone, winds against canvas, nails scraping flesh, gold set in wood, blood on metal, sun on rock, cloth on tangled grass, and so on. This sensuous style applies to describing the inanimate, and also, as we have seen, is a means of presenting different emotional states. Obvious examples are the treatment of Orestes' illness, or Hecuba's grief, or Heracles' madness through their observable physical symptoms. Many single metaphors which are used to describe violent action or severe distress have a strongly physical cast to them, as for instance in the word καταξαίνω, where the process of carding wool is applied to jagged rocks lacerating flesh, or in διακναίω, which Aristophanes uses of scraping the colour off a boat, which is used as an expression for wearing down the soul.[2] It is as if 'reality' is first communicated through its physical impression, shutting out until later any more abstract assessment of what is involved. It is odd that a poet who seeks through the imagination to awaken what is initially an emotional or physical response, should so often have been labelled as nothing more than an uncompromising intellectual who regarded the emotions with detached curiosity. If that attitude is partially and necessarily present in the careful observation and analysis of emotions, at least the attempt to communicate them to an audience and thereby ellicit response, implies a concern for human problems which goes beyond mere detached curiosity.

In the sense that dramatic reality is thus communicated in Euripides' plays through imagery, some answer has been made to those critics mentioned earlier, who would have preferred to see him writing in prose. For of all poetic devices, imagery is the furthest from prose, and yet it is used extensively by this dramatist in all modes, and in some, notably the monody and the messenger speech, with the important purpose of conveying new truths in regions not previously explored by dramatists. There remain however one or two more criticisms which it is worth mentioning by way of summary in this last chapter.

These criticisms are voiced by those who acknowledge in Euripides a flair for visual imagery, but who deny that he uses it properly. Their views may be briefly summarized. Masqueray believed that Euripides had a perceptive flair for visual detail which obsessed him to such an extent that the main road constantly got lost in an endless pursuit of footpaths. 'Il semble avoir la vue du myope qui s'arrête sur un détail, le scrute, l'étudie, et néglige les fonds lointains, qu'il n'aperçoit qu'à travers un brouillard.'[3] The second view is that of Delulle which runs on slightly different lines. Euripides was blessed with a certain associative sensibility, which he let run riot in a kind of vague visual impressionism totally lacking in sharp edges. It may seem to resemble painting, but really it does not. 'L'image, chez Euripide, ne peint pas, elle évoque.'[4] He thus attributes to the poet a gift for the picturesque and no more, since there is lacking in his opinion both concentration and vitality. The third is a different view again which might be represented as follows. Euripides' acuteness of observation was such that it led him into a sort of painful

clarity that borders on the simple-minded. Since one can almost invari-
ably understand what he is saying at any given point, his imagination, in
the shape of his images, is lacking in ambiguity and his work therefore in
complexity.[5] All these judgements have partial truth to them and are
unfair for this reason. One could call them myopic in the sense that they
do not take into account the total work, as it must finally be assessed from
correlation of different modes and styles, combined as they are within
the compass of one play. Imagination, as was said earlier, must ultimately
be judged not from the isolated stylistic unit, but from the way this
this is worked into the whole fabric.

No doubt the minutiae the messenger speeches contain would
demonstrate very nicely the charge of myopic vision on the poet's part
if that was all there was of the plays. Every recorded detail would seem
to have a magnified significance which would indeed be baffling if
nothing existed beyond the speeches themselves. But as it is, the eye-
witness account of the messenger must be memorable enough for its
impact to reach to the end of the play, and to stir up memories of action
which took place earlier. It is not irrelevant therefore to single out such
tiny points of detail as the slackening claws of a dying bird, or to note
that Pentheus was still wearing shoes when he died, since such observations, as they do in modern reports of crimes, make more easily imaginable a violent and, on the face of it, improbable death.[6] In the dying
convulsions of a bird, there is a potentially poisoned youth. Mention of
Pentheus' shoes ironically recalls the extreme care he took in dressing up
for the disastrous expedition to the mountains. Small pictorial details are
in this sense dramatically active. Moreover, in the sharpness of outline
with which they are drawn, they force the hearers to see with the
reporter's eyes and preclude escape into any more reassuring vagueness.
It is precisely because there is no natural inclination to follow the poet
down these bizarre paths, and because one has to nevertheless, that the
tragic event is brought close. As a matter of fact however, the particular
examples Masqueray cites to illustrate his point about top-heavy detail
are not from the messenger speeches but from lyric. 'Que nous importe',
he writes 'que les lavandières de l'Hippolyte et de l'Hélène fassent
sécher, elles ou leurs compagnes, des vêtements de pourpre sur des
pierres sur l'herbe, sur les roseaux, quand elles apprennent les événements
qui les décident à se diriger vers le théâtre ?'[7] Doing the washing may be
new material for tragedy, but as we saw in an earlier discussion, it is not
irrelevant to the total action. The scenes referred to are organically
functional in that they establish a norm against which to judge more

clearly the abnormal situation of the heroine.[8] The small visual details are necessary to the building up of mood appropriate to this norm. Euripides was the first tragedian to recognize compatibility between sights such as he must have observed every day and heroic myth, and was also the first to go out of his way to use them to interpret myth itself. Household tasks and household objects become believable occupations and environments through which to interpret his heroes' actions. In that sense they are not stray details which happen to catch his random associative fancy, but a necessary part of his own dramatic equipment.[9]

The charge of picturesque vagueness is associated mainly with those decorative romantic choral odes which set out to evoke moods of escapism, happiness, longing or nostalgia. These are thought to be evidence of Euripides' sentimentalism. 'Colour is laid on thickly' writes Earp, for instance, of the second *stasimon* of the *Helen*, 'but with an impressionistic brush, and the outlines are not very clear.'[10] He concludes that here the dramatist was working from 'fancy', and simply embroidering conventional ornament. Such a judgement, however, fails to take into account the mood of the whole play which requires, unlike others, a certain romantic lightness of tone. To find fault with this ode without taking into account the fantasy elements of the plot generally, is somewhat like saying that the language of *The Tempest* is unsuited to *King Lear*. In other cases, and perhaps more commonly, a single ode may be thought sentimental without any further consideration as to whether it is intended to contrast ironically with what precedes or follows. The Dawn chorus of the *Phaethon*, as we saw earlier, was an instance of such contrast.[11] What appears if one only looks at the choral song, is a vague and romantically evocative description of early morning. What emerges when one considers it in full context, is that by its juxtaposition to a very different mood on the part of Phaethon, it forms part of a wider and profoundly realistic design, composed of many disparate elements.

Most of the tragedies combine in some way or other such differing elements and styles – 'realistic, romantic, sharply etched, impressionistic, austere or colourful'. Not that these are comprehensive, or mutually exclusive categories. The 'romantic' in mood may be precisely rendered, and the so called 'realistic' impressionistically so. What matters is that full meaning can only emerge from some final correlation of these elements as they are deployed according to the demands of mode, situation and character. On the level of imagery alone, such a correlation may be made for instance from an assessment of the different types of pictorial language used to describe Orestes' madness. Electra's descriptions are graphic but clinically precise, those of the chorus are decorative with elements of fantasy. Both styles are necessary to present a contrast between new and old beliefs, and to allow an assessment of the new in the light of the old. Heracles' exploits are described in imagery of pictorial fantasy by the chorus, in sceptical rhetoric by Lycus, and in terms of 'factual' pictorial narrative by the messenger. Again, all are necessary to a final assessment of his action and character, and this emerges in the closing scenes of the play where Heracles himself converses with Theseus. In this dialogue, earlier views, and the styles underlining them, are rehearsed and sorted. The labours are reviewed, thus recalling the first decorative *stasimon*; the scepticism of Lycus finds echo in some of Heracles' own doubts; the madness is faced as fact in a way which confirms the messenger's account. Finally, a new view of Heracles is formed which is a selective assimilation of previous elements in the tragedy. The courage which enabled him to perform the labours is retained, but reapplied to a new situation, namely to the decision to live. Thus where the old labours ended in Hades, the new trials which brought madness have ended in an affirmation of life. These are only two examples of the way in which apparently disparate styles form the preparatory basis for a final judgement or resolution. But they do make the point that Euripides, so far from being 'myopic' and ignoring 'les fonds lointains', was, on the contrary, composing with a view to the totality of the drama. Paradoxically, the apparent separation of modes and styles is designed only to facilitate an ultimate correlation between them which is larger than the sum of their parts, just as the separate sharply divided edges of a crystal allow the whole to shine more brightly than if the shape were uniformly curved.

This question of correlation, of fitting together the separate pieces, which begins as an imaginative exercise on the part of the poet and ends as a response demanded from the audience, may provide some clue as to how to meet the third view mentioned above, that Euripides' imagery is over-clear in expression. For again it is only if one does not look beyond the individual passage, in which an image occurs, that clarity is liable to seem over-clarity. It is certainly true that, taken singly, hardly any of Euripides' images are incomprehensible or even obscure. They seem to have a perspicuity as absolute as that of Homer's.[12] But only on the surface. For the fact that this is drama, not epic narrative, makes a decisive difference. Instead of a neutral epic narrator to explain the action in terms in which one unequivocally believes, there is a whole range of characters among whom the dramatist shares himself and behind whom he personally stands obscured. Earlier dramatists had perhaps put more of themselves into the 'neutral' chorus, which was not a character in the same way as the others onstage. But Euripides altered this practice by making his chorus more of a character in the sense that he gave it committed and frequently biased points of view. One cannot therefore, even here, search for the author as a detached commentator. As we have seen previously, Euripides frequently adapts language to suit the differing viewpoints of his characters. Any one image is likely to express an attitude which may not be shared and may even in some cases be misinterpreted by another character. The final estimation again lies beyond the individual utterance. This is particularly true in those cases where the poet is attempting to show characters whose emotional state is puzzling to others. What appear to one character as literal utterance may be made to seem metaphor to others. When for instance Agave refers to Pentheus' mangled head which she carries on a stick, as successively a newly cut vine, a lion and a bull calf, her relatives seeing the human head can only assume that she is imagining things.[13] To the audience who know everything, Agave's language is the poet's metaphorical way of expressing the nature of delusion. Cassandra in the *Troades* sees in her hand a marriage torch to light her fictitious wedding ceremony, whereas the chorus and Hecuba see merely an ordinary torch in danger of falling from her grasp.[14] To the audience who see both perspectives, there is another dimension still, since this firebrand can hardly fail to remind them of the torch Hecuba dreamt she gave birth to when she was expecting Paris. This is mentioned both in the first play of the trilogy and later in this play as a symbol of doom to the whole Trojan house. All levels are therefore incorporated into this one image, literal, deliriously imaginative or historically symbolic; but only if one is the audience does one see all at once. Onstage, the interpretations are split between different characters. In the *Orestes*, the multiplicity of level in terms of language is illustrated even more clearly. Orestes describes the Furies in pictorial terms of creatures flying towards him with bows and arrows.[15] How is one to interpret this vision? The chorus seem to treat it literally, to judge by the way in which they continue the kind of imaginative language used by him during his fit.[16] They see black-skinned monsters darting through the air demanding blood for blood. Electra and Menelaus, on the other hand, take a less traditional line. They are quite clear that Orestes' language was purely imaginative, resulting from a delusion. 'Even if you are not ill,' says Electra, 'you think you are, and that brings fatigue and helplessness.'

$$\kappa\mathring{a}\nu\ \mu\grave{\eta}\ \nu o\sigma\mathring{\eta}s\ \gamma\grave{a}\rho,\ \mathring{a}\lambda\lambda\grave{a}\ \delta o\xi\acute{a}\zeta\eta s\ \nu o\sigma\epsilon\widehat{\iota}\nu,$$
$$\kappa\acute{a}\mu a\tau os\ \beta\rho o\tau o\widehat{\iota}\sigma\iota\nu\ \mathring{a}\pi o\rho\acute{\iota}a\ \tau\epsilon\ \gamma\acute{\iota}\gamma\nu\acute{\epsilon}\tau a\iota.^{17}$$

'Your imagination has made you ill,' says Menelaus, 'but what were the things you imagined like ?'

$$\mathring{\epsilon}\kappa\ \phi a\sigma\mu\acute{a}\tau\omega\nu\ \delta\grave{\epsilon}\ \tau\acute{a}\delta\epsilon\ \nu o\sigma\epsilon\widehat{\iota}s\cdot\ \pi o\acute{\iota}\omega\nu\ \mathring{\upsilon}\pi o;^{18}$$

At this, Orestes temporarily sane again, replies 'I thought I saw what looked like three women appearing in the night.'

$$\mathring{\epsilon}\delta o\xi'\ \mathring{\iota}\delta\epsilon\widehat{\iota}\nu\ \tau\rho\epsilon\widehat{\iota}s\ \nu\upsilon\kappa\tau\grave{\iota}\ \pi\rho o\sigma\phi\epsilon\rho\epsilon\widehat{\iota}s\ \kappa\acute{o}\rho as.^{19}$$

This is a long way from Aeschylus' Orestes, whose picturesque vision is accepted unanimously by himself and all other characters onstage as reality. Indeed the Furies then appear in person at the beginning of the *Eumenides* to confirm his vision. There is no question of metaphor there, whereas in Euripides' *Orestes*, Menelaus' use of the word φάσματα alone shows that the tension in the dramatic situation is no longer how to fight a reality, but how to interpret language as a clue to a mental state. The poet shows through contrasting stylistic means and use of image a situation of great psychological complexity. Ambiguity is then not lacking to him as a dramatist. It is merely that his way of presenting it is different from that of other poets, and as far as imagery goes, it is to be found not in the use of a single image or figurative expression, but in the composite view which may be derived from the use of several different images distributed between various characters.[20]

Granted however that certain criticisms which spring from too narrow an attention to some parts of the plays without due regard to the whole, may be answered in these terms, can it still be said that there is in this dramatist's work anything which might plausibly be called a consistently maintained view of life ? The usual assumption is that there is not. It is perhaps because Euripides' imagination has been so successful in representing the diffuseness and inconsistency which make up human life, that he has been in danger himself of being called inconsistent or contradictory, as if the exploitation, for dramatic purposes, of the contradictions working as part of human nature necessarily sprang from similar contradictions in his own thought. Large as this question is, and properly beyond the scope of this study, some light may be thrown on it, I believe, by observation of the language of imagery and its interpretation. For varied and uneven though Euripides' work is, one cannot help noting in the use of descriptive and figurative language certain recurring characteristics which point if not to a systematic philosophy, at least to an underlying view of the world which finds implicit expression through the nature of the images chosen, in a large number of plays. The two most significant of these characteristics are, first their secular, and second their sensuous qualities. The two are related.

One grows accustomed in Aeschylus to a constant sense in the language of divine presence or transcendence. By this I mean primarily a feeling of the animate in inanimate things, or of hidden forces lurking in places and motivating human actions. Aeschylean imagery is full of this sense of the interpenetration of divine with human. Not only do Furies and Daemons stalk the earth, but the landscape itself is perceived almost as if it were a live presence. Rivers 'pour out strength from their temples', the sea has 'jaws,' marshes 'stare like Gorgons', and mountains 'brood'.[21] Personification is both forceful and accepted as natural. Divine phenomena are also represented in terms of secular landscapes, so that the mind of Zeus for instance is explained as a mass of tangled pathways where it is difficult to see clearly, and his will is said to blaze like fire on a dark night;[22] Ares' activities are thought of as the reaping of harvest in a field, and Insolence blossoms on the earth like a flower.[23] In such an outlook, divine and secular are inextricably interwoven because personification is still a vigorous force with the power to frighten those who walk abroad unwarily. Such a way of seeing things is quite alien to Euripides. It is not that he does not go in for personification as part of poetic expression, nor that he has banished gods forever from appearing as forces in the lives of men. It is a question of difference in emphasis and of a new kind of separation between these forces and the secular world. Personifications, for instance, although they habitually describe cosmic elements such as Sun, Night, Moon and Stars, more often decorate than terrorize, and their function is, as we have often seen, the fairly restricted one of setting a particular mood in a particular context. Andromeda's appeal to the chariot of Night, or Electra's description of the Sun in its chariot turning to meet the single horse upon which Dawn is riding, do not contain much primitive awe.[24] They are there in the one case to create a mood of not too serious romantic despair, and in the other to adorn an old myth in a sufficiently picturesque way to make it memorable. One wonders how the personification of the Sun in his chariot in the *Ion* squares with the god's actual appearance in the prologue.[25] Surely the answer is that it does not. The personification here is a simple literary convention which joins with others to convey, paradoxically, a much more impersonal impression of inanimate light which symbolises Apollo's influence.[26] The separation here between the persona of the god as he appears on the stage, and the sense of abstract power which is communicated through literary devices, notably the language of light, is comparable to the separation between the anthropomorphic figure of Aphrodite in the *Hippolytus*, and her more abstract power which is conveyed again through images, particularly in the choral odes.

But if the old force of personification, as Aeschylus' audience understood it, has disappeared, new kinds of imagery come into prominence to replace it. In Euripides' hands, landscape, once freed from its animating mythical inhabitants, acquires significance in its own right. It becomes valued precisely because its inanimate qualities make it something remote from human misery and despair. Euripides' heroes and heroines who express a wish to fly up into the desert air, or to plunge into the sea depths, or to escape to lonely forests, do so precisely because such places are empty of people. Like that of the fawn in the well known simile from the *Bacchae* their pleasure is in non-human solitude.

$$ἡδομένα$$
$$βροτῶν ἐρημίαις σκιαρο –$$
$$κόμοιό τ᾽ ἔρνεσιν ὕλας.^{27}$$

And even when this romantic wish is not allowed to provide consolation, one finds in Euripides that places, or if one prefers, environments, are depicted with the sharpness of a natural observation which enables an audience to picture the total setting before contrasting and relating it to the human behaviour going on in or near it. This setting is secular and perfectly comprehensible. It is not haunted by the mysterious gods and powers one associates with Aeschylus, but is intended to provide natural background for, and sometimes, as we saw earlier, intelligible explanations of human behaviour.

This concentration upon the external aspects of setting is not, as might conceivably be thought, poor compensation for an inner spirit which is lacking to this poet. It is simply the foundation for a new way of looking at the world. For what matters now is not which unseen divine influences lurk in the shadows to trip men up,[28] but how significant is the way in which men themselves interpret the things they see around them. The senses are indispensable in this process of interpretation. That Euripides' attention to the physical aspects of environment, as they are seen and felt by his characters, is fundamental to his whole outlook, is suggested not only by the way in which he emphasizes the sensuous aspects of landscape, but also by the way in which he approaches his characters. For here too the sense perceptions are invoked as criteria for judgement. Observed appearance becomes dramatically important, how a woman wears her hair, what clothes she goes about in, whether she wears jewels or constantly looks in the mirror; what people's faces look like – smiles, tears, wrinkles, blushes, pallor, frothing at the mouth, rolling eyes, all such minutiae are carefully recorded because they are part of the total conception of dramatic character. Andromache sums up Hermione on the basis of such evidence, as Electra does Helen or Pentheus Dionysus. Other characters, Hecuba or Phaedra or Antigone, for instance, describe their own appearance in such a way that conclusions as to their total state are drawn from their description. The fact that ghastly misjudgements may arise from opinions formed by such external evidence in no way diminishes the poet's estimation of this evidence as a significant and operative factor in those opinions. He is surely implying not that such criteria are infallible (this is after all tragedy), but that they are the only evidence we have. In both people and environments, he recognizes the necessity and also the frailty of relying on what the eyes see, the ears hear, or the fingers touch. Banish a divine superstructure and this is all you have. How shall the women of Troy not be reluctant to leave behind their known possessions and familiar sights, when they have not, as Aeschylus' Orestes had, for instance, in leaving Argos for Delphi, or Delphi for Athens, any hope of a final divine solution to their troubles? One of the main generating sources of dramatic energy in Euripides' plays comes either from this sense of separation from a known visual and well remembered environment, or else from a disastrous miscalculation of evidence presented by their senses, or sometimes both. In the latter category belongs, for instance, the Nurse's miscalculation of the symptoms observed in Phaedra's illness, Pentheus' gross misjudgement of the relation between Dionysus' languid appearance and real power, or the Trojans' misguided attraction to the splendid appearance of the wooden horse. Examples of the dramatic use of separation from a known environment were cited earlier in chapter II. The degree of intensity with which it is represented varies from play to play, and ranges from the most generalized nostalgia to the sharpest visual realism. In all cases, the emotional force is conveyed through the vivid descriptive details of the language. It is in this sense that imagery is able to act as a clue to attitudes which far exceed the immediate context.

For what comes from the apprehension of the senses evoked by descriptive language, as it is applied to what often seem tiny details, is a concentration of strong emotion, and this strong emotion is part of Euripides' tragic realism. It is not, I think, melodrama, that when at the end of the Medea, Medea shows Jason the bodies of their children she has just murdered, he utters an instinctive wish simply to look closely on them and touch them.

> δός μοι πρὸς θεῶν
> μαλθακοῦ χρωτὸς ψαῦσαι τέκνων.[29]

Medea refuses, and by denying him sight and touch in this way, for she immediately takes the bodies with her to Athens, she is hurting her husband with a calculated depth which comes from her own similar experience when she said goodbye to them before the murder. She too then had simply wanted to touch them and feel their breath on her cheek. The point is reinforced by the phrase she uses for their soft textured skin, which is identical to the one Jason uses.

> ὦ γλυκεῖα προσβολή
> ὦ μαλθακὸς χρὼς πνεῦμά θ᾽ ἥδιστον τέκνων.[30]

This small incident shows the degree to which Euripides made his characters cling to the visible and tangible experiences which are part of every day life. It is part of an outlook which sees emotional concern and responsibility for judgement as no longer dependent on divine aid prompted by any kind of instant theology, but as bound to contemplate without such help the material and human environment. Through the texture of the poetic language itself, in particular the imagery, one sees working a new assessment of this human and inanimate environment in terms of its valuation through the senses.

Notes to the Text

Chapter I

1 Some of the reasons underlying the decline of verse as a universally acceptable form for drama are analysed by M. E. Prior, in the first chapter of *The Language of Tragedy*.

2 Obvious examples are the sung lyrics and ballads in *Mother Courage*, *The Threepenny Opera* and the *Good Soldier Schweik*, the parodies of classical poems in *St Joan of the Stockyards* and the verse passages of many prologues. H. Arendt discusses some of these effects in 'The Poet Brecht', in P. Demetz, *Brecht*, Twentieth Century Views (pp. 48, 49).

3 Masks precluded observable nuances of facial expression, and scenery did not become elaborate until late fifth century and after. On masks see T. B. L. Webster, *Greek Theatre Production* (p. 38 sq.), and on scenery, *ibid.* (p. 14 sq.); A. M. Dale, 'Seen and Unseen on the Greek Stage' in *Wiener Studien*, LXIX, 1956 (pp. 96–106) suggests ways in which language supplies details which scenery did not provide.

4 The fact that comic writers other than Aristophanes, such as Telecleides, Phrynichus and Eupolis, parody tragedy, suggests that the tradition of literary parody was securely enough established to ensure continuing appreciation.

5 These at least are the questions implicit in the famous literary contest between Aeschylus and Euripides in the last part of the *Frogs*. See particularly Radermacher, ed. *Frösche*, 2nd ed., Vienna, 1954, on the test of iambics at 1119–1250, (p. 304 sq.), and that of lyric 1261–3 (p. 315 sq.). See also W. B. Stanford's note on 1264 sq. and on 1309–22, ed., *Frogs*, London, 1965 (pp. 177 and 182).

6 E.g. H. Weir-Smyth, *Aeschylean Tragedy* (p. 2) 'Sophocles is indeed the greater artist, but Aeschylus is the greater genius.' (p. 11), 'Not the exquisite refinement of the art of Sophocles, nor Euripides' portrayal of man as he is, can vie with the massive imagination linked with moral grandeur that distinguishes their predecessor.' For an estimation of such comparisons which go back to the ancient tradition in the life of Aeschylus (see W. B. Stanford, *Aeschylus in his Style* (pp. 12–13).

7 The strongest recent statement of this kind of criticism may be found in the introduction to A. J. A. Waldock's book, *Sophocles the Dramatist*, Cambridge, 1966 (p.vii). 'The assumption upon which this book is written is that Sophocles was first and foremost a dramatist. This assumption seems to me confirmed by nearly every line he wrote. It is shaken only by an occasional stanza in

which it is evident that Sophocles the dramatist has for the moment and without any reservations yielded to Sophocles the lyric poet, in which Sophocles seems to become oblivious of his drama and writes verses that actually conflict with it.' Although less extreme, there are other titles which suggest a similar emphasis, e.g. S. M. Adams, *Sophocles the Playwright*; H. D. F. Kitto, *Sophocles: Dramatist and Philosopher*.

8 R. Lattimore, *P.G.T.* (pp. 104–5, of more explicitly 109–11) although he, more than most, analyses Euripides' poetic qualities on their own terms.

9 M. Croiset, *H.L.G.* (pp. 358–9).

10 A. Lesky, *History of Greek Literature* (p. 403).

11 The prolonged fashion for, and the one-sidedness of, this kind of criticism has been discussed by A. Rivier in the introduction to his book, *Euripide*, 1944 (p. 10 sq.). His own work and that of Conacher, Ströhm, Zürcher and others have done much to offset the bias of earlier approaches, but there is still room for more work to be done on the language.

12 Classic cases are *Hel.* 1301 sq.; *I.T.* 1234 sq.; *Electra* 432 sq. (see Ch. II, pp. 20–21). Few, however, would surely subscribe to the very extreme judgement of Croiset: *H.L.G.*, III (p. 359) 'les parties chantées ne pouvaient être que de jolis caprices de la muse lyrique, mêlés ça et là à ceux de la muse dramatique.'

13 Some of the sources of obscurity in Aeschylus' style are analysed by W. B. Stanford, *Aeschylus in his Style* (Ch. VI, pp. 126–37), although he denies that this has in any way lent the poet grandeur in translation.

14 *I.T.* 1244 sq. for instance, a simple description of a snake, yet artfully depicted through careful word order and use of compound adjectives, or *Alc.* 579–87 where again the language and subject matter of Apollo leading the wild creatures from their lairs to dance to his music are simple, but also artfully composed in positioning of words, and in the choice of one or two carefully placed compound epithets (see Ch. II, pp. 19–22).

15 H. Delulle, *Les Répétitions d'Images chez Euripide* (p. 25).

16 A., *Poet.* 22, 1459a. (See also *Rhet.* III, 10, 1410b, where he recognizes its cognitive function to reveal truths which might otherwise remain hidden.)

17 W. B. Stanford, *G.M.* (p. 41).

18 Modern theories of metaphor discussed by Stanford, *G.M.* (p. 78 sq.).

19 C. Spurgeon, *Shakespeare's Imagery* (p. 5); M. E. Prior, *The Language of Tragedy* (pp. 11–12); U. Ellis-Fermor, *The Frontiers of Drama* (p. 79); W. Clemen, *The Development of Shakespeare's Imagery* (see esp. p. 97 sq.).

20 Aesch., *Ag.* 737 sq., translated by R. Lattimore.

21 See Fraenkel's commentary and especially pp. 343–5. H. Lloyd-Jones, *H.S. Cl. Ph.*, 73, 'Agamemnonea III', p. 99 sq. has recently questioned the common view held by Fraenkel and others, that these four nominal phrases all refer metaphorically to Helen. He reads Porson's δ' in preference to Hermann's τ' which Fraenkel adopts, and thus recognizes a clear separation between the first phrase and the other three. The first he takes to refer to a

general feeling of false security within Troy itself, while the others he takes to refer to different aspects of Love, Ἔρως.

Both τ' and δ' present special problems, yet it is hard to see what this interpretation adds, since Helen is still implicitly the common factor to all four phrases in the sense that both the illusory calm and the manifestations of Ἔρως are to be traced to her. She has been the subject of the previous *strophe* and *antistrophe*, and if she can be symbolically described there in a number of metaphorical metamorphoses including a lion cub, which is itself identified with the inanimate ἄμαχον ἄλγος and μέγα σίνος, it seems unlikely that φρόνημα should be barred here from referring to a person in the way that L-J. suggests. Surely these lines continue the metaphorical series, indicating this time a shift from the immediate sphere of home δόμοις to the wider one of Troy and the Trojans Πριαμίδαισιν. From being an ἄμαχον ἄλγος οἰκέταις she becomes a destructive agent to the Trojans as well. There is continuity of image also between ἱερεύς τις Ἄτας and Ἐρινύς.

It is odd moreover, if L-J. is right, that Ἔρως is the referent of the last three nominal phrases, that its prominence is not marked by an earlier reference instead of its position in the middle of the last phrase where it looks like an ordinary noun in the genitive case closely linked to ἄνθος and exactly parallel to the ὀμμάτων βέλος above. L-J.'s interpretation must destroy the structural balance of these lines, yet it is this, as Fraenkel points out, which underlines the sense common to all four descriptions, namely the beguiling mildness which conceals a destructive agent. ἀκασκαῖον and μαλθακὸν in identical positions at the beginning of the line, qualify their respective nouns with similar meanings of 'gentle' and 'mild'. The intrinsically pleasant associations beginning and ending the series, φρόνημα. . . γαλάνας and ἔρωτος ἄνθος, are each qualified by adjectives which mitigate these associations, 'νηνέμου suggesting the abnormality of a windless calm which precedes a storm and δηξίθυμον the psychologically destructive power a beautiful thing may have.

The probability that all four phrases are metaphorical ways of describing Helen's arrival in Troy and of what she brought with her, seeming tranquility, wealth, amorousness and beauty, does not preclude the possibility of other associations provoked by these words. In fact ambiguity and complexity of association are just what one would expect of metaphor. The temper of windless calm may thus also, and quite appropriately, recall Aulis, and the luxury and delight in gold, the Trojan's own predilections for opulent living. But neither of these alters the importance of Helen's agency in Trojan destruction.

22 W. Cowper, *Task*, ii. 285–93.

23 Wallace Stevens, 'On Poetic Truth', *Opus Posthumous. Poems Plays and Prose* (p. 237).

24 William Carlos Williams, *Collected Earlier Poems*, XXI, London, 1967 (p. 277).

25 'glazed' perhaps contains some slight metaphorical quality.

26 Philip Larkin, *Love Songs in Age* in *The Whitsun Wedding*, London, 1964 (p. 12).

27 Pi., *Pyth.* I, 23–4.

28 Pi., *Ol.* VI, 52 sq. Pindar's use of light and colour is discussed by F. Dornseiff, *Pindar's Stil* (p. 43).

29 Compound adjectives borrowed from lyric poets include: λεύκιππος, *Hel.* 639; λιπαρόζωνος. *Pho.* 175; οἰνωπός, *I.T.* 1245, *Hyps.* 64, III, *Ba.* 438, *Cretans*, 15, *Pho.* 1160, *Or.* 115; ποικιλόνωτος, *H.F.* 376, *I.T.* 1244–5; ποικιλόπτερος, *Hipp.* 1270; χρυσοφαής, *Hec.* 636, *Hipp.* 1276; χρυσοκέρως, fr. 270–2; πάγχρυσος, *I.T.* 167, *Ion* 124, *Hec.* 528, *Med.* 840; χρυσόδετος, *Pho.* 805.

30 Compounds of light and colour appearing for the first time in Euripides: αἰολόχρως fr. 593.4; ἀλλόχροος, *Hipp.* 175; ἀλλόχρως, *Pho.* 138, *And.* 879; ἀργυροειδής, *Ion*, 95, *I.A.* 752; ἀργυρόρρυτος, *H.F.* 386; γλαυκο]φαής, *Hyps.* 1.II.4; δονακόχλοος, *I.T.* 399; ἠλεκτροφαής, *Hipp.* 741; κυαναυγής, *Alc.* 261; κυανέμβολος, *Electra* 436; κυανοειδής, *Hel.* 179; κυανόχρως, *Pho.* 308; κυανόχροος, *Hel.* 1501; λευκήρετμος, *I.A.* 283; λευκόθριξ, *Ba.* 112; λευκοκύμων, *Or.* 992; λευκολόφας, *Pho.* 119; λευκόπηχυς, *Pho.* 1351, *Ba.* 1206; λευκόπους, *Cyc.* 72; λευκόστικτος, *I.A.* 222; λευκοφάης, *I.A.* 1054; λευκόχρως, *Pho.* 322; μελάμβροτος, fr. 228.3, fr. 771.4; μελάγχρως, *Hec.* 1106, *Or.* 321; μελάμπεπλος, *Alc.* 427.819.843, *Ion* 1150, *Or.* 457; μελαμφαής, *Hel.* 518; μελαναυγής, *Hec.* 153; μελανόπτερος, *Hec.* 705; μελανοπτέρυξ, *Hec.* 71; μελεγγραφής, fr. 627; ξουθόπτερος, *H.F.* 487, fr. 467.4; ποικιλοδέρμων, *I.A.* 226; ποικιλόθριξ, *Alc.* 584; πολιόχρως, *Ba.* 1365; πολυποίκιλος, *I.T.* 1149; πυρσόθριξ, *I.A.* 225; πυρσόνωτος, *H.F.* 397; πυρσώδης, *Ba.* 146; σκιαρόκομος, *Ba.* 875–6; φοινικόλοφος, *Pho.* 820; φοινικοσκελής, *Ion* 1207; φοινικοφαής, *Ion* 163; χιονόχρως, *Hel.* 215; χλοεροτρόφος, *Pho.* 826; χλοηφόρος, *Pho.* 647.653; χλωρόκομος, *I.A.* 759; χρυσανταυγής, *Ion*, 890; χρυσεοβόστρυχος, *Pho.* 191; χρυσεόκυκλος, *Pho.* 176; χρυσεόνωτος, fr. 159; χρυσεοπήνητος, *Or.* 840; χρυσοκόλλητος, *Pho.* 2; χρυσεοσάνδαλος, *I.A.* 1042, *Or.* 1468; χρυσεόστολος, *H.F.* 414; χρυσεοφάλαρος, *Tro.* 520; χρυσήρης, *Ion* 157, 1154, *I.T.* 129; χρυσορόης, *Ba.* 154, *H.F.* 315; χρυσότυπος, *Electra* 470; χρυσώψ, *Ba.* 553.

31 *I.T.* 1244 sq.

32 Compare Pi., *Pyth.* IV, 249; *Ol.* VI, 45.

33 Adjective clusters, e.g. *Hel.* 1501–2; *I.A.* 218–66; *Pho.* 322 sq., 120, 638 sq., 784 sq., 175–8; *Hel.* 179 sq.; *H.F.* 375–6, 396 sq.; *Ion* 887–92; *Androm.* fr. 114; *Or.* 960 sq.; *I.T.* 1244 sq.; *Hec.* 152–3, 458–73; *Tro.* 536 sq., 799 sq.

34 A point made by H. R. Fairclough, *The Attitude of the Greek Tragedians toward Nature* (pp. 40–1). He shows that there are proportionately more words expressive of colour, and a wider range of colour within them, in Euripides, than in either of the two other tragedians.

35 Pliny, *N. H.*, XXXV. 29. Ancient descriptions of the techniques of shadow painting are contained in J. Overbeck, *Die Antiken Schriftquellen 1641–1730*.

Briefly they may be summarized as the use of a wider colour range, and the application of colour in overlaid flecks and splashes rendered in such a way as to suggest modelling and shading, and the changing tones of colour under the influence of light. This technique may be seen in miniature on a white lekythos in the Museum at Hamburg. Hamburg. Inv. 1898, 21. Beazley *A.R.V.* 562/119. See also M. Swindler's comments on another lekythos from Berlin, in *Ancient Painting* (fig. 375 and pp. 226–7, see also Ch. III, n. 70)

36 P. Oxy. XXVII, no. 2459, frag. 1. The Sphinx was sometimes depicted with coloured wings in painting (see A. Trendall, *Phlyax Vases*, no. 115, London, 1967).

37 *Hec.* 152–3; *Tro.* 548–50; *Ion* 889–90; *Cretans*. D. L. Page, *G.L.P.*, p. 74. Technical that is, in the sense of being interested in the way things work, in this case light reflection and the changes in colour brought about when light acts upon it. A child's eyes for instance are said to reflect the light in the way a mirror does. *Hyps.* fr. 1.ii.3 sq. (see Bond's note). The light reflections contained in mirrors are described as extending backwards without limit, *Hec.* 925–6 χρυσέων ἐνόπτρων λεύσ / σουσ' ἀτέρμονας εἰς αὐγάς. Paley's interpretation of ἀτέρμονας still seems the most plausible here in a much disputed passage, although N. Collinge in *C.Ph.*, 1954, 35–6, has reviewed the controversy and introduced a new interpretation of his own. Like the French Impressionist painters, Euripides' descriptions of changing colour are both impressionistic and precise. They arise from a wish to record how light acts upon colour. Thus in *Ion* 887 sq. the light given off from Apollo's gold hair affects the tone of objects near it, in this case crocus petals. In the *Cretans* passage, the bull projects from his eyes and flaming red hair a glow so brilliant that it seems by contrast to cast his cheek into shadow and deepen its colour.

38 *Cretans*. D. L. Page, *G.L.P.*, p. 74. The questions here are rhetorical; 'was it that he was handsome? etc. etc. The notions of light and dark are surely complementary to each other, not separate, as Page makes them. There is no punctuation in 15, and to assume it as he does in his translation is to leave a disjointed phrase (for it cannot go with the next line, which introduces a new point) consisting of syntactically isolated participle and noun. Taking 14–15 as one unit, the nom. masc. partic. περκαίνων may be taken in close conjunction with ἐξέλαμπε and both have a personal subject. This is common with verbs of light, and one might compare *Hel.* 1130–1 δόλιον / ἀκταῖς ἀστέρα λάμψας (he caused a treacherous light to shine on the shore), or *Ion* 887–8 where Apollo himself is said to flash χρυσῷ χαίταν μαρμαίρων. σέλας is a cognate acc. with ἐξέλαμπε (cf. Aesch. fr. 300.4, ἐν ᾗ πυρωτὸν φέγγος ἐκλάμψαν φλόγα τήκει πετραίων χίονα; *Hel.* 1126, πυρσεύσας φλογερὸν σέλας; Eur. fr. 330.3, λαμπρὸν ἐκλάμπει σέλας). σέλας describes brilliant sparkling light, and is most often used of fire or lightning as for instance at Aesch., *Ag.* 281, 289. It is therefore an appropriate word to use here and preserves the metaphor hinted at in πυρσῆς 'fiery red'. οἰνωπός is the word used to describe flushed complexions and ripening grapes. περκαίνων

an *hapax leg.*, is an appropriate word to use in its environment, since the variant from περκάζω in the context of grapes which are beginning to ripen, means 'to turn dark' (cf. Theophr. *C.P.* 3.16.3 ὅταν ἄρχωνται περκάζειν οἱ βότρυες or Chaerem. 12.2 ὀπώρα ἄκραισι περκάζουσα οἰνάνθαις It can also mean to 'turn dark' in an active sense, as at Diosc. 5.2. περκάζει τὴν σταφυλήν. The active περκαίνων gives such good sense here that one is perhaps justified in taking it so, particularly since there are no other instances of the word to throw any further light on its use here. It is also possible however to take it intransitively as Hesychius evidently does, to judge from his explanation of it as διαποικίλλεσθαι, a word which often suggests the blending of multi-coloured elements (see Plato, *Laws* 693d. 863a.); the blending in this case being the change of colour under the influence of reflection. This passage has many features in common with others mentioned. The serpent at *I.T.* 1244 also looked οἰνωπὸς in the shade. The change in tone from πυρσῆς to οἰνωπὸν (note their parallel position at the beginning of two successive lines) and from bright light to shadow σέλας ... ἐξέλαμπε / περκαίνων resembles the change from χρυσωπὸν to κυανωπὸν in the Oedipus fragment. The alternating effects of light and shade are mirrored by the interlocking word order σέλας / οἰνωπὸν / ἐξέλαμπε / περκαίνων as they are also at *I.T.* 1244 sq., where κατάχαλκος is sandwiched in between σκιερᾷ and δάφνᾳ.

39 Aesch., *Ag.* 355 sq., translated by R. Lattimore.

40 R. Lattimore's translation of *Tro.* 1060 sq.

41 Imagery is listed by content of the images in many of the older studies, e.g. those of Delulle, Pauer, Schwarz, Rappold, Hoerman. Imagery grouped in terms of a basic idea is the principle employed more recently by J. Taillardat, *Les Images d'Aristophane*, Les Belles Lettres, Paris, 1965.

42 These are conveniently collected in the preface of Nauck's edition of Euripides, Vol. I, 1900.

43 *Hel.* 1501.

44 Similes and Metaphors drawn from painting and sculpture, e.g. at *Hec.* 560–1, 807; *Androm.* fr. 125; *Pho.* 128–9; *Hel.* 262–3, fr. 618.

Chapter II

1 'Lyric Dimension' is Lattimore's term. His discussion of choral action with particular reference to Aeschylean drama is to be found in the introduction to his translation of the *Oresteia. Complete Greek Tragedies*, Chicago, 1959, Vol. I.

2 A. M. Dale in 'The Chorus in the action of Greek Tragedy', an essay in *Classical Drama and its Influence* (pp. 18–19), draws attention to the lack of *dianoia* in the choral role. This does not of course mean that it did not have a didactic function.

3 Soph. *O.T.* 873; *Aj.* 157; *O.T.* 1186–8; *Antigone* 332 sq. I do not mean to imply that Sophocles' choral odes are always built round a few quotable

precepts. Their function as a whole is to develop themes which occur in the dialogue, and the structure of each ode must ultimately be judged by its place in the total context. Such themes may sometimes be expressed through figurative metaphor (there are examples in the odes quoted above) or through pictorial description of scene, as for instance in *Aj.* 596 sq. or *O.C.* 678 sq. Nonetheless they do not, on the whole, consist of that extended sensuous clarity which characterizes so many Euripidean odes (see following discussion) and which itself has the function of acting as implicit moral or emotional comment.

4 H. D. F. Kitto, *Greek Tragedy* (p. 193), with particular reference to *Med.* 1081 sq.

5 On the non-detached role of the Euripidean chorus see G. M. A. Grube, *The Drama of Euripides* (p. 101).

6 Eur., *Hec.* 911–13. *Tro.* 539–40. *Ba.* 150, 142.

7 *Hipp.* 752 sq.

8 *Alc.* 438 sq. The fact that this is to some extent a traditional image (see A. M. Dale's comments on this passage) still does not alter its function in this context.

9 The importance of social and material environment in Euripides' treatment of action and character has recently been stressed in an essay by H. Diller in the Fondation Hardt series, *Euripides Entretiens*, Vol. VI (pp. 89–105).

10 *Alc.* 575 sq.

11 *And.* 274 sq.

12 The theme of the *Judgement of Paris* is a familiar one in Euripidean lyrics (cf. *Hec.* 644 sq.; *Hel.* 357 sq., 676 sq.; *I.A.* 182 sq., 573 sq., 1283 sq.). Some of the same descriptive features appear there as here, Paris the herdsman for instance (he is βουκόλος at *I.A.* 574, 1292; βούτας at *Hec.* 646); the rustic setting (the word βουστάθμους is used at *Hel.* 359), the mountain spring for the goddesses to bathe in (*I.A.* 182 ἐπὶ κρηναίαισι δρόσοις and 1294 λευκὸν ὕδωρ ὅθι κρῆναι . . . κεῖνται). But the stress is mostly upon the romantic decorativeness of the scene; there are roses and hyacinths *I.A.* 1296 sq., diverting music *I.A.* 576, sleek cattle and snow-white heifers *I.A.* 573 sq. The austere loneliness of Paris introduced here is a new feature.

13 T. W. Stinton in *Euripides and the Judgement of Paris* (pp. 16–17), points out the stress upon rusticity and seclusion as it is brought out by the pairs of synonyms and the uniqueness of some of the vocabulary.

14 Although Stinton may be right that the women's machinations here are not directed specifically at Paris but at each other.

15 *Med.* 824–45. D. L. Page in his commentary on the *Med.* (p. 134) draws attention also to the remarkably close structural logical and artistic connections between the two stanzas.

16 *Electra* 432 sq.

17 *I.A.* 164–302. Part of it is most probably not by Euripides, see D. L. Page, *Actors' Interpolations in Greek Tragedy*, Oxford, 1934 (pp. 141–7).

18 The colour is emphatically brought out in the rare compound κυανεμβόλοισιν and the sinuous movement of the dolphin leaping echoed, as Aristophanes' parody in *Frogs*, 1314 suggests, in the musical treatment.

19 Brightness is stressed both in the compound verb κατέλαμπε and in the participle φαέθων.

20 *I.A.* 218–26. Here four new compound epithets placed in contrast, χρυσοδαιδάλτους, λευκοστίκτῳ, πυρσότριχας, ποικιλοδέρμονας, appeal strongly to distinguishing perceptions of colour.

21 The 'actual' positioning is echoed in the order of the words. Πρωτέσιλαον – Παλαμήδεα are placed at either end of the sentence and enclosed between them is the description of counters and board.

22 Exekias. *A. B. V.* 145/13, Pfuhl. *M. und Z.* 229. Eretria Painter, *A.R.V.*2 1248.9(7). Richter and Hall, 143–4. Blacas krater. Swindler, *Greek Painting* 343. Furtwaengler-Reichold, *G.V.*, 126.

23 Other possible cases are the Demeter ode in the *Hel.* 1301 sq. and the Apollo ode in the *I.T.* 1234 sq. On the odes of the *Electra*, and the Demeter ode in the *Hel.* and the extent to which they should be regarded as embolima see J. D. Conacher's comments in *Euripidean Drama* (pp. 210–2, with note 23, and p. 300). It is perhaps significant that in his discussion of the *I.T.* he mentions the connections of the first and second *stasima* to each other, and to the main themes of the play, but omits mention of the third. These cases seem to me to be the most patently difficult to justify on grounds of total dramatic relevance. Opinions have differed very widely on how many others approach irrelevance (see Ch. I, n.11, p. 3).

24 Some form of scene painting may well go back to the pre-Periclean theatre, see T. B. L. Webster, *Greek Theatre Production* (p. 13 sq.), but elaborate effects did not come in until the last part of the fifth century when perspective was invented. Verbal description seems in many cases to make clear what scenery did not. A. M. Dale, *Seen and Unseen on the Greek Stage*, Wiener Studien, LXIX, 1956 (pp. 96–106), discusses examples.

25 Grube, *Drama of Euripides* (pp. 107–10).

26 *Hel.* 179 sq. Lattimore's translation admirably brings out the strong contrasts of colour and the sense of texture suggested by the phrases ἕλικα τ᾿ ἀνὰ χλόαν and ἀμφὶ δόνακος ἔρνεσιν.

27 *Hipp.* 121 sq. It is surely a question of appropriateness here as well as the difference between style in early and late Euripidean lyric. Fantasy can take a frothy dithyrambic style, whereas the sort of realism demanded by the plot of the *Hipp.* cannot.

28 R. P. Winnington-Ingram, 'Hippolytus...' in *Euripides Entretiens* (pp. 174–5), alludes to Euripides' development of the circumstantial conditions which foster Phaedra's love, as these emerge in her rhesis at 373 sq. The irony of the contrast between the chorus' situation and Phaedra's, which the descriptive language conveys in the first *strophe* and *antistrophe*, is increased, as Mrs Easterling points out to me, by their mistaken but natural assumption in the second *strophe* and *antistrophe* that Phaedra's illness can still somehow be explained in terms of normal ailments which they themselves understand.

29 *Ion* 184 sq.

30 The metaphor is reminiscent of Pi., *Ol.* VI, 1–4, and *Pyth.* VI, 14, except that Euripides has gone one stage further in adding the epithet καλλιβλέφαρον.

31 For the frequency of Heracles' labours as a theme in fifth-century sculpture at Athens and elsewhere see F. Brommer, *Herakles*, Münster-Köln, 1953, pp. 5–6.

32 Phaethon, Nauck² 773. The MS reading at line 28, πόιμνας is hard to make any sense of. Professor Handley has suggested πόιμναις which could easily have been corrupted into ποίμνας under influence of the -ας in σύριγγας above. ποιμνᾶν is suggested by J. Diggle, *Euripides' Phaethon*, p. 58.

33 In the sense, that is, of a series of main clause structures without subordination. In fact the word order is varied in the Greek to avoid beginning each sentence with the same syntactical item. My translation does not preserve this variation.

34 T. B. L. Webster *Greek Art and Literature* (p. 164).

35 On the plot generally see T. B. L. Webster, *The Tragedies of Euripides* (p. 220 sq.) and on the place of the *parodos* (pp. 222–3).

36 *Ion* 714 sq., 492 sq.

37 *Hel.* 1301 sq.

38 *Hec.* 444 sq.

39 *Hel.* 210, 349; *I.A.* 179; *I.T.* 399–400.

40 *Alc.* 452; *Tro.* 801 sq.

41 *I.T.* 1098 sq; *Ion* 919 sq; *Hec.* 458–61.

42 Lattimore, *P.G.T.* (pp. 117 and 119–20) draws a contrast between 'persistent themes' and relief scenes, although he does not treat the latter in any detail as part of a total organic structure.

43 *I.T.* 107, 260 sq., 300.

44 *I.T.* 123–5.

45 *I.T.* 218–20. This translation inevitably misses the precise sense of the intentional juxtaposition in ἀξείνου-ξείνα. Perhaps 'friend' and 'friendless' might approach it.

46 *I.T.* 392 sq. Here the repetition as in κυάνεαι at 392 and the compound adjectives εὔυδρον δονακόχλοα (399), περικίονας (405) draw attention to texture or colour.

47 *I.T.* 407–12; 421–38.

48 This passage is distinguished by a precise use and arrangement of words evocative of many different sense effects. Texture is suggested by the successively mentioned nouns, pine oars, rocks, waves, pebbles and spray. The compound adjectives δικρότοισι and λινοπόροις strengthen this appeal. A sense of movement is underlined by the one idea implicit in the three variations of the same root word, συνδρομάδας-δραμόντες-δρόμους. Colour is

suggested in the single epithet λευκὰν appropriately ambiguous so that it may be held to refer either to the seashore whitened by sand, or to the white sea-birds which cluster on it -πολυόρνιθον. Sound is evoked both directly in words such as μέλπουσι and indirectly through alliteration, e.g. of σ sounds in the phrases πλησιστίοισι πνοαῖς / συριζόντων and αὔραις ⟨σὺν⟩ νοτίαις which suggest the swishing of a boat through the water.

49 I.T. 1089 sq.

50 Conacher in *Euripidean Drama* (p. 307), points out the effectiveness of the continuity of bird imagery in these two sea-odes.

51 *Tro.* 511 sq. The word ἐπικήδειον which means 'appropriate to a funeral' has been restored from the Σ to 511 to replace the much more mundane word in the MSS, ἐπιτήδειον. That this restoration is right is suggested not only by the comments of the Σ but also from the fact that the same word occurs earlier in the trilogy in a similar context in the *Alexandros* fr. 16.12. Snell. Hermes Einz. V.

52 *Tro.* 531–50. This passage contains many problems of interpretation. I follow the text of Murray who keeps the MSS reading θέα, i.e. θέᾳ indicating sight, rather than the emendation of Musurus θεᾷ alluding to the goddess Athene. This reading has the advantage of underlining the importance of the spectacle which plays a large part in the deception of the over-credulous Trojans. Since Athene is referred to at 536, 541 and 526 there is no need of a further reference to her in this line. There is a parallel for the phrase in *And.* 1086–7. τρεῖς μὲν φαεννὰς ἡλίου διεξόδους / θέᾳ δίδοντες ὄμματ' ἐξεπίμπλαμεν. Does ἄζυγος ἀμβροτοπώλου at 536 describe Athene or the wooden horse? Hermann took it to be the latter, but to call the horse 'immortal' would have little point here unless in the sense of 'indestructible' for which there is no precedent. Since the single epithet ἄμβροτος is always applied to gods and goddesses, it is most likely that the compound here refers to Athene and that it means not as *L.S.J.* 'with immortal steeds' but simply 'immortal', the last part of the epithet preserving the metaphor of ἄζυγος. Conington on *Aen.* II, 31 sq. may be right in saying that 'innuptae Minervae' owes its inspiration to this phrase, but if so, is it not more likely that those words refer to this line, not 535, and that far from being an argument for θεᾷ, an echo of the notion in θέᾳ δώσων may be heard in 'stupet' and 'mirantur'?

The objection to the reading of the MSS. V.P. at 538 λίνοισι is that it involves taking κλωστοῦ as being from the noun κλωστής in the sense of 'web' – 'with the encircling flax strands of web' – a meaning which would be unparalleled since the word usually means a 'spinner' and then is rare. Bothe's λίνοιο is derived from the comment of the Σ. κλωστοῦ λίνου ἀμφιβόλοις suggesting that κλωστοῦ should be interpreted as an adjective from κλωστός 'spun'. L.S.J. quote some late examples of its use. This is perhaps slightly preferable since the palaeographical change is a small one. On -οιο genitives in Euripides see D. L. Page on *Med.* 135, Barrett on *Hipp.*

848–51, also *Telephus* fr. 18, 19, 20 P. Berol. 9908 col. II. Handley and Rea (p. 11).

At 550 the text has suffered some corruption. Two syllables are needed if the line is to correspond with 530 δόλιον ἔσχον ἄταν (ithyphallic clausula in iambo-trochaic context). Parmentier accepts the text as it is and simply indicates that two syllables are missing. He translates 'et dans les maisons l'illumination resplendissante de la fête fit s'éteindre la clarté sombre des feux qui bientôt s'endormirent.' His contrast therefore is not of dark against light, but of one brightness eclipsing another. The objection to his view is that he has to supply 'de la fête' to which there is no specific reference in the text. Murray conjectures ἄκος, drawing a parallel with Aesch. *Ag.* 17 and Soph. *Aj.* 362. The meaning is then that the brightness of torchflares gleams in the darkness (this is expressed by μέλαιναν αἴγλαν) and acts as a guard or remedy against sleep. Euripides describes the effect of brightness and blackness in similar terms elsewhere, notably at *Hec.* 153, and for this reason Murray's solution seems preferable to the interpretation of Parmentier in the Budé edition.

53   For φόνιος in the sense of blood see line 16 of this play, also *Hel.* 1089; *Supp.* 77; *Hec.* 1281. Paley's translation in his note on 537 shows that he takes it in this sense.

54   See Ch. III, p. 51. and Ch. VI, p. 118.

55   *Tro.* 551–60.

56   Lattimore's translation of 562–7 catches the sense although it does not precisely reproduce the force of the startling double metaphor 'decapitating devastation', which produces a 'crowning triumph' of bastard children. See the comments of Kirchoff in his edition for the correct interpretation of this metaphor.

57   *Hec.* 905 sq. and esp. 924 sq.

58   Domestic scenes, women with mirrors, women dressing, or talking to their maids, e.g. *A.R.V.*² 1250 34 (27), 1250 33 (26), 1248 4 (4). Interior scenes are frequently marked on white lekythoi by the hanging of objects on the wall, e.g. Pfuhl. *M. und Z.* II. 549–57.

59   *Tro.* 814–8, Lattimore's translation. The text of these lines is fraught with difficulty. τυκίσματα in 814 is the correction of τεκίσματα P. τυκτίσματα V. The scribes missed this rare word, which is found only in Euripides, although τύκος, the usual word for a chisel, is common in prose. 818 as it stands does not correspond with 807 in the *strophe* ἀμετέραν τὸ πάροιθεν ὅτ᾽ ᾽ἔβας ᾽αφ᾽ ῾Ελλάδος (the metre is dactylo-epitrite throughout *strophe* and *antistrophe*). Since there is no visible corruption in 807, one has either to follow Dindorf in arbitrarily bracketing ὅτ᾽ ἔβας ἀφ᾽ ῾Ελλάδος and accept φοινία αἰχμά as a gloss in 818, or leave 807 intact, accept Musurus φονία for φοινία in 818 and print as Parmentier does, or obelise the text. Since no sense can be made of either περὶ V. or παρὰ P in the line above, 817 (both Parmentier and Murray obelise this), this seems the best course until a plausible conjecture can replace, or an explanation be found for the presence of these words.

60 κανόνων echoes the use of κανών in the prologue 5–6. On τύκισμα see note 59 above.

61 Tro. 1173 sq.

62 πυργόω at 612 and 844 (see Ch. VI, p. 117).

63 Tro. 1060 sq.

64 Ba. 135 sq.

65 P. Vellacott's translation (Penguin edition) of Ba. 105 sq. This translation, although it seems to me to be one of the better ones of this passage, still does not capture all those stylistic traits of the Greek which lend special force to the sense; the repeated βρύετε for instance with its religious and poetic associations (see Dodd's note on 107), or the centrally placed single compound verb καταβαγχιοῦσθε which the translator renders by an eight word periphrasis. He does attempt to reproduce the strong stop in the middle of 114, which draws attention to the new sense of movement. But the effect of the staccato αὐτίκα and the subsequent dactyllic rhythms on the insistently repeated εἰς ὄρος are still lost in the English version.

66 Pho. 784 sq.

67 W. Kranz, Stasimon 242.

68 e.g. R. Lattimore, P.G.T., p. 110.

69 Med. 824 sq. My translation departs slightly from the usual translation and text of these lines. It is based upon Reiske's emendation of χώρας for the MSS χώραν and understands it as a genitive not with καταπνεῦσαι (see Page's notes on this passage), but with αὔρας meaning breezes of, or native to, the land. Apart from the grammatical difficulty of taking the text as it stands, (see Page's notes) is the added one of sense, i.e. the awkwardness of having Cypris breathe breezes, not vice versa. It is surely the function of breezes to escort (see Hec. 544, Phaeth. 86, Pho. 1712, Pi. Pyth. IV. 203), and to occur in the environment of the verb πνέω (see Homer. Od. 5. 469., Hdt. 2.19., and metaphorically Eur. Electra, 1148). There is no parallel, on the other hand, for a goddess breathing breezes. (See Verrall's notes on the Excursus to his edition of the Med., p. 121–2.) It would seem odd in a context where αὔρας and καταπνεῦσαι occur together to take αὔρας as the object. καταπνέω governs an accusative in Rhesus 387. Surely this stanza is describing the attendants of Aphrodite, namely the Breezes, the Αὔραι, who should be capitalized as the single Αὔρα is in Hec. 444 and Phaeth. 86, who escort the goddess in this sentence as the Ἔρωτας do in the next. To take Αὔρας and Ἔρωτας as the subjects of καταπνεῦσαι and πέμπειν respectively (for πέμπω in the sense of 'escort' see Eur. Electra, 434; Pi. Ol. IV.4; Nem. IX 52) and Κύπριν as the object, qualified, in both cases, by the parallel participles ἀφυσσομέναν and ἐπιβαλλομέναν, seems to follow Verrall's general principles without the disadvantages of his drastic emendations. The only change is from χώραν to χώρας and a capital A for αὔρας.

In view of the strongly pictorial qualities of this description, a quality which Verrall points out in his commentary and Page implicitly recognizes by comparing an attic lekythos in which Eros and the personified Harmonia are depicted together, it seems much more likely that παρέδρους should be interpreted literally here as 'sitting next to' and not figuratively as editors usually understand it. The Loves are then imagined as sitting at the elbow or shoulder of the female figure Σοφία; this is a characteristic position for them on red-figure vases which depict just such personifications as this. On an aryballos by the Meidias painter for instance, A.R.V.² 45(l.10). Nicole VII.1., a winged Eros sits on the shoulder of Aphrodite who is seated in the centre of the vase; she is surrounded by personified qualities depicted as female attendants, Eunomia and Paideia on one side, Peitho and Eudaimonia on the other.

70 R. Lattimore, P.G.T. (pp. 118–9).

71 H.F. 348 sq.

72 E.g. on a red-figure hydria in the Metropolitan Museum attributed to the Meidias painter is a scene showing Heracles in the garden of the Hesperides. (Brommer. Herakles 30. N.Y. Met. Mus. 24.97.5.) In between Heracles and one of the maidens, stands a tree with a spotted serpent gracefully wound round it. It is painted white with dark spots, and is thus differentiated from the tree whose leaves and apples are red. The artist has emphasized the curving lines of the snake in relation to the upright tree and the figures standing in repose beside it. An Attic alabastron in the Museum at Nauplia has a similar scene. Brommer. Herakles. 29. Naup. 136. In both these versions of the legend, the artist has chosen to stress the decorative elements rather than any violent action. There is no sign of Heracles killing the snake as in many older versions.

73 I.T. 452 sq.

74 Hipp. 732 sq.

75 Hel. 1479 sq. The theme of migrating cranes is Homeric as A. M. Dale points out in her commentary upon this passage. But there is a unique touch in the personalized address to the birds flying overhead and the precisely observed details as they emerge for instance in the description στοχάδες, with its slight metaphorical cast (the word is used of fencing in a straight row), the lyric compound δολιχαύχενες and the apt ἐφεζόμεναι – the same verb Homer uses at Il. III.152 to describe grasshoppers settling on a bush.

76 Ba. 403 sq.

77 Ba. 430–2.

78 T. B. L. Webster has already pointed this out. The Interplay of Greek Art and Literature (pp. 9–10).

Chapter III

1 Ion 95; I.A. 752; Hec. 1106; Or. 321.

2 Mention of escape, e.g. Hipp. 836–8; Ba. 403–15; of domestic tasks, e.g. I.T. 221–8; Hec. 466–74; of dancing, e.g. Tro. 325 sq.; Tro. 551–5.

3 Euripides' originality in developing the original *Kommos* form is stressed by Masqueray, *Théorie des Formes Lyriques* (p. 203 sq.) and by Décharme, *Euripide et l'Esprit de son Théâtre* (pp. 495–6).

4 *Frogs* 1309 sq.; 1331 sq.

5 At 1314, 1349.

6 1331, 1361 (cf. Eur. *Hel.* 518); *Hec.* 473; *Hipp.* 559; *Ion* 212, 716.

7 *Med.* 440; *Or.* 1376–7. (cf. *Ion* 796); *H.F.* 69; *Hec.* 1100; *I.T.* 844; *And.* 1219.

8 For the kingfisher motif cf. Eur. fr. 856.1. Nauck², the source for this parody, and *I.T.* 1090 sq.; for dolphins, cf. Eur. *Electra* 435–7 whence these lines are borrowed; for the bloom on the grape cf. Eur. *Ba.* 261, 383; fr. 146.3. The *Σ* to *Frogs* says 1320 and 1322 are borrowed from Eur. *Hyps.*

9 *Frogs* 1331–2.

10 *Ib.* 1334–5.

11 *Ib.* 1335.

12 *Ib.* 1336–7.

13 *Ib.* 1338–9 (for the serpent's bloody gaze cf. *Ion* 1263), 1340. The tonal contrasts which appear here throughout in the ingenious variation of words for darkness and light, and in the implied colour contrast between φόνια and μελανονεκνείμονα are, as has already been noted, common in Euripides both in one word compounds such as μελαναυγής, μελαμφαής and also in more extended passages, e.g. *Tro.* 547–50; *Alc.* 438–54; *Hec.* 151 sq. etc.

14 *Ion* 82–183, 859–922.

15 The three stages are 82–111, 112–43, 144–83. Max Imhof's discussion of this monody in his commentary on the play, 1966 (pp. 19–21), is useful and perceptive, particularly as far as structural elements are concerned, although he has no detailed comments to make on the role of imagery in creating what he acknowledges to be a presentation of Ion's inward attitude of mind.

16 *Ion* 82–8.

17 E.g. *Ion* 1148–9; *Electra* 464 sq., 866; *Or.* 1001 sq.; *Pho.* 1562–3; *I.A.* 156–8; *Phaeth.* 2 (see Ch. VI, note 34).

18 *Pho.* 1–3, translated by Elizabeth Wyckoff.

19 *Ion* 95, 163, 157, 146.

20 See p. 49.

21 *Ion* 112 sq.; paean refrains at 125–8, 141–3. See Owen's note on the form and language. The climax of the part enclosed within these refrains is Ion's acknowledgement of Apollo as his father.

22 See Owen's note on 112.

23 Note the repeated idea in both παναμέριος and κατ' ἦμαρ.

24 *Tro.* 308–41. (On the symbolic role of the torch in this scene see p. 53 and also Ch. VII, p. 125.)

25 *Ion* 144 sq.

26 On the probability that swallows are meant at 171 sq., see Owen's note.

27 It is true that the birds are seen by Ion as the bearers of omens from gods to men (180), but the point is that they are *other* gods who do not impinge upon

Ion's particular devotion to Apollo. His attitude is similar to that of Hippolytus who will take only Artemis seriously as the object of his worship.

28 Owen in the introduction to his edition (p. xxiv), tends to give this impression.

29 *Ion* 859–922. For a general discussion of this monody see Imhof's commentary, 1966 (pp. 36–8), and Friederich *Euripides und Diphilos* (pp. 17–23).

30 For the motif handled as a term of praise see *I.T.* 1235; *H.F.* 687 sq.; *Hec.* 462.

31 *Ion* 887–92. It is probable that the apparently epexegetic ἀνθίζειν here which is difficult to translate, and where editions give very little help, means not 'to strew or deck with flowers' as *L. S. J.* render it, but 'to use for dyeing or colouring'. This is the meaning in A. *H.A.* 5.15, 18 and gives some purpose to Creousa's action. She was gathering crocuses to collect the saffron from them for dyeing.

32 Verrall, *Euripides the Rationalist* (pp. 147–8). 'Piety, to be intelligent, must prefer here the obvious explanation which omits Apollo and presumes the criminal to have been some unknown man.'

33 Words such as μομφάν, 885, which precedes this description and ἀναιδείᾳ, which immediately follows it. In this contrast, the epithet λευκοῖς, 'bare' or 'pale' wrists, becomes not a merely ornamental epithet, but a qualitative adjective stressing Creousa's helplessness.

34 Wilamowitz in his edition of the play (p. 127).

35 The *Hec.* is an exception to this general convention, and it is significant perhaps that her monody is in anapaests, and has not yet developed the metrical complexity of the late monodies.

36 *Hipp.* 58–87.

37 *Hec.* 59–97; *Tro.* 98–152.

38 *Frogs* 1332 in the passage already discussed generally on p. 44.

39 *Hec.* 68–72.

40 *Tro.* 686 sq.

41 Nautical metaphors at 102–4, 118, 137 and continued in the ensuing lyric dialogue at 162 in close conjunction with literal descriptions of Greek ships waiting to receive women captives.

42 *Tro.* 112–9.

43 The Σ on *Frogs* 536 gives the meaning, cf. Homer *Od.* 12, 421; Eur. *Hel.* 1573. This, however, is the only instance of the word's metaphorical use, as Breitenbach *Untersuchungen* (p. 145) points out. The full effect of the metaphor is enhanced by detailed description of physical discomfort felt in separate parts of the body. ἄκανθα seems to be used with special emphasis as if νῶτον itself were not enough. It is commonly used of a fish spine, Aristoph. *V*.969 or a snake's backbone, Hdt. 2.75. In prose it is used of the human backbone. Hdt. 4.72; Hp. *Art.* 14, but the only other place it occurs in verse is Eur. *Electra* 492 where, as here, it refers to the curved, double-bent spine of an old person.

44 The last lines of the play 1331-2 contain a reference to the Greek ships as the women move forward to embark.

45 *Hipp.* 198-266.

46 Barrett comments upon Phaedra's suppressed wishes, 208 sq., in his edition of the play (p. 200). On the imagery see C. P. Segal, 'The Tragedy of the Hippolytus', *H.S.C.Ph.*, LXX, 1965 (esp. p. 124).

47 *Tro.* 308-41; *Electra* 112-66.

48 *Tro.* 348-9.

49 Note particularly 309-10, and 320-1 where the meaning of ἀναφλέγω πυρὸς φῶς / ἐς αὐγάν ἐς αὔγλαν seems to be 'I make my torch's flame blaze into brightness and glowing radiance', presumably by waving it as she dances (cf. *Ba.* 145-9).

50 *Electra*, 140 sq.

51 *Ib.* 150-6 (see also discussion Ch. VI, p. 102 and note 29).

52 As Denniston points out in his commentary on these lines.

53 *Electra* 175-87.

54 See the farmer's remarks at 64 sq. and 77 and Denniston's comments on 77-8.

55 *Electra* 314-8.

56 *Ib.* 1069-73.

57 Kranz, *Stasimon*, p. 243.

58 *Pho.* 1485-92.

59 *Ib.* 306-9.

60 Particularly Kranz (see note 57), and Schadewaldt, *Monolog und Selbstgespräch* (pp. 162, 221).

61 Masqueray, *Théorie des formes lyriques* (p. 170, cf. also p. 129).

62 E.g. *And.* 825-65; *Tro.* 235-91; *Alc.* 244-79; *Pho.* 103-92, 1335 sq.; *Electra* 1147 sq.

63 *Alc.* 244-79; *Pho.* 103-92.

64 See A. M. Dale in her edition of the play on 252.

65 On Admetus' attitude see the comments of Hadley and Dale on 246-7.

66 *Sept.* 375-676.

67 *Pho.* 110-1 (cf. *Hyps.* fr. 1.ii 30-1).

68 At 110, 175-6. There is no direct reference to the Sun (at 175 it is merely the Moon's relative) and even if Hermann is right to keep a variation of the MS. L. reading at 169, ἁλίου still comes within a simile and is not a direct statement. It is most likely however that ἡλίου crept into the MSS from a gloss, since the phrase describing Polyneices' shining armour as 'blazing like the rays of dawn' makes perfectly good sense in itself. The presence of mist or mere half-light is suggested by 161-2 where Antigone is obviously having difficulty in seeing anything but the mere outline of Polyneices. 167 suggests a sudden change when his armour glistens and makes him ἐκπρεπής.

69 *Pho.* 127-30. On the several different interpretations of ἀστερωπός see Pearson's note on 128. The word is appropriate for two reasons. It draws attention to the literal brightness by which Hippomedon's armour (e.g. his

breastplate) is distinguished on the battlefield, and it illustrates his general pre-eminence as a warrior.

70 *A.R.V.*² 1338 1.(i). Pfuhl *M. und Z.* 574. Swindler (1929) 376, who describes the artist's rendering of the giant's metal body as follows: 'The gleaming bronze of the giant's body is rendered in white and modelled by means of shading in diluted brown varnish.' The choice of subject, which involves rendering the reflection of light off a metal surface, is an indication of the kind of problem which interested artists at this time.

71 Although highlighting – 'splendor' as opposed to 'lumen' – was not properly mastered until the fourth century, Pliny *N.H.* XXV. 29 (see A. Rumpf, *J.H.S.*, 1947, vol. 67, p. 10 sq.), artists were experimenting in the last quarter of the fifth century with applications of white and gold even on red-figure vases to give an illusion of reflected light and perspective. On the vases of Meidias for instance, necklaces, trappings of horses, diadems, flames, wings and other details are often rendered in gold or white. As time went on white was applied in larger patches to give a sense of perspective by light.

72 An implication of highlighting that is, simply because the aspects the poet selects for comment through epithets is reminiscent of white and gold as it is picked out to suggest light in painting (see esp. lines 146, 119, 168, 172).

73 191, 175, 177-8. The Sun has a gold belt on the Vienna bell Krater *A.R.V.*² 1318, Vienna 1771; Hahland: *Vasen um Meidias* 19a. Sun and Moon appear together on the Naples Krater *A.R.V.*² 1338, Naples 2883; Pfuhl *M. und Z.* 585. Hahland 9a, and the Blacas Krater, London B.M.E. 466. Swindler, (fig. 343). The reading 'Αελίου which Murray adopts, and which was clearly recognised by the Σ, has been questioned by some editors, notably Nauck who conjectured ἁ Λατοῦς, Wecklein and Méridier/Chapouthier, all of whom accept this in favour of the MSS reading. It is true that the Moon is usually the sister not the daughter of the Sun, but the Σ answer this objection by quoting Aeschylus as saying that the Moon is the daughter of the Sun because she derives her light from him. The other objection to the MSS reading is that λιπαρόζωνος by analogy with other -ζωνος compounds (see Powell's note) should refer to a woman and not a man. But if ζώνη is used of a man's belt, as it is at Xen. *An.* 1.6.10, 4.7.16, and more important, of the belt of Orion, which consisted of three stars, at *A. Meteor,* 343b 24, there is not only no reason why the compound should not apply here, but it also seems the appropriate word to use of a personified heavenly body.

74 *Pho.* 161-9.

75 The implication of μορφῆς τύπωμα is that the outline promises more than the eye can actually see. τύπωμα means the moulded shape of an object as it is formed or made in a mould (cf. Soph. *El.* 54). Therefore it is a word which suggests volume. The passive of ἐξεικάζω implies an image as opposed to the real thing. Cf. Aesch. *Ag.* 1244 where it is used of mere semblance or

representation in contrast to the real truth, and *Sept.* 445 where it describes the representation of a fire-bearer, not an actual fire-bearer. E. Fraenkel comments on the word in both passages in his note on *Ag.* 1244. Here Antigone sees the *image* of Polyneices' form 'portrayed as in a picture' as Powell translates it, that is to say the mere etched suggestion of an outline implying the hollow shape which is μορφῆς τύπωμα. Parrhasios, Euripides' contemporary (on his date and style see Rumpf *A.J.A.*, 1955, 67, p. 1 sq.), was a master of contour and outline. According to Pliny he drew figures in relief in such a way that they appeared to fold back and hint at more than was actually there (*N.H.* XXXV. 67. 68). Perhaps Euripides was thinking here of these new experiments with contour and outline. The somewhat laboured words suggest the attempt to express an unfamiliar concept.

76 The metrical change here and its significance is discussed by Masqueray, *Théorie des formes lyriques* (pp. 241–2).

77 This point was first suggested to me in a discussion of my thesis by Professor R. P. Winnington-Ingram.

78 E.g. Kranz, *Stasimon* p. 236. Décharme, *Euripide* (pp. 518–9). Aristophanes was of course the first to seize upon it as a point of caricature.

Chapter IV

1 As well as being outside the immediate family circle and an employee rather than a royal personage, the messenger is a detached observer in the sense that either his participation in the events he describes is not extensive, or that where he does take part, his own participation does not affect the comprehensive and objective quality of his reporting. The role of the messenger in the action described in the speeches of the *Ba., I.A., Electra, And., Med., Hipp., H.F.,* for example, is minimal. In the *Supplices* 719 sq. and *Heracl.* 847–8, the personal reactions of the messenger do not affect the fulness of his report, or his grasp of the whole scene.

2 In the absence of colourful compound adjectives for instance (φοινικοσκελεῖς at *Ion* 1207 is a rare exception) or in colour contrasts (again ξανθός / οἰνωπός at *Pho.* 1159–60 is a rare exception) χρυσός and ξανθός occur fairly commonly, but κυάνεος, χλωρός, χλοερός, φοῖνιξ, πορφύρεος, κροκόεις, γλαυκός do not appear at all in the messenger speeches.

3 Contrast Sophocles' practice with messenger-type characters in the *El.* and *Trach.*, or the highly subjective style of the Guard in the *Antig.*

4 ἄγγελος appears in the *Med., Supplices, H.F., I.T., Electra, Hel.* (twice), *Pho.* (twice), *Or., Ba.* (twice), and *I.A.*

5 Moral platitudes for instance at the end of the messenger's speech in *Med.* 1228 sq., *Heracl.* 863 sq., *Ba.* 1150 sq. Personal judgements or advice at *Hipp.* 1249 sq., *Androm.* 1161 sq., *Supplices* 726 sq., *H.F.* 1014 sq., *Electra* 857 sq., *Ba.* 769 sq.

6 τλήμων: e.g. *Med.* 1204., *Hipp.* 1177., *Ba.* 1102, 1117., *Or.* 947., *Electra* 850.

τάλας: e.g. *H.F.* 973, *Pho.* 1429. δεινός, e.g. *Med.* 1214, *Hipp.* 1218, *Androm.* 1135, *Supplices* 704, 715, *H.F.* 978, *I.T.* 1372, 1379, 1394.

7 The quasi-formulaic devices in messenger speeches have been discussed by Ludwig, *Sapheneia* (pp. 11–29) and G. Erdmann, *Der Botenbericht bei Euripides* (p. 179 sq.)

8 R. Lattimore, *P.G.T.* (p. 129).

9 Novelists, that is, or ballad writers. Contemporary novelists, it is true, may have abandoned the conventional forms, but here are the opening words of three famous novels selected more or less at random. 'A wide plain, where the broadening Floss hurries between its green banks to the sea . . .' (*A Mill on the Floss*). 'In that pleasant district of merry England which is watered by the river Don, there extended in ancient times a large forest covering the greater part of the hills and valleys which lie between Sheffield and the pleasant town of Doncaster' (*Ivanhoe*). 'While the present century was in its teens, and on one sunshiny morning in June there drove up to the great iron gate of Miss Pinkerton's academy for young ladies on Chiswick Mall a large family coach' (*Vanity Fair*). An elementary form of scene-setting is also the traditional opening to many ballads, e.g. *Faber Book of Ballads*, ed. Matthew Hodgart, London, 1965, pp. 77, 81, 94, 111, etc. This may also be seen in adaptations of the old ballad form in poems such as Auden's *Bristol Street* or *It was Easter as I walked in the public gardens.*

10 *Supplices* 650 sq., translated by Frank Jones, Chicago series.

11 *I.T.* 260 sq., translated by Witter Bynner, Chicago series.

12 *Electra* 774 sq., translated by Emily T. Vermeule, Chicago series.

13 Who comes to the main point of Orestes' victory at 687 after only eight lines and then proceeds to give the details.

14 *Supplices* 650 sq.

15 *H.F.* 925 sq.

16 *Med.* 1165–6 (see Page's note on 1166).

17 *Hipp.* 1194 sq.

18 *Ion* 1207–8. φοῖνιξ and compounds imply red-purple, rather than blue-purple and can include a range of shades from scarlet to dull reddish brown (see A. E. Kober, *Use of Color Terms*, pp. 93–5).

19 *Hel.* 1569 sq. Note the shift from τὰ πάντα to πλήσασα . . . 'Ελένη

20 *Ba.* 726–7, 1084–5 (cf. *And.* 1132 sq., *Electra* 802, *Pho.* 1192, see also note 22).

21 *Med.* 1202–3 (cf. *H.F.* 950, *Hipp.* 1216–7, 1243–4, see also note 22).

22 *Supplices* 719 sq. (cf. *Pho.* 1164 sq.). For a fuller discussion of the relation of the messenger's view to his audience, and to his material, and for more examples of changes of perspective see Erdmann, *Der Botenbericht bei Euripides* (pp. 89–90).

23 *And.* 1117 sq. On the use of individual words in this passage, A. R. F. Hyslop's notes in the Macmillan series are the most helpful.

24 Cf. also *Ba.* 737, 740, 747.

25 *Ba.* 677 sq.

26 See Dodd's note on 677-8.

27 Arrowsmith's translation of *Ba*. 692 sq.

28 *Ba*. 726-7.

29 Winnington-Ingram, *E.D.* (p. 93).

30 *Anaphora* and effective repetition for instance at *Ba*. 1065, 1118-20; *And*. 1131; *Med*. 1188-9; *H.F*. 989.

31 Concentration of verbs in one or two lines: instances at *Ba*. 763; *Electra* 843; *H.F*. 981, 999-1000; *Heracl*. 821; *Supplices* 700, 717, 719-20; *Ion* 1204.

32 Rare words for example at *H.F*. 992 (μυδροκτύπος is an *hapax legomenon*) 946 (συντριαινόω 'to shatter with a trident' occurs only in one other place).

33 Philostratus, *Imagines* II. 23. 2. That Euripides' messenger speech is in his mind is suggested by the reference in the paragraph immediately preceding this one (see also Fairbanks' note 1, p. 233, Loeb edition).

34 Chaeremon's *Oeneus* Nauck² fr. 14. Dodds refers to this fragment in his note on *Ba*. 683, but does not discuss it in any detail.

35 For a recent discussion (and a kinder view) of the language of this fragment see C. Collard in forthcoming *J.H.S.*, 1970.

36 ἡ μὲν . . . τῆς δ' . . . ἄλλη . . . ἄλλης . . . ἡ δὲ . . . in Chaeremon (cf. *Ba* αἱ μὲν . . . αἱ δὲ (684-5), ἡ δὲ (689), αἱ δ' (692), αἱ δ' (699), ἄλλη (706).

37 Similes from painting see Ch. I, note 41. Contrasts of light and dark have been discussed throughout. The word ἀντηύγει is used by Euripides at *Or*. 1519 and in a fragment from the *Oed*., P. Oxy. XXVII. 2459 1 + fr. 540 (cf. also *Ion* 890). Lines 14-15 are reminiscent of *Ion* 887-90. Of the metaphors ἐξομόργνυμι occurs metaphorically at *Ba*. 344 in a very emphatic passage; ἐξεπισφραγίζομαι does not exist in Euripides (but cf. ἐκσφραγίζομαι, *H.F*. 53).

38 There is monotony too in the pictorial devices used. Note repetition of λευκός at 1, 6, of φαίνω at 2, 5, 10, of λύω at 2, 4 and also of the idea of dark against light at 6, and 14-15.

39 M. Croiset, *H.L.G.*, Vol. III (p. 402). For a considerably less severe view see G. Norwood, *Greek Tragedy*, London, 1920 (p. 33).

40 Eur., *Hipp*. 1198 sq., David Grene's translation.

41 It is of course appropriate since Poseidon is god of the sea, both that there should be extensive description of his domain at this point, and that part of his power should manifest itself in some portent from it. The symbolic role of the sea generally in the play in relation to both Aphrodite and Poseidon has been discussed very fully by C. P. Segal, 'The Tragedy of the Hippolytus', *H.S.C.Ph.* 1965 (esp. pp. 120 and 142-4).

42 Seneca, *Phaedra*, 1035 sq. 'Cornibus' seems superior to 'orbibus' in 1038, since it suits the variegated catalogue of different physical items, and avoids repetition with 'oculi' below. Although I have adopted the punctuation of most editions in 1040-1, I am not sure that it does not make better sense to put a strong stop after 'relucent', to read 'insignis', and to delete the semi-colon after 'nota'. 'Caerula nota' then refer to markings on the neck as

mentioned at 1036. 'Its eyes belched out flame one minute and glowed the next. Its splendid neck, marked by a clear blue line, supported great muscles.'

43 The treatment of the mangling of Hippolytus' body for instance, 1085–1108, is much longer and more elaborate than in Euripides' speech.

44 Ornamental that is, in the sense of 'gratuitously decorative' and not only in Bergson's terms of inherited Homeric vocabulary. For his definition of the term see *L'Epithète Ornementale* (p. 18).

45 See *Ba.* 487 after Dionysus has led the king into the trap of his own suspicions.

46 Erdmann, *Der Botenbericht* . . . (p. 67 sq.). He nonetheless seems to me to underplay the connections with epic. The speech in the *Pho.* for instance is full of echoes from epic imagery. cf. *Pho.* 1151 with *Il.* 16. 750; *Pho.* 1152 with *Il.* 13. 655 or 23. 220; *Pho.* 1380 with *Il.* 17. 725; *Pho.* 1154 with numerous Homeric similes of storms.

47 *Ba.* 748, 1056; *Pho.* 1380, 1154; *H.F.* 992 (a simile different in form from most); *Med.* 1200.

48 *Electra*, 777 sq.

49 *H.F.* 953, Arrowsmith's translation.

50 See Agave's address to her companions "Ω δρομάδες ἐμαὶ κύνες at 731, Winnington-Ingram, *E.D.* (pp. 94 and 130).

51 *Ba.* 726, 1091, 1103, 1146. Although the prefix συν- is so common as often to have no special emphasis, the context, the repetition of συν- and the rareness of the words with which it is compounded (συνεργάτης and συγκύναγος particularly) suggest that it may have weight in these instances.

52 B. Brecht, 'A Dialogue about Acting' in *Brecht on Theatre* (p. 27).

Chapter V

1 *I.T.* 72–5.

2 T. B. L. Webster, *Greek Art and Literature*, p. 187, draws attention to description of characters' appearance as a trend of realism particularly characteristic of the last twenty or so years of the fifth century. He has counted 40 instances, but of those he mentions only two are Sophoclean, and of these, *El.* 664 is so brief and general as hardly to belong with the rest.

3 Brief references to mean appearance, e.g. at 191, 451–2, are not developed beyond a phrase or a couple of lines. On the other hand, there is extensive description of Electra's emotional stress, especially in the lyric dialogue she has with the chorus at 121 sq.

4 The classic instance is at *Acharnians* 415 sq. where Aristophanes alludes to Euripides' use of τρύχη in general at 418 (cf. Euripides' *Electra* 185. 501; *Pho.* 325; *Tro.* 496) and in particular the λακίδας πέπλων of the *Philoctetes* (423), the δυσπινῆ πεπλώματα of the *Bellerophon* (426) and the ῥακώματα of the *Telephus* (432). (See too *Frogs* 1061 sq. and Van Leeuwen's notes on 837 and 1063.)

5 See E. W. Handley's remarks on rags in his edition of the *Telephus* (p. 29);

     Hel. 416–7, 421; *Tro.* 506–9.

6 Even if it was only a slight modification, such as plainer styles or duller colours. Unfortunately there is no surviving evidence on this point. What does seem clear is that *complete* realism was out of the question (cf. T. B. L. Webster, *Greek Theatre Production*, p. 39).

7 *And.* 719–20.

8 *Tro.* 1194–9. ἡδύς seems originally to have been used of impact on the senses of taste, sight, smell, touch, etc. (cp.*L.S.J.*) hence I have translated here 'pleasant to my sense'.

9 *Tro.* 1173 sq.

10 *Med.* 1071–5. *Pho.* 1699. This is a point also developed in Ch. VII, p. 129–30.

11 *Or.* 128–9.

12 *Electra* 487 sq., note particularly the selective use of epithets and nouns here to describe physical features of the body, e.g. ῥυσῷ ποδί (490), διπλῆν ἄκανθαν (492), παλίρροπον (which only occurs here) γόνυ (492). Or the force of ἄκανθα (see Ch. III, note 43).

13 *Med.* 92, 24, 27 sq.

14 *Hipp.* 274–80.

15 *Electra* 239, 241, 304 sq.

16 *Or.* 385–91. Arrowsmith's translation ἀμορφία in my opinion would better be rendered by 'disfigurement' rather than 'alteration'.

17 *Or.* 219 sq.

18 πέλανον of clotted blood at *Alc.* 851. *Rhet.* 430, of honey at fr. 467.5, of gum in the eyes Heliod. ap. Stob. 4. 36.8; and of offerings to the Gods *Ion* 706; *Tro.* 1063.

19 ἀφρώδης of blood. Hp. *Aph.* 5.13. ἀφρός as froth or slaver at the mouth, rather than sea-foam, is a medical term also Hp.*Aph.* 2.43.

20 πινώδης of the grease in wool. Hp. *Mul.* 2.185. πιναρός cf. *Electra* 184. Eupolis 251. It is also used of unwashed wool Aretaeus ὀξέων νόσων θεραπευτικόν I.I.These adjectives seem to imply a certain greasy sheen since the word πίνος is also used of the shine on bronze statues, as well as the natural grease in wool. Plut. 2.395b.

21 *Alc.* 947. From 'without rain', αὐχμηρός came to mean 'without being washed'.

22 *Chrysippus* 842 N².

23 *Oed.* 548 N².

24 *Med.* 516–9; *Hipp.* 925–6; *Electra* 558–9 (cf. *H.F.* 669–70).

25 The connection survived in the well known phrase καλὸς κἀγαθός. On ἀρετή as a union of all the excellences, including beauty, in Homer cp. Jaeger *Paideia* I. chapter i. He is, however, concerned in tracing into later times the continuity of such ideas, rather than looking for discontinuity.

26 *Il.* II, 216–20 transl. E. V. Rieu.

27 *Il.* III, 156–8 transl. E. V. Rieu.

28 *Or.* 479–80.

29 *H.F.* 867–70, 931–4.

30 *H.F.* 1102, 1395, 1378–82, 1399.

31 *H.F.* 1231–4 (Arrowsmith's translation).

32 *And.* 147–53 (see Paley's note on ἀπαρχάς).

33 *And.* 207–8.

34 *Tro.* 1022 sq.

35 *Tro.* 987–97.

36 ἐκμαργόομαι and ἐγκαθυβρίζω occur only here. κατακλύζω is quite common in other authors but is used once elsewhere in Euripides in a metaphorical sense at *Or.* 343.

37 That the theme of Eastern extravagance was traditional in no way affects the originality of its use.

38 *Ba.* 233 sq., 453 sq.

39 *Thesm.* 134 sq. (see Rogers' note on 135).

40 *Ba.* 216–25.

41 *Ba.* 233–41 (reading οἰνωπός Barnes' conjecture, see Dodd's note).

42 *Ba.* 343–54.

43 *Ba.* 453–60.

44 *Thesm.* 134 sq. On representations of Dionysus in art as a youthful effeminate figure, see Dodd's note on *Ba.* 453–9.

45 Winnington-Ingram, *E.D.* (p. 46).

46 Pi. *Pyth.* VIII. 87. Tyrtaeus 11.36.

47 Dodds on 343–4.

48 *Electra* 303 sq. See Denniston's commentary for discussion of the precise sense of words, especially αὐλίζομαι, στερήσομαι, ἀναίνομαι, ἐγγενῆ, σέσηπεν.

49 *Electra* 1071 sq.

50 *Electra* 1140.

51 *Electra* 1023, translated by Emily Townsend Vermeule. Chicago Series.

52 Denniston points out that the delayed name gives a pathetic effect. The central position of διήμησ' in between λευκὴν and παρηῖδα also mirrors the sense and is impossible to reproduce in English.

53 Plut. *de Audiend. Poet.* 3=Overbeck *Schriftquellen* 1708 cites Parrhasios as an example of an artist who sought 'out of the way subjects'. γράφουσι δὲ καὶ πράξεις ἀτόπους ἔνιοι, καθάπερ ... Παρράσιος τὴν Ὀδυσσέως προσποίητον μανίαν.

54 Euphranor's comment upon Parrhasios' painting of Theseus comes from Plut *de glor Ath.* 2=Overbeck *Schriftquellen* 1704. The Theseus cup by Aison (see Pfuhl. *Masterpieces*, p. 81, fig. 107) is perhaps a reflection of Parrhasios' Theseus.

55 Xen. *Mem.* 3.10.1=Overbeck *Schriftquellen* 1701 which A. Rumpf *Parrhasios A.J.A.*, LV, 1951 (pp. 1–12) compares with Pliny *N.H.* XXXV. 69 'pinxit (Parrhasios) demon Atheniensium argumento quoque ingenioso; ostendebat namque varium, iracundum, iniustum, inconstantem eundem exorabilem;

clementem, misericordem, gloriosum, excelsum, humilem, ferocem, fugacemque et omnia pariter.'

56 Lucian 5.6, 7. He gives Zeuxis the highest prase, 'ὅτι ἐν μιᾷ καὶ τῇ αὐτῇ ὑποθέσει ποικίλως τὸ περιττὸν ἐπεδείξατο τῆς τέχνης.'

Chapter VI

1 W. Breitenbach, *Untersuchungen* (pp. 164, 289).
2 H. Delulle, *Les Répétitions d'Images chez Euripide* (pp. 24–5, 27, 46).
3 B. Altum, *Similitudines Homeri* (pp. 71–3).
4 K. Pauer, *Die Bildersprache des Euripides* (p. 168).
5 Breitenbach for instance cites all the similes and metaphors which occur in lyric passages by content. He distinguishes between those which appear to be new, and those which do not, but does not enter into discussion of context. Pauer cites according to image-content and play, but still does not take account of context. Delulle does consider images in their context, but the range of his study is narrow in its restriction to bird imagery only. Pot, who deals solely with nautical imagery, discusses context where there are important textual cruces, but does not venture into wider placing of contexts.
6 The prominence of nautical imagery in the Medea has been noted and commented upon by E. Blaiklock, 'The Nautical Imagery of Euripides' Medea', *C.Ph.*, L., 1955, pp. 233–7 (see also Pauer, 1935, p. 6; Pot, 1943, p. 99).
7 *Med.* 278–9; 768–70.
8 *Med.* 522–5.
9 *Med.* 79.
10 *Med.* 1138.
11 Metaphorical uses of κάμνω, e.g. at *Electra* 1358, *Ion* 363, *I.T.* 1119, *Hec.* 306, *H.F.* 101, 293, *I.A.* 966, etc.; of κάλως, e.g. at *Med.* 278, 770, *H.F.* 837, 478; of λιμὴν at *Med.* 769, *Or.* 1077, *And.* 891, 749.; of ἐξαντλέω, e.g. at *Cyc.* 10, 110, 282, *Supplices* 838, fr. 454.3; of κλυδών, e.g. at *Hec.* 116, *Ion* 60, *Supplices* 474, *H.F.* 1091. etc. The middle of μεθορμίζω appears to be used only at *Med.* 258, 442. Pot's study demonstrates this. (See especially the index of terms and passages in which they occur pp. 94–101.)
12 E.g. *H.F.* 837 (see also Aristoph. *Equ.* 756, Plato, *Protag.* 338 A).
13 E.g. *And.* 891. ὦ ναυτίλοισι χείματος λιμὴν φανεὶς / Ἀγαμέμνονος παῖ Aesch. *Ag.* 899 where Agamemnon is γῆν φανεῖσαν ναυτίλοις παρ' ἐλπίδα. λιμὴν is used to describe friendship at Soph. *Aj.* 683. ἑταιρείας λιμήν.
14 ἐξαντλέω, e.g. at *Cyc.* 10, 110; *Supplices* 838, fr. 454.3. ἀντλεώ, e.g. Aesch. *P.V.* 375; *Cho.* 748; Soph. *El.* 1291. διαντλέω, e.g. Pi. *Pyth.* IV, 522.
15 See Ch. III, p. 51–2.
16 *Hipp.* 73–81. On the difficulties of translating the exact sense of 'Αἰδώς see Barrett's note on 78.

17   See Barrett's note on 79–81; also C. P. Segal, 'The Tragedy of Hippolytus,' *H.S.C.Ph.*, LXX, 1965.

18   Barrett draws attention to the placing of ἀκήρατον and also its echoing of 73.

19   *Hipp.* 245, 250–66.

20   Metaphors of mixing are common in general even if ἀνακίρναμαι is not. κιρνάω is used with κόμπον in Pi. *Isthm.* V. 25 in the sense of mixing a cup of praise. κεράννυμι is extremely common in the sense of mixing (metaphorically) so as to get the right blend, e.g. Pi. *Pyth.* V. 2, X, 41 etc. There is one possible very close parallel to this passage if Porson's emendation of *Med.* 137 is right. στέργηθρον, which according to Dioscorides 4.92 was the plant from which love charms were concocted, is commonly used of love itself, e.g. Aesch. *Cho.* 241, *Eum.* 192. *P.V.* 492. μυελόν as a metaphor of strengthening is common, e.g. Homer *Od.* 2.290, 20, 108; *Il.* 22, 50; Aesch. *Ag.* 76, although the meaning here seems to be rather the innermost part. For συντείνω in the metaphorical sense of 'brace' see Plato *Laws* 800 d. ἁρμονίαις συντείνοντες ... τὰς ψυχάς. ὠδινέω as a metaphor for mental anguish is very frequent, e.g. Soph. *Aj.* 794, *Trach.* 325; Eur. *Heracl.* 644; Plato *Theaet.* 148 E. 210 B. (For πολεμέω with abstract things cf. also Soph. *O.C.* 191; Eur. *Ion.* 1386.

21   *Hipp.* 589 καὶ μὴν σαφῶς γε τὴν κακῶν προμνήστριαν/τὴν δεσπότου προδοῦσαν ἐξαυδᾶ λέχος. Barrett notes the emphatic quality of the introductory particles which precede this image.

22   *Hipp.* 1171–2. πῶς καὶ διώλετ'; εἰπὲ τῷ τρόπῳ Δίκης/ἔπαισεν αὐτὸν ῥόπτρον αἰσχύναντ' ἐμέ; On the precise meaning of ῥόπτρον see Barrett's note on these lines.

23   *Hipp.* 539–40.

24   *Hipp.* 541 sq.

25   *Hipp.* 526–7.

26   *Hipp.* 530–4. Light is chosen for this image as Barrett points out because its reach is farther than anything else known to man.

27   νοσέω, e.g. *Med.* 16; *And.* 548, 950; *H.F.* 273, 34, 542; *I.T.* 536; *I.A.* 411, 1403; *Pho.* 867, 66, 472, fr. 202.2, 141. 3, etc. δάκνω, e.g. at *Med.* 1370, 1345; *Electra* 242, 291; *Heracl.* 483; *H.F.* 94; *Hipp.* 1313, 696; *I.A.* 385, 689; *Ba.* 351; *Pho.* 383, fr. 572.4, 316.6, etc. κάμνω see note 11. κνίζω, e.g. *Med.* 568, 599, 555; *I.A.* 330; *And.* 209. Phrases with βάρος, e.g. βάρος κακῶν *Hipp.* 878. πημάτων βάρος, *Supplices* 818. βάρος ψυχῆς, *Alc.* 353. πλούτου βάρος, *Electra* 1287. ὄλβου βάρος, *I.T.* 416. Metaphorical phrases involving κλύδων, e.g. at *Hec.* 116; *Ion* 60; *Tro.* 696; *H.F.* 1091; *Pho.* 859; *I.T.* 316; *Med.* 362 (cf. *H.F.* 1087; *Hipp.* 822; *Supplices* 824).

28   *Hec.* 807–8. γραφεύς, the reading with the best MS authority, has been daggered by Murray who substitutes βραβεύς. But there seems no warrant for this. γραφεύς makes perfectly good sense as a unique and precise simile. Hecuba wants the full extent of her grief to be realized. This can only be done by a contemplation of it in its full perspective. The simile describes

this process as comparable to the way a painter gets the full measure and perspective of his work by standing back from the canvas and looking at it objectively. This might apply to any painter and any paintings but it is perhaps particularly appropriate to the illusionistic art of Euripides' own day, since this was experimenting with effects of perspective. cp. Plato *Theaet.* 208 E where ἀφίσταμαι is also used of standing back and contemplating illusionistic painting. Euripides brings the visual arts into a number of his similes e.g. *Hec.* 560–1, *Pho.* 128–9, *Hel.* 262–3, *Androm.* fr. 125.

29 *Electra* 151–6. Paley comments on the 'remarkable uniformity' of style in this little *mesode* without saying in what it consists. This impression surely comes partly from the regularity of the *glyconic* line, with resolutions in the first foot and partly in the sustained unity of the image itself, maintained syntactically in one extended sentence beginning with the οἵα which introduces the simile.

30 Swans are the subject directly or indirectly of similes also at *H.F.* 110, 692; *Ba.* 1365.

31 *I.T.* 47–57.

32 *H.F.* 777–80.

33 *Androm.* fr. 114 N².

34 *Ion* 82–5 (cf also 122, 1146 sq.), *Or.* 1001 sq; *Electra* 464 sq, 866; *Pho.* 1, 1562–3; *I.A.* 156–8; *Phaeth.* 2 etc. Similar pictorial personifications are to be found on vase paintings of this period. See especially the Blacas crater F.R. *Gr. V.* Plate 126. Swindler, *Ancient Painting*, fig. 343. Night in a chariot: see *J.H.S.* LXV 1945 Plate 7b; also Furtwängler, *Sammlung Sabouroff* Taf. 63. B.M. *E.* 776.

35 *H.F.* 860–3.

36 *Ion* 1262–8.

37 *Ion* 877. ἀλγέω is commonly used of both physical and mental anguish so it is hard to say which is the predominant notion here. The personification of ψυχὰ is strengthened here by a compound verb, unique in form and appropriate to people, not things, i.e. κακοβουλευθεῖσ'. Its meaning seems to be close to that of ἐπιβουλευθεῖσα. The view of both Paley and Owen that the form is designedly irregular to avoid the connotation 'foolish' which the natural formation by analogy with the adjective κακοβουλευθεῖσ' would have, seems highly likely. Owen renders 'victim of a vile conspiracy'.

38 Breitenbach, 1934, pp. 163–4.

39 *Ba.* 1107–8. Winnington-Ingram, *E.D.* draws attention to the psychological confusion in the women's minds (pp. 131–2). The ambiguity is continued into the next scene where the head of Pentheus undergoes various metamorphoses in Agave's deluded vision.

40 *Tro.* 118, 1258–9 (see Ch. III, p. 51 and Ch. VII, p. 125).

41 *Tro.* 1176 (see p. 159 and note 92), 1121.

42 *Ba.* 1136; literally 'every hand, covered in blood as it was, played ball with Pentheus' flesh'. The word διεσφαίριζε appears only in this passage. *Tro.*

564. καράτομος ἐρημία. Kirchoff in his edition was the first to interpret the meaning of this metaphor in its content.

43 Delulle, 1911 (p. 35) makes a list of repetitions in both the same and in different plays. He makes a valid distinction between effective echo within the same play, and weak repetitions or dramatic cliché in different plays (see esp. pp. 46, 49 sq).

44 *Pho.* 1423, 1154, 1380, 1151 (see Ch. IV, p. 73).

45 *Or.* 1330. ἀνάγκης δ᾽ ἐς ζυγὸν καθέσταμεν. Euripides has substituted the common word ζυγόν for the more precise λέπαδνον.

46 *And.* 630 (cf. Homer *Il.* 6.344, 356 where Helen calls herself a 'bitch'.)

47 *Ba.* 977 (see Winnington-Ingram, *E.D.* on the use of this word in the play, p. 94).

48 *And.* 447, 1116. This compound is first used by Soph. *O.T.* 387. ῥάπτω alone at 911, πλέκω with μηχανή 66, 995, words with μηχανο- base: 85, 548, 770, 983.

49 ζεύγνυμι is especially common as a metaphor for marriage, e.g. *Phaeth.* 112. fr. 24.1; *Ba.* 468; *Tro.* 676; *Hel.* 1654; *Ion* 949, 907, etc.

50 *H.F.* 454–5. The ignominiousness of the yoking is enhanced, as Wilamowitz points out in his note on this passage, by the inclusion of disparate elements within it, i.e. νέοι as well as γέροντες.

51 *H.F.* 1375–6.

52 *H.F.* 1403, Wilamowitz comments on the effectiveness of this image in its context.

53 *H.F.* 445–6.

54 *H.F.* 478–9.

55 *H.F.* 629–33, 1423–4.

56 *H.F.* 629–33. The ἐφολκίς was a small boat which was often towed behind warships or freighters (see Wilamowitz on 631).

57 *H.F.* 1423–4.

58 *H.F.* 1425–6.

59 *H.F.* 110, 692–3.

60 Time is a racetrack at 777. Its negative and positive power is also stressed through personification at 506, 805, where it is said 'not to know how to preserve hopes', and to have 'revealed the preeminent strength' of Heracles.

61 See Ch. VII, p. 127.

62 See Ch. IV, p. 73.

63 *Ba.* 1064–7. Dodds is surely right in his interpretation (following Sandys) that these lines refer to the drawing out with peg and line of a cartwheel rim, and not to the use of the pole lathe (see his note on 1067). He draws attention to the way the description is enhanced by unique triple repetition of the verb.

64 Dodds calls κυρτός purely ornamental, taking it as a weakness in the description. But since the audience or reader must still have the tree in mind as being

bent only with great effort, its effect really goes beyond the wheel rim to which it strictly refers, and therefore makes it more than a mere formulaic adjective.

65 *Supplices* 714–7. ἐπικείμενον κάρα κυνέας 'and heads having helmets set upon them' (see Paley's note).

66 See Ch. V, passim.

67 *Ba.* 688, 459, 352, 231, 958. (On the metaphor of ἐν ἄρκυσιν at 231 see Winnington-Ingram's note, *E.D.*, p. 74, and on hunting metaphors in general *ib.* p. 90 n.1. and p. 74 n. 1.)

68 *Ba.* 455–6, 236 (see Ch. V, pp. 89–90).

69 *Ba.* 354, 344 (see Ch. V, p. 89).

70 *Ba.* 957–8 (Arrowsmith's translation).

71 *Ba.* 487; Hp. *Vict.* 1. 15.

72 *Hec.* 907.

73 *Hec.* 910–11.

74 *Hec.* 911–13.

75 On the frequency of cloud metaphors to describe large numbers of people, see Garzya's note on this passage. Troy's towers are a στέφανος also in Pi. *Ol.* 8.32, and at *Tro.* 784 where Euripides uses the metaphor again.

76 *I.A.* 1051–2. The metaphor of colour here, 'golden hollows of cups', is similar to one in a fragment of Aristophanes 165, where a cup is said to be κυανοβενθῆ 'deep-blue-depthed'.

77 *Or.* 988. The 'winged racing of steeds' as England translates in the second of the two alternative versions he proposes (see his note on 987–94). ποτανὸν is an emendation of Porson's, universally accepted as a correction of τὸ πτανὸν codd.

78 *Pho.* 1485–6. βότρυς is in ͺHomer a bunch of grapes: the clusters then come to be applied to curls grouped round the face. On the connection of βότρυς to βόστρυχος see Pearson's note on this passage.

79 *Ba.* 862–76.

80 Dodds draws attention to the boldness, for a Greek poet, of a colour word applied to an abstract noun. χλωρός is however a qualifying epithet of fear in the *Il.* and *Od.* and at Aesch. *Suppl.* 566, Eur. *Supplices* 599.

81 On the metaphorical use of ἀέλλαις here see ͺDodd's note. He translates 'gusts of swift racing'.

82 The place of this ode in the play as a whole is discussed by Winnington-Ingram, *E.D.* (pp. 105 sq.).

83 1204–6. Tyrrell compares Tennyson's 'Time, a Maniac scattering dust . . .'

84 *Tro.* 190–6.

85 The garland image is used repeatedly in the play to indicate the paradox that victory is really with the defeated, and defeat with the victorious Greeks. Its implication throughout is double-edged, e.g. at 223, 401, 565, 784, 803, 937, 1030, 1144, 1223.

86 ἐρημία is personified at 26–7, 97, 563–7.

87 Bacchic frenzy is the common way of describing madness in tragedy; here it recurs at 170, 341, 367, 408, 172, 307, 349, 415.

88 *Tro.* 555–6.

89 *Tro.* 560.

90 *Tro.* 563–7 (see Ch. II, note 56).

91 *Tro.* 820–38.

92 *Tro.* 1173–7 translated by Lattimore.

93 ἐκγελάω is used by Plato at *Rep.* 473 C to describe a breaking wave γέλωτι . . . ὥσπερ κῦμα ἐκγελῶν.

94 *Tro.* 844–5. As Tyrrell points out, the reference here is not to physical building.

95 *Tro.* 612–13. Lattimore's translation.

96 See Ch. III, p. 51–2.

97 Shipwreck images at 162, 677. The wooden horse looks like a ship at 537. Other ship images at 569, 686–96, 1258.

98 *Tro.* 686–96.

99 *Hipp.* 1004–5.

100 Descriptions of gold at *Tro.* 520, 820 sq., 1107. Simile at 432.

Chapter VII

1 *Tro.* 560; *Hec.* 911; *Tro.* 1295 sq., 1320, 557–9. (The general point was discussed in Ch. I, p. 9 sq.)

2 καταξαίνω *Ion* 1267 (cf *Hipp.* 274); *Pho.* 1145; *Med.* 1030; *Tro.* 509; *Supplices* 503. διακναίω, Aristoph. *Clouds* 120; *Heracl.* 296 (cf. *Electra*, 1307); *I.A.* 27; *Alc.* 109; *Med.* 164.

3 Masqueray, *Euripide et ses Idées* (p. 71).

4 Delulle, *Les Répétitions d'Images* (p. 25).

5 *Sapheneia*, or Clarity, as it is applied to Euripides, is in fact the principle upon which W. Ludwig bases his book, as his title *Sapheneia* suggests. Admittedly he applies it structurally rather than verbally, and takes clarity of rhetorical organization to be on the whole a virtue and not a vice. But his conclusion (pp. 137–8), where he attributes to the poet the over-riding aim of clarity as something Euripides had in common with the sophists and rhetoricians of his day, implies this as a fundamental principle in all his work. On a purely stylistic level see the blistering comments of Euripides' lyric style by W. Breitenbach, *Untersuchungen*, pp. 290–1, and also p. 292, where he contrasts it unfavourably with the greater grandeur of Pindaric, Aeschylean and Sophoclean diction. 'Die euripideische lyrische Diktion zeichnet sich gegenüber der seine Vorgänger durch Klarheit und Leichtverständlichkeit aus'. Twice in this paragraph he uses the term 'einfach' and sums up 'Rätsel-artiges Andeuten erstrebt er nicht'. See also the remarks of Earp, *The Style of Aeschylus* (p. 81) who speaks of the 'greater simplicity' of Euripides in relation to Aeschylus.

6   *Ion* 1207–8; *Ba.* 1134.

7   Masqueray, *Euripide et ses Idées*, p. 71.

8   See detailed discussion in Ch. II, pp. 21-2.

9   This point has been neatly made by E. Fraenkel, *De Media et Nova Comoedia Quaestiones* (p. 15).

10 *Hel.* 1107 sq.; F. R. Earp, *The Style of Aeschylus* (p. 78).

11 In Ch. II, pp. 23-4.

12 The stylistic connection between Euripides and Homer has been noted before. See Breitenbach, *Untersuchungen* pp. 268 sq.

13 *Ba.* 1170, 1174, 1185.

14 See discussion in Ch. III, p. 53.

15 *Or.* 273–4.

16 *Or.* 321-3.

17 *Or.* 314–15 (see Paley's note).

18 *Or.* 407.

19 *Or.* 408.

20 This is a point which Breitenbach in his assessment of Euripides' use of metaphor, does not allow for.

21 Aesch. *P.V.* 720–1, 726; *Ag.* 302 (see Fraenkel's note); *Supp.* 795. 'Brooding' is perhaps the best translation of οἰόφρων.

22 *Supp.* 93–5, 88–90.

23 *Supp.* 638; *Pers.* 821-2.

24 *Androm.* frag. 114 N². (See discussion Ch. VI, p. 103. *Or.* 1001 sq.)

25 *Ion* 82 sq.

26 See discussion in Ch. III, pp. 47-9.

27 *Ba.* 874-6.

28 This characteristic Aeschylean attitude is neatly expressed by the chorus at *Pers.* 107–15.

29 *Med.* 1402–3.

30 *Med.* 1074-5.

Bibliography

This is intended to be a select bibliography, including for the most part those works which have been cited more than once. Edited texts are listed by play titles, books and articles are listed alphabetically by author.

Editions of Texts

Euripidis fabulae, ed. G. Murray, Oxford, 1900.

Euripide, L. Parmentier, H. Grégoire, L. Méridier, F. Chapouthier, J. Meunier. Ed. Budé, Paris, 1925–61.

Euripidis Tragoediae, ed. A. Kirchoff, Berlin, 1867.

Euripides. Ausgewählte Tragödien, ed. N. Wecklein and R. Prinz, Leipsig, 1878–1902.

Euripides' plays edited F. A. Paley, 3 vols., Bibliotheca Classica, 1851.

The Complete Greek Tragedies, edited D. Grene and R. Lattimore, Chicago, 1955.

Euripides, transl. Philip Vellacott. Penguin editions. London, 1953, 1954.

Alcestis, ed. W. S. Hadley, Cambridge, 1934; A. M. Dale, Oxford, 1954.

Andromache, ed. A. R. F. Hyslop, London, 1900.

Bacchae, ed. E. R. Dodds, Oxford, 1944.

Electra, ed. J. D. Denniston, Oxford, 1939.

Hecuba, ed. F. W. King, London, 1938.

Helen, ed. A. M. Dale, Oxford, 1967; ed. A. C. Pearson, Pitt Press, Cambridge, 1903.

Heracles, ed. U. von Wilamowitz-Moellendorff, Berlin, 1899.

Hippolytus, ed. W. S. Barrett, Oxford, 1964.

Hypsipyle, ed. G. Bond, London, 1963.

Ion, ed. A. S. Owen, Oxford, 1939.

Iphigeneia in Anlis, ed. E. S. Headlam, Cambridge, 1939; E. B. England, London, 1891.

Iphigeneia in Tauris, ed. M. Platnauer, Oxford, 1938.

Medea, ed. A. W. Verrall, London, 1881; ed. D. L. Page, Oxford, 1938.

Orestes, ed. N. Wedd, Cambridge, 1942.

Phaethon, ed. J. Diggle, Cambridge, 1970.

Phoenissae, ed. A. C. Pearson, Pitt Press, Cambridge, 1875; ed. J. U. Powell, London, 1911.

Telephus, ed. E. W. Handley and J. Rea, *The Telephus of Euripides*, Institute of Classical Studies, Bulletin Supplement V, 1957.

Troades, ed. R. Y. Tyrrell, London, 1897.
Nova Fragmenta Euripidea, ed. C. Austin, Berlin, 1968.

Books and Articles

S. M. Adams, *Sophocles the Playright*, Toronto, 1957.

J. T. Allen and G. Italie, *A Concordance to Euripides*, London, 1954.

B. Altum, *Similitudines Homeri*, (*cum Aeschyli, Sophoclis, Euripidis comparantur*), Berlin, 1855

J. D. Beazley, *Attic Black-Figure Vase Painters*, Oxford, 1956; *Attic Red-Figure Vase Painters*, Second edition, Oxford, 1963.

L. Bergson, *L'Epithète Ornementale*, Uppsala, 1956.

E. Blaiklock, 'The Nautical Imagery of Euripides' Medea', *C.Ph. L.*, Chicago, 1955, p. 233 sq.

B. Brecht, 'A Dialogue about Acting', in *Brecht on Theatre*, transl. J. Willett, London, 1964.

W. Breitenbach, *Untersuchungen zur Sprache der euripideische Lyrik*, Stuttgart, 1934.

W. Clemen, *The Development of Shakespeare's Imagery*, London, 1951.

J. D. Conacher, *Euripidean Drama*, Toronto, 1967.

J. D. Conington, *P. Vergili Maronis Opera*, Vol. II, London, 1883.

M. Croiset, *Histoire de la Littérature Grecque*, III, Paris, 1929.

A. M. Dale, 'Seen and Unseen on the Greek Stage', *Wiener Studien*, LXIX, Graz. Böhlhans, 1956, pp. 96–106; 'The Chorus in the Action of Greek Tragedy', in *Classical Drama and Its Influence*, ed. M. J. Anderson, London, 1965.

P. Décharme, *Euripide et l'Esprit de son Théatre*, Paris, 1893.

H. Delulle, *Les Répétitions d'Images chez Euripide*, Louvain, 1911.

H. Diller, 'Umwelt und Masse als Dramatische Faktoren', in *Euripide: Entretiens*, Fondation Hardt, Geneva, 1960, p. 87 sq.

F. Dornseiff, *Pindar's Stil*, Berlin, 1921.

F. R. Earp, *The Style of Aeschylus*, Cambridge, 1948.

U. Ellis-Fermor, *The Frontiers of Drama*, London, 1964.

G. Erdmann, *Der Botenbericht bei Euripides*, Kiel, 1964.

H. R. Fairclough, *The Attitude of the Greek Tragedians toward Nature*, Toronto, 1897.

E. Fraenkel, *De Media et Nova Comoedia Quaestiones*, Göttingen, 1912.

W. H. Friederich, *Euripides und Diphilos*, Munich, 1953.

A. Furtwaengler and K. Reichold, *Griechische Vasenmalerei*, Munich, 1904-1932.

G. M. A. Grube, *The Drama of Euripides*, London, 1941.

W. Hahland, *Vasen um Meidias* Berlin, 1930.

W. Hoerman, *Gleichnis und Metapher in der griechischen Tragödie*, München, 1934.

Max Imhof, *Euripides' Ion. Eine literarische Studie*, Berne, 1966.

W. Jaeger, *Paideia*, transl. G. Highet, Oxford, 1939.

H. D. F. Kitto, *Greek Tragedy*, London, 1961; *Sophocles: Dramatist and Philosopher*, London, 1958.

A. E. Kober, *The Use of Color Terms in the Greek Poets*, New York, 1932.

W. Kranz, *Stasimon*, Berlin, 1933.

R. Lattimore, *The Poetry of Greek Tragedy*, Baltimore, 1958.

A. Lesky, *History of Greek Literature*, trsl. by J. Willis & C. de Heer, London, 1966.

H. Lloyd-Jones, 'Agamemnonea III', *H.S. Cl. Ph.* 73, 1969, p. 99 sq.

W. Ludwig, *Sapheneia*, Tübingen, 1935.

P. Masqueray, *Euripide et Ses Idées*, Paris, 1908; *Théorie des Formes Lyriques de la Tragédie grecque*, Paris, 1895.

A. Nauck (ed.), *Fragmenta Tragicorum Graecorum*, Leipsig, 1926, 2nd edition.

J. Overbeck, *Die Antiken Schriftquellen*, Leipzig, 1868.

D. L. Page, *Actors' Interpolations in Greek Tragedy*, Oxford, 1934.

K. Pauer, *Die Bildersprache des Euripides*, Breslau, 1935.

E. Pfuhl, *Malerei und Zeichnung der Griechen*, Munich, 1923; *Masterpieces of Greek Drawing and Painting*, London, 1955.

E. Pot, *De Maritieme beeldspraak bij Euripides*, Harderwijk, 1943.

M. E. Prior, *The Language of Tragedy*, New York, 1947.

J. Rappold, *Beiträge zur Kenntnis des Gleichnisses bei Aischylos, Sophokles und Euripides*, Vienna, 1886.

G. Richter and L. F. Hall, *Red-Figured Athenian Vases in the Metropolitan Museum of Art*, New Haven, Conn., 1936.

A. Rivier, *Essai sur le Tragique d'Euripide*, Lausanne, 1944.

W. Schadewaldt, *Monolog und Selbstgespräch*, Berlin, 1966.

C. P. Segal, 'The Tragedy of the Hippolytus', *H.S. Cl. Ph.*, LXX, 1965, 117 sq.

C. Spurgeon, *Shakespeare's Imagery*, Cambridge, 1965.

W. B. Stanford, *Aeschylus in his Style*, Dublin, 1942; *Greek Metaphor*, Oxford, 1936.

Wallace Stevens, *Opus Posthumous. Poems, Plays and Prose*, London, 1959.

T. W. Stinton, *Euripides and the Judgement of Paris*, London, 1965.

M. Swindler, *Ancient Painting*, New Haven, 1929.

A. W. Verrall, *Euripides the Rationalist*, Cambridge, 1895.

T. B. L. Webster, *Greek Theatre Production*, London, 1956; *Greek Art and Literature 530–400 B.C.*, Oxford, 1939; *The Interplay of Greek Art and Literature*, London, 1949; *The Tragedies of Euripides*, London, 1967.

H. Weir-Smyth, *Aeschylean Tragedy*, California, 1924.

R. P. Winnington-Ingram, *Euripides and Dionysus*, Cambridge, 1948; Hippolytus, A Study in Causation in *Euripides Entretiens sur l'Antiquite*, Fondation Hardt, Geneva; 1960, 169 sq.

I. Index of Poetic Texts cited

II. General Index

[This index excludes the authors cited in the Index of Poetic Texts]